BELIEVING IN GOD

BELIEVING IN GOD

A Philosophical Essay

by
Gareth Moore, op

T & T CLARK
EDINBURGH

Copyright © T & T. Clark Ltd, 1988

Typeset by Saxon Printing Ltd., Derby
Printed in Great Britain by
Billing & Sons Ltd, Worcester

for

T. & T. CLARK LTD
59 George Street, Edinburgh EH2 2LQ

First printed 1988

British Library Cataloguing in Publication Data

Moore, Gareth
Believing in God
1. Christian doctrine. God
I. Title
231

ISBN 0 567 09498 7

To My Mother

CONTENTS

PREFACE

This book started life as a dissertation for the qualification of *Sacrae Theologiae Lector* in the Order of Preachers. It is meant to be a sketch towards a philosophical understanding of Christianity. It is merely an introduction, suggesting a general approach and covering a very wide area. Some points which deserve to be gone into thoroughly have been treated only generally, sometimes merely suggested. What I have written here is perhaps not so much a book as a programme, an outline for a number of possible books. I do not aim to do anything so large as 'philosophy of religion' in general, if there is such a thing. My method has been to look at some of the ways language about God is generally used by Christian believers. Christians believe many different and opposed things. The examples I have taken for discussion by and large, though not entirely, express beliefs and attitudes I am familiar with and sympathetic to, and which I take to belong to the mainstream Christian tradition. Because I have also wanted to stick largely to the centre I have relied heavily on scripture as a source (not, of course, that this guarantees orthodoxy, but scripture is fundamental to all but the most far-flung Christians). However, my concern is with what it is for Christians to believe the things they do, not with the truth of a particular range of beliefs. So the philosophical approach I follow, if it is valid at all, is applicable to heterodox as well to orthodox beliefs, and I occasionally look at examples of beliefs that are wildly unorthodox (and which I hope nobody actually holds). It will also become clear that religions quite other than

Christianity might benefit from being looked at in a similar way.

It will be obvious, if only from the fact that I quote him so much, that I have been much impressed and influenced by Wittgenstein. In using him so much I have hoped to encourage those who have not read him to do so. There may be other influences on me that are equally clear to the knowledgeable reader. If I do not acknowledge them, it is only because they are not obvious to me.

All references to works of Wittgenstein are to paragraph numbers unless a page is explicitly referred to. All the translations from the Bible, and the one from the Koran, are my own. My thanks are due to The Brynmill Press, Retford, for permission to quote from Wittgenstein's *Remarks on Frazer's Golden Bough*; to Basil Blackwell, Oxford, for all other works of Wittgenstein quoted; to Oxford University Press for E. E. Evans-Pritchard's *Witchcraft, Oracles and Magic Among The Azande*; to SCM Press, London, for Antony Flew and Alasdair MacIntyre's *New Essays in Philosophical Theology*; and to Faber and Faber, London, for James M. Clark and John V. Skinner's *Meister Eckhart: Selected Sermons and Treatises*.

Thanks also to Michael Doyle op, Marcus Hodges op, Tadeusz Kwasnica op and Peter Johnson op, who read through various portions of the script; to Brian Davies op, who made many helpful criticisms; to Michael Daly and Mark Dowd; and to Fergus Kerr op, who re-introduced me to Wittgenstein, and who helped and encouraged me at all stages of the work.

CHAPTER 1

INTRODUCTION

A Question

What is it to believe in God, the Christian God? One way to answer this question would be to show how we would explain Christian belief to somebody who did not understand it. I do not mean, how we would convince somebody of the truth of Christianity, but rather how we would bring him to understand what it is that Christians believe to be true, and what it is for them to believe it. The way we would explain it, what would count as an explanation, would very much depend on who we wanted to give the explanation to. If somebody ignorant of Christianity or perplexed about it asked us to explain it to him, the way we would go about it would depend on the kind of ignorance or perplexity in question. If the questioner were, say, a believing Jew or a Muslim, then perhaps all we would need to do would be to ask him to read a few books of Christian doctrine and spirituality, the creed, the New Testament, and so on, and then to familiarise him with the kind of rituals that Christians perform, get him to visit a few church services. A Jew or a Muslim, we may expect, already has some understanding of the basic ideas and concepts used in Christianity. He knows what it is to believe in God, for God to command certain actions and for people to perform them in obedience to the will of God; he knows what it is to love God and fear him, to seek him, to pray, to worship, to perform religious rituals, and in general to lead a religious life, a life lived in the light of God. So all we would have to do in such a case is to show him by various means what

1

Christians think God is like, what *Christians* say of God, what *Christians* believe to be the will of God, the way *Christians* worship.

The situation would be quite different with somebody whose ignorance was more fundamental, somebody who came from a background without any religion that bore any similarity to ours, or with no religion at all, and who had never in any way come into contact with anything like our religion before. Such a person would not be able to understand the clarification of Christianity that we would offer to a Jew or a Muslim. He would not know what it is to believe in God, to pray, worship, obey the commandments of God, and the rest. That is to say, he would not know what is meant by those expressions, and what part they play in people's lives. He would not know what people are talking about when they say that God commands certain things to be done and forbids others, that God is loving and merciful, and so on. We would not only have to describe Christianity to him, but we would also have to explain the words that we use in describing Christianity, or lead him to understand them in some other way. We know that this can be done, since people do come to understand Christianity, and come to understand it, moreover, from such a position of radical ignorance. *Everybody* who understands Christianity once started off from a position of complete ignorance of what we mean by "believing in God", since they once started off completely ignorant of what is meant by *any* word or phrase, ignorant, that is, of how any word or phrase is used in English. If it is possible to learn what it is to believe in God, how?

A Problem
Let us assume such a person, somebody who wants to learn about Christianity from a position of this fundamental ignorance. Normally we get to know about religious

concepts gradually, as we learn the rest of our language. But to make things clearer and easier, let us say that this person is not a child without any language at all. He has a normal grasp of English and knows of many of our secular institutions and social customs, but he knows nothing at all about Christianity. He was born into an isolated community of logical positivists, in which he was taught only those things that made obvious secular sense. He was kept well away from any contact with religious ideas and practices. All his contacts were monitored and all his books censored to make sure that he never so much as saw or heard the word "God". He never saw a church or any pictures of one, never saw any rituals of a religious kind, and was successfully brought up not only without any religious ideas of his own but without even knowing that there was such a thing as Christianity or any other religion. He was raised to be the first of a new breed of the scientific, the logical, the sensible, free from any taint of superstition. During the day he, together with the rest of the community, would study mathematics or some other approved subject, and in the evening they would all gather round the hearth and read to each other propositions of natural science. But one day Otto (for such is his name), feeling that there must be more to life than this, escapes his enlightened mentors and finds himself wandering around in our town, where we come across him and furnish him with a place to live and means of support. He begins to explore the town and, among other things, goes into churches and sees the way people speak and act there. In response to his curiosity we set about trying to describe Christianity to him. We get him to read the Bible and books of doctrine and spirituality, volumes of church history, etc.; we also encourage him to carry on going into churches to learn more about what people do there, and also to watch these same people as they go about their daily lives.

In this way he begins to learn, both through instruction and through his own observation, something about the concepts of God, of obedience to God, of prayer and worship, of heaven and hell, and so on.

We can expect him to have some trouble following what is going on. Apart from the baffle inherent in particular Christian notions, such as incarnation, the real presence of Christ in the sacraments, the Trinity, and so on, he is liable to encounter a more general difficulty: Christians speak of God as of a very important and powerful human being, or at least as of somebody very like a human being. He makes things, he makes his creatures do things, he loves, hates, forgives, rewards and punishes, he lays down commandments for them to follow, and so on. He acts very much like a human king or despot, and is in fact sometimes referred to as a king in the Christian sacred scriptures and other writings. And people react to him much as one would react to such a person. They do their best to do what he commands them to do, they listen to his words and read them. They in turn talk to him in a number of ways: they ask him for things they need, go to him for guidance, praise him, thank him, ask his forgiveness. They trust him to look after them, to protect them and act for their good, though sometimes they may feel that he has let them down badly and come to hate him and rebel against him. They sometimes approach him with the kind of ceremony appropriate to a great and powerful monarch. They perform ritual gestures of self-abasement before him, bowing, kneeling or prostrating; they perform other ritual actions and speak at the proper times using certain prescribed words. What perplexes Otto about all this is that, while Christians speak of God as a person who, they say, does many things, and while they behave towards him in many ways as a person, *there is nobody there called God.* They speak of God doing things when he can see nobody doing anything. In their churches they say they are speaking to God, but there is obviously nobody there to speak to; they speak into thin air. They kneel, but they kneel before nobody. They talk of obeying, but there is nobody they are obeying, unless it be somebody like a bishop or a minister, somebody who is not God. They perform many actions that Otto is quite familiar with, and by and large they speak words that he knows, since he also is a competent speaker of English. But they perform these familiar actions and speak these familiar words in circumstances and in ways quite unlike any in which he has seen them performed and spoken before.

For example, when he was growing up and learning English in the positivist commune he learned what it was to speak to somebody, and part of what he learned was that if you were speaking to somebody, then, unless you were using some apparatus, like a telephone, that carried your voice out of your presence, the one you were speaking to had to be in the same place as you, in your presence. – It is a fact about the way the words "speak to" are used that, barring the use of special apparatus, talking is only called "speaking to" somebody if there is somebody there. When he was being brought up he was taught to be respectful to others and sometimes to bow before them; but then the others had to be there before him for him to bow to. So an important part of learning to speak to people and to bow to them was for him (as it is also for us) learning what counts as there being somebody there, when it can properly be said that there is somebody there. Principally, people are said to be there when they can be *seen* (though sometimes when they can be heard or felt). If there is doubt about whether there is somebody there, the doubt can be resolved typically by looking, but sometimes by listening or feeling – in general, by using the senses. When there is somebody there, you can, by testing like this, generally establish that there is somebody there, if there is a doubt about it; and, importantly, you can also often establish with certainty that there is nobody there when there is in fact nobody there. Again, Otto was taught to obey commands, but then he had to be able to tell when somebody was giving him a command, and though there were a number of ways he could do this, the central case was when he could see somebody standing before him and speaking to him in a particular way. He also had to be able to determine who it was who was giving him a command, for he was only to obey Freddie, the leader of the commune, and his deputies. That again he would mostly do by seeing who it was standing before him and talking to him, though he might sometimes do it by recognising a familiar voice or a signature. There are ways of establishing the identity of people who are talking to you.

But the words and actions of Christians do not hang together with circumstances in the same way. Though they say and do many things that Otto is used to or recognises, they do them in apparently quite inappropriate circumstances, circumstances made inappropriate specifically by the *absence* of anybody before them. Though they may say they are talking to God in the way that Otto might have talked to Freddie, yet quite obviously, by all the tests that Otto has learnt, there is nobody there for them to be talking to. And though they talk of God in very much the way they might talk of a man, there seems to be no such man about the place.

If Otto saw just one man speaking and acting like this, his simplest way of dealing with the situation would be to say that the man was mad. For this is indeed just the kind of thing that madmen do: they hallucinate, think people are there when they are not; they talk to people who are not there; they behave in ways quite inappropriate to the

6

circumstances, suddenly kneeling down or prostrating, taking off their shoes and putting them on again, spreading out their arms, crying out, wearing funny clothes, etc. They perform activities he cannot make sense of. But Otto discovers that there are thousands, millions of people who act like this, who speak when there is nobody there to speak to, and who describe this as "speaking to God"; who kneel before nobody, talk of "kneeling before God"; and so on. He discovers, moreover, that most of them are quite normal and sane in the rest of their activities. They are perfectly able to distinguish between the presence and the absence of other people and do not normally speak to others when they are not there to be spoken to (and if they ever do they can recognise that they have made a mistake). And they do not for most of their lives go round making gestures of greeting, submission, etc., in inappropriate circumstances. In general, they show themselves competent users of language and of gesture. It is only when this word "God" is involved that they speak and act so strangely.

Moreover, it is not as if the actions and words that they perform and say in such a problematic way were random. While some Christians insist on a lot of spontaneity, for many of them there are actually books prescribing what is to be done and said, and there are even special buildings made for people to come together to do and to say all this, to speak to and reverence somebody who is not there. And these people confidently and systematically teach their children to do the same things and say the same things in the same inappropriate circumstances. This is all too widespread and too institutionalised to count as madness, apart from the fact that the people give no other indication of being mad. And if they are not incompetent either, some other explanation has to be found.

One possible explanation that might present itself to Otto is that, though he is in general a competent user of English, still he is yet young and has led a sheltered life, and there may be uses of words that he has not yet learned, uses that he will be quite able to learn given enough time living with people among whom they are current. And the same goes for all these strange gestures, which seem to be linked in some way with these unfamiliar uses of language. He may think that they are simply alien to him, different from what he is used to, and that in time they could become familiar to him and he at home in them, able and willing to use them as those around him do; or at least he could come to understand how other people are at home in them. For he has grown up and has seen others growing up, and he knows that, in general, uses of language and gesture and of rituals and customs are things that have to be assimilated over a period, perhaps by means of deliberate training; he knows that he himself has done so previously, so that he may well do so again. He may think, in short, that in order to understand Christianity he has to extend his command of language; and that would in turn involve learning to see the sense of new ways of behaving.

A Straightforward Answer

But, it might be objected, Otto's problem can be resolved in a much quicker and more straightforward way. His problem, what makes it so difficult for him to understand what Christians say about God and how they act towards him, is that there seems to be nothing or nobody called God for them to talk about and to act towards. What he needs now is not to see this as some new use of language quite unlike any other he has encountered before; what he needs is simply new information. This absence of anybody called God, which makes all these words and gestures so puzzling, is only a *seeming* absence. The one Christians speak of, the one they speak to and reverence, is in fact there all the time, only you cannot see him. God is invisible. And not just that; you cannot bump into him or touch him, for he is intangible, neither does he make any sound. And he doesn't smell, either. In fact, he is absolutely undetectable by any of our senses, and cannot be found even by our most sophisticated scientific instruments. And that is not just because our senses are not keen enough, or our instruments not yet sensitive enough. No sense could ever detect God, neither will he ever register on any of our instruments, no matter how good we make them. The invisibility, the intangibility, the general undetectability of God, these are not a matter of our contingent limitations; they are actual properties of God. If you like, God has no body. (It is true that we shall, by grace, see God when we die, or at the end of time, but we do not quite know what we mean when we say that; it will certainly not be a bodily seeing, our bodily eyes seeing a visible body.) He it is who made us and all heaven and earth, who gives us commandments, protects us and guides us, who loves us, who sent his Son to save us, who promises us rewards if we obey him but also threatens us with punishments if we do not. That is why we do our best to obey him, and why we worship him. He is the one to whom we speak in church, and before whom we kneel. (Well, not strictly *before*, since God is everywhere, and so also behind us when we kneel; so admittedly one does, as a Christian, have to learn uses of gesture that are a little different from secular uses.) So Christians do not use language in a different way from non-Christians. They are just better informed. They realise that there is this thing or person around whom they call God, whereas others do not. Or at least, Christians believe that there is this extra being, even if their belief should turn out to be false.

Belief

Much of that is right, and is in fact only a reminder of what Otto should have remembered from his reading of scripture, for there God is more than once spoken of as invisible. For example:

> Since the creation of the world the invisible things of God – his eternal power and godhead – can be clearly seen in what he has made. (Romans 1:20)

> Christ is the image of the invisible God, the first-born of all creation. (Colossians 1:15)

> To the king of the ages, the immortal, invisible and only God, honour and glory for all ages. Amen. (1 Timothy 1:17)

> By faith Moses left Egypt, not afraid of the king's anger; for he endured as if seeing the invisible one. (Hebrews 11:27)

But a clarification of Christian belief of the kind given above is liable to be understood as claiming that there is one more being around than Otto thinks, only one who is invisible, intangible, and the rest. When Otto read the scriptures initially, his scepticism was aroused, for he had never heard that anybody had made the earth or governed the fate of all nations and individuals; neither had he seen or otherwise caught whiff of this being. Nevertheless, he may have tried to keep an open mind, and said something like this: "If these Christians can show me this thing or person called God, I will be very surprised, but, if they do, I will have to believe the evidence of my senses". But now when he hears that there is no evidence of the senses, he is surely likely to become incredulous: just what is the difference between this being's existing and its not existing? What

10

grounds has Otto for believing that the universe contains one more (very peculiar) thing than he ever thought it did, apart from just being told so?

Of course he, like everybody else, has come to believe many things just because he has been told they are so. This is the way that most of our education works; Norwegian trade officials may learn what are the major imports and exports of Norway by standing on Norwegian quaysides over a long period to see what goes in and out, but we do not; we learn it by reading about it in newspapers or geography textbooks or Norwegian government trade statistics, or by being told it by somebody we have reason to believe is competent to tell us. This is normally how we find such things out. In learning to do things like this we also learn what it is to find something out; we learn *what is called* finding out a country's major imports and exports. So that, if we are later asked to find out what are the major imports and exports of Burma we will know roughly what to do and what not to do. We will know, if we have learned properly, that the process we call finding out the major imports and exports of Burma will involve any one of a number of operations, like reading official Burmese trade statistics, asking informed Burmese people, and so on. But we will also know that it will *not* involve, say, throwing dice or writing down the first word we think of.

If learning how to find out things involves learning what counts as ways of finding them out, it also entails learning what count as grounds for our believing the things we claim to have learned, what counts as a proper answer to the question, "How do you know that?" And what are called "ways we find out things" are closely related to what are called "grounds for believing things". If I am asked, "How do you know Norway exports a lot of wood?" – if I am asked my grounds for saying, believing or claiming to know this much about Norwegian trade – my answer will be something like "I was taught it at school", or "It was in today's Financial Times", or "The Norwegian ambassador happened to mention it to me last night at dinner". These count as grounds for my saying such a thing because they also count as ways in which I might find it out. But if I offer as an answer, "I get a warm feeling if I say Norway exports a lot of wood", that will not be accepted as a ground for my belief, because when we are taught how to find out facts in geography the methods do not include paying attention to the warmth of our feelings.

We should note, too, that different things count as grounds for different people in different situations. It might be enough for *me* to say, "The Norwegian ambassador told me so", but it certainly would not be enough for the Norwegian Minister for Overseas Trade, still less for his subordinates. For them it would have to come down to invoices and bills of lading, and perhaps even visits to the dockside to inspect what goes on.

So being taught things, or otherwise coming to learn them, also involves the process of learning what we count as ways of finding them out and what we count as grounds for saying them. This goes too for questions of the existence of people and things. Otto has never been to Australia, he has only heard about it, in the way that most of us have; but he has also been told that somebody has actually been there and seen the place, he has spoken to people who say they have been there, he has received postcards that were posted there, he has seen films made on location that show famous Australian sights. That is to say, as well having acquired a belief that there exists this place called Australia, he has also been given grounds for believing it. As well as this belief, he has acquired the concept of a ground for such a belief. He has learned that being told that somebody has been to

12

Australia, the fact that Australia is marked in all atlases, and a number of other such things, count as grounds for believing that Australia exists; that is what we *mean* by grounds in this case. He also knows that different kinds of thing count as grounds for different beliefs. If he is told that a certain sub-atomic particle exists, he will not expect to be shown photos of it as he might expect to be shown photos of Australia. Or if he does, he will be corrected; such grounds do not exist for belief in this particle. He may be shown a photo of the trace of such a particle, be told the elementary facts about particle accelerators, bubble chambers, etc., and in this way he will be taught that this photo counts as evidence for the existence of that particle. Thus one of the things that serves to differentiate between kinds of belief or between belief in the existence of different kinds of thing, is the answer to the question what counts as grounds for the belief.

Now Otto's trouble can be put like this: He has been told and has read that God exists, and from what he has been told and what he has read God seems either to be or to be very much like a human being, a person. So he expects the grounds for believing in the existence of God to be like the grounds for believing in the existence of a human being. He expects it might be possible to see him, or at least pictures of him, to hear his voice, to touch him if he gets close enough, or failing that to talk to somebody who has met him. Now when he is told that none of these things is possible, he learns that this belief in the existence of God does not have the kind of grounds he expected it to have, the kind it ought to have had if the language he had heard and read about God was to be understood in any way familiar to him. So he is perplexed about what *kind* of belief this 'belief in the existence of God' is supposed to be. He has not yet learned what counts as grounds for belief in the existence of God. So his difficulty goes deeper than that of a lack of evidence for the existence of God. He does not even know what such evidence would look like, what would *count* as evidence for the existence of God; he only knows that the kind of thing that would normally count as evidence for the existence of somebody is not available in the case of God. And that is not just because it is particularly hard to come by, but because what is normally evidence for the existence of somebody does not count as evidence for the existence of God: it is a mistake to look for such evidence in the first place.

Belief & Evidence

One course a believer might take here is to supply Otto with grounds for believing that this extra being really does exist. He might say something like this: We know that everything we see around us must have a cause for its existence; things don't just come into being spontaneously. So the whole world must have some cause, which is itself uncaused; and that is what we call "God". Or: whatever moves must be moved by something; but it cannot be that everything is moved by something else, since then the motion would never get going in the first place; so there must be some unmoved mover, and that is what we call "God". Or again, the world shows evidence of design, so it is likely that somebody intelligent designed it, and that somebody we call "God". And so on. (But if more than one argument is used, it also has to be shown that, if they each establish the existence of some being we didn't know was there before, they all establish the existence of the *same* being.)

There are, however, well known difficulties in all this. It is doubtful whether such 'arguments for the existence of God' actually ever succeed in establishing the existence of anything, however subtly they may be presented. But regardless of the problematic nature of the individual arguments, there are two difficulties in this philosophical approach that

14

deserve special mention. One of the troubles that atheists may have with it is not that the evidence adduced by Christians appears too weak to support their claim that God exists, but that it seems not to be evidence at all. The problem might be put like this: Even if the Christian can supply what he calls evidence, still he can supply *only* evidence; he cannot present the sceptic with the thing itself, with God. The smell of burning wood, smoke and ash in the air, are normally taken as evidence of a fire nearby. It might be said they make us want to say, "There's a fire somewhere". Here we can say that the evidence for the existence of the fire is also the ground of our belief that there is a fire; if somebody said to us, "Why do you think there's a fire?" we would provide grounds for our words by pointing out the evidence: the smoke, the smell and the ash in the air. And then maybe, if it is important to us, we check by looking for the fire; and then if we actually discover it we know we were right.

Occasionally, what we call evidence for the existence of a fire nearby might be there, and yet there may be no fire. Perhaps it is all stage effects – for some reason somebody wants us to think there is a fire. Or the smell is produced by some plant new to us, the smoke is really pollen, and the ash merely dust thrown up by the wind. But that could not happen all the time, otherwise the connexion between smell, smoke, and ash on the one hand, and fire on the other, could never be set up. We would not react to the smell, the smoke and the ash by saying, "There's a fire somewhere". They would not count as evidence for the existence of a nearby fire; we would not *call* them evidence. So we could never point them out as grounds for our saying, "There's a fire", and we could never mistakenly or through deceit come, on the basis of them, to think there is a fire somewhere when there is not. If we could never actually discover a fire, there could be no such thing as evidence that there is a fire.

Now it may be said: the Christian can only supply the sceptic with what he calls evidence for the existence of God, not with the thing itself. And if the existence of God really were a hypothesis based on evidence, then this consideration would be an important criticism of the Christian. There is here no equivalent to, "There is a smell of burning, and smoke – and see, here is the fire!" We cannot say, "Here are things in motion, here are things that exhibit design – and see, here is God!" There is in this sense no discovery of God, as there might be of the fire. (It is of course possible to speak of discovering God, but *this* is not the way those words are used.) And normally, if evidence does not lead to discovery, we are led back to the phenomena that we initially counted as evidence, to reinterpret them, to find another explanation for them. Now they no longer count as evidence in this case in the way we originally thought they did. If we can find no fire, we look for some other explanation of the smell, the smoke and the ash, and we no longer think of them as evidence for any fire, since, as far as we can discover, there *is* none (and we may be able to make *quite certain* that there is no fire). So it might be argued that we should say about motion, signs of design, and the rest, "All these phenomena lead us to the hypothesis that there is a being we might call God, we think of them as evidence for the existence of God. But when we look we do not in fact discover anything we might call God. So we have to come to terms with this absence by going back to the phenomena and reinterpreting them. We have to find some other explanation of them, if we can, since it has turned out that there is in fact no God, and so that hypothesis has to be dropped".

But that belief in the existence of God is not a hypothesis is shown by the fact that this is not a serious criticism. It is objected, "We do not in fact discover anything we might call God". But it is not 'in fact'. The Christian does not *fail* to produce God, where he might have succeeded. For the Christian is committed, upon pain of idolatry, to rejecting any and every candidate that might be presented as the discovered God. (This is true of Christians. There might well be discoverable gods in other religions.) So it is not that he fails in the task of producing God. Rather, in Christianity, there *is* no such task. For the Christian is committed to finding what the atheist too expects to find – *nothing*. The disagreement between the Christian and the atheist does not lie here, in their expectations. Their disagreement is not like a disagreement over what might be the results of an experiment, what might be discovered, what might be apparent to the senses or register on our instruments.

We say that God is invisible, intangible, etc. These traditional attributes of God have their part to play in theology and in the spiritual life of Christians. Treating the existence of God as a hypothesis makes them look like makeshifts for the purpose of preserving the hypothesis from falsification, as if they said, "God is there all right, as the evidence indicates, but the reason you can't discover him is that he is invisible, etc., not accessible to your senses or detectable by your instruments". But that cast-iron defence of the 'hypothesis' only serves to make it idle, a kind of joke, like saying, "There is a green, three-legged, ten-foot tall woman in the middle of the road, only you can't detect her because she is invisible, intangible, etc." And one would still be left with the problem why any phenomena could be understood as evidence for this hypothesis. But in fact these traditional epithets say (or one use of them is to say): There is no such thing as discovering God. Whatever you discover, it is not God. God is not this, not that. God is 'totally other'(than what you might find), 'transcendent' (outside the realm of the discoverable).

One consequence of this is that the meaning of the word "God" cannot be explained by pointing to something and saying, "That is God". We can do this with, say, the word "chair". Pointing out a chair to somebody and saying, "That is a chair; that is the sort of thing we mean by 'chair'" could be part of an explanation of the word "chair", and normally would be. We might also point to a chair and say, "'Chair' is the name of that sort of thing". But "God" works differently. The relation between the word "God" and God is not the relation between name and thing named. In this sense, God is not a thing. When we hear talk of God, and before we learn how it actually works, we may be misled by it; we may actually expect to come across a person or thing named by the word "God", just as we might expect to come across a thing named by the word "chair". This is a false expectation and has to be corrected. Here is a place where we might introduce talk of God as a *spirit*. This move would be analogous to that described by Wittgenstein when he is talking about the use of the phrase "point to the shape of a thing":

> And we do here what we do in a host of similar cases: because we cannot specify any *one* bodily action which we call pointing to the shape (as opposed, for example, to the colour), we say that a *spiritual* activity corresponds to these words. Where our language suggests a body and there is none: there, we should like to say, is a *spirit. (Philosophical Investigations* 36)

This remark may well be intended as a criticism of the procedure, but it will do equally well simply as a comment on one of the ways the word "spirit" enters the language and is used. And so also as a warning: when you hear the word "spirit" do not look for a single thing of which you would say that *that* is the spirit. Here, there is no one thing named; the relation of the word "spirit" to a spirit is not to be construed on the model of the relationship between a name and the thing named. We might say, then, following Wittgenstein's example, that God is a spirit, and that is not to say that God is made out of strange and rarified stuff, but to make a logical point, a point about the use of the word "God": that it is mistake to look for something to label "God". One way to put this would be to say that a spirit is not a kind of thing.

It is a misconception, then, to think of God as similar to a human being, a person, except without a body, or invisible and undetectable. It makes God too like people, in that it neglects the fact that the differences between them are not merely material, but logical. If God were just like a human being, except for being invisible, more powerful, more knowledgeable, better, and so on, we would find not only that we often use the same words both about God and about people – which we plainly do – but also that we use them *in much the same way*. But in fact, if we actually look at the ways we use words when we are talking about God, we will see they are often crucially different from the ways we use those same words when we are talking about people. The principal aim of this book is to point out some of those differences as they crop up in major areas of our talk about God.

We speak of God in the absence of anything (any thing, person) that is called God. This is a plain fact that Otto observes. If this is not madness, neither is it because we have knowledge of the existence of some omnipresent being whom unfortunately we are unable to show to anybody (or to ourselves). Rather, the word "God" is used in unusual ways. In particular, establishing the presence of anything that we might call God is irrelevant to our speaking of God, since there is nothing that we might call God. Not that we want to say that God is absent: for most purposes, we want to say that God is present everywhere, at all times. (We have a use for this expression and others like it; though sometimes we may also want to say that God is absent; we may find a use for the sentence "God is absent", for instance in great misfortune or desolation.) But God would be absent, there really would be no God, if God were (supposed to be) a thing. But the presence of God is not the presence of a thing (or person) called God, a thing undetectable because invisible, intangible, bodiless. There is not one more thing in the universe than atheists think. On the contrary, for Christians no such extra thing could count as God.

Jesus

But there is an obvious objection here. It appears not to be true that Christianity is like this, that it rules out the task of discovering God. While it might be true of Judaism and Islam, it seems obviously false as applied to Christianity. In John's gospel (20:28), does not the disciple Thomas, confronted by the risen Christ, exclaim, "My Lord and my God"? And Christians do, on the whole, follow Thomas; they say that Jesus Christ is God, and he is a historical figure who was once visible, tangible, and so on, who lived in a particular place at a particular time. So Christians do have a use for talk about an identifiable God.

This is true and important. But there are two things to be said here. First, alongside talk of Jesus as God there remains in Christianity a great deal of talk of the invisible God, in contrast to Jesus. This too is an important element of Christianity, which requires attention. When philosophers have produced arguments for the existence of God it is not that they have argued for the existence of Jesus, and in this they are surely right. Second, though saying that Jesus is God is of course of central importance to Christianity, it is a

20

logically secondary use of the word "God". You could not explain the meaning of the word "God" by pointing to Jesus Christ (if he were still around to be pointed to). To call him God is an extension of the use of the word, and a paradoxical one at that; it might be called a creative misuse of it. At any rate it is a use that presupposes an already existing one. (Jesus himself uses the word, and not of himself.) Given the primary use of the word, "Jesus Christ is God" is not a sentence that lies ready to hand with an obvious sense. It is rejected by, for example, Jews and Muslims not just as false but as obvious nonsense, since, of course, Jesus Christ is visible, tangible, etc., and God is invisible, intangible, etc. According to the primary use of the word "God" Jesus is not even someone who might be God, but fails to be; *nobody* might be God. So even Christians recognise it is an extraordinary thing to say that he is God. In a similar way, the vowel *a* is not something that might be pink, but fails to be; to talk about the colour of a vowel is to extend language, make it take a new turn, a move which others might resist and declare to be obvious nonsense. Compare this remark of Wittgenstein:

> It's just like the way some people do not understand the question: "What colour has the vowel *a* for you?" – If someone did not understand this, if he were to declare it was nonsense – could we say that he did not understand English, or the meaning of the individual words "colour", "vowel" etc.? On the contrary: Once he has learned to understand these words, then it is possible for him to react to such questions 'with understanding' or 'without understanding'. (*Zettel* 185)

Similarly, to say "Jesus is God" or "It is absurd to suppose that Jesus or anybody else might be God" is possible only when we have learned the primary uses of the

21

word "God". For this reason I shall stick mainly to trying to elucidate some of these primary uses, which is already work enough. That means that I cannot pretend to give here even a rough outline of how Christian language as a whole works; I omit much of what is most characteristic and most important, and only occasionally allude to some of the things involved in speaking of Jesus Christ as God.

Believing Religiously

A second reason why some Christians have been unhappy with the philosophical approach is that it makes it look as if the majority of Christians, those who hold the faith because they have been brought up to do so, are in some way second-class believers, because they believe without sufficient rational grounds, and that because they have had neither the wit nor the leisure to pursue a particular kind of philosophy of religion. One could then ask, among other things, why, if such a particular philosophical approach were logically fundamental to Christian belief, the scriptures do not contain philosophical arguments but demands to repent and believe the gospel. That is to say, this philosophical approach appears to misrepresent the nature of Christian belief, which is counted as a *virtue*, something to be nourished and held to, rather than a hypothesis which may or may not have been established by means of particular arguments. Some remarks of Wittgenstein on the special nature of Christian belief are relevant here:

> If the question arises as to the existence of a god or God, it plays an entirely different role to that of the existence of any person or object I ever heard of. One said, had to say, that one *believed* in the existence [of God], and if one did not believe, this was regarded as something bad. Normally if I did not believe in the existence of something no one would think there was

anything wrong in this. Also, there is this extraordinary use of the word "believe". One talks of believing and at the same time one doesn't use "believe" as one does ordinarily. You might say (in the normal use): "You only believe – oh well...." Here it is used entirely differently. (*Lectures and Conversations on Aesthetics, Psychology and Religious Belief*, p.59f.)

Again, though here the subject is belief in Christ:

> Christianity is not based on a historical truth; rather, it offers us a (historical) narrative and says: now believe! But not, believe this narrative with the belief appropriate to a historical narrative, rather: believe, through thick and thin, which you can do only as a result of a life. *Here you have a narrative, don't take the same attitude to it as you take to other historical narratives!* Make a *quite different* place in your life for it.... This message (the Gospels) is seized on by men believingly (i.e. lovingly). *That* is the certainty characterising this particular acceptance-as-true, not something *else*. (*Culture and Value*, p.32e)

Some of this is exaggerated, but the fundamental idea is important. This idea, that religious belief plays a quite different role in the believer's life from that which philosophical arguments for the existence of God would appear to presuppose, is something I want to develop at length; in a sense it is the theme of this whole book. But some general points about religious belief can be made now.

First, religious belief is not just belief in God; or, if you like, belief in God is never just belief that there exists a being that it would be reasonable to call God. Believing in God typically means having a whole complex of beliefs and attitudes. It involves, for example, believing that there is some kind of meaning or purpose to it all, even if you can't

23

say what it is; it means believing in certain teachings, and probably in the authority of particular teachers or books. It means subscribing to particular values, accepting one range of practices as good and right and another as wrong; perhaps also adopting a number of customs, not because they are somehow better than other customs, but just because they are the customs associated with this religion. It may involve believing that certain historical statements are true; say, that some particular person said and did such and such things. It may involve believing in propositions of natural science, such as that the earth came into existence in a particular way, that present-day species did not evolve from earlier ones, and so on. It may involve subscribing to philosophical-sounding beliefs about the Nature of Man, believing that certain philosophical arguments are sound, or that certain propositions can be proved by argument. Different religions and religious believers vary in the way they mix these elements, but it would be difficult to understand somebody who said he believed in God and whose belief had none of them. Certainly any belief in God that wanted to pass for a form of Christianity would have to have some form of the mix.

One consequence of this is that, since religion may involve all sorts of beliefs, it is probably a mistake to try to separate off a class of 'religious beliefs' as distinct from all others. The belief, for instance, that the world was formed in six days in roughly 4004 BC looks like a straightforward proposition of history or astronomy or geology. It is not obviously religious in content; it does not contain the word "God" or any other standard religious vocabulary. It is quite possible to imagine an atheist holding such a belief, even an atheistic astronomer or geologist. Yet it is crucial to some people's religious belief. It may even be crucial to the belief of a Christian scientist. Suppose a Christian geologist has this belief. Is his a religious belief, or a scientific one? Both? Or if a Christian historian believes that Christ rose from the dead on the third day after his crucifixion, is that a religious belief or a historical one?

It is perhaps not so much the content of a belief that makes it religious as the way in which it is believed. There is a religious attitude to the content of belief, as there is what we might call a scientific or empirical attitude. There is a different relationship in each case between what is believed and why it is believed, which means also that there is a different relationship between what is believed, the evidence for it, and the grounds for believing it. One thing (among others) that characterises what we call "religious belief" is that it is clung to; whatever its source, it is an authoritative word, not a hypothesis that may be changed if the evidence appears to require it. Changing religious belief means overcoming the power of an authority. To this we may oppose 'scientific belief', belief which we adopt because of the weight of evidence in its favour, and which we are ready to drop if the balance of probability shifts. Here the authority of a tradition or a scripture or a teacher is irrelevant. For example, to the man to whom religious questions mean nothing, whether the world was formed in six days or not will (unless he has some other stake in the matter) perhaps be a mildly interesting question, but no more, and he will change his opinion on the subject with ease, as he is led by the evidence. The committed Christian (of a certain type) will treat the same belief in an entirely different way, as will the committed atheist. Perhaps these two types of belief never occur in a pure state. People do abandon or change their religious beliefs, despite the importance of authority, if they come to think they are untenable – if the beliefs come to seem absurd, or morally outrageous, or perhaps if the evidence against them appears too strong. But what counts as being absurd or what counts as being sufficiently strong counter-evidence has no independent authority to define it. To an atheist (or certain kinds of Protestant) it may seem absurd to call a consecrated host the body of Christ: the evidence of the senses is that it is obviously ordinary bread. To the Catholic – who also has senses, just as good as the atheist's – it is not an absurd belief. (And they may be one and the same person, at different times.) Or to a Catholic the ancient Christian belief in the wrongness of contraception, however traditional, however widely held and however solemnly proclaimed by voices that he or she normally holds authoritative, may come to seem unacceptable because of its morally repugnant consequences.

On the other hand, people may also sometimes believe propositions of science despite strong counter-evidence, even when they are doing science, because some authority, say a physics professor, says they are true. Nevertheless, this attitude is more typical of religious belief, and is not recommended in science. In science it is considered a bad thing if the personal influence of a professor is so strong as to inhibit proper criticism of his pet theory, if he has the status of a guru, so that his theory becomes a dogma. This does not only apply to individuals. The received wisdom of a whole scientific community may similarly resist challenge, make it difficult to pursue lines of enquiry that threaten it. And this is said to be bad for science. On the other hand faith, holding on to what is taught even in spite of apparently strong evidence against it, is considered a virtue in religion. And something similar goes for what is apparently evidence for belief. Typically, what is believed is believed independently of discovery or proof. Thus one who produces what he thinks is a cast-iron proof of the existence of God does not therefore come to believe in God; and his conclusion is not

Can you teach faith? You can examplify but is that teaching or learning?

26

where his argument just happened to lead him. The proof supports an already existing belief.

One way to develop this might be to say that in religion there is an important distinction between grounds and evidence. That the Bible says the earth was created in six days is certainly not evidence that that is what happened; evidence might come from something like radio waves or very old rocks. It is the kind of thing we would have to ask scientists about. But for the religious believer the words of the Bible are certainly *grounds* for believing that is how it happened. (Different believers will have different ideas on whether they are strong or convincing grounds.) That the pope says contraception is wrong is, again, not *evidence* that it is wrong; but for a Catholic or mainstream Christian it is certainly grounds for believing it is wrong. In a scientific, empirical outlook, on the other hand, there is a much closer identification between grounds and evidence. So a Catholic woman may at the same time hang on the words of the pope and yet be ready to challenge the foremost authorities in her own scientific field.

A second and related point about religious belief is that, in the central case, it is *doctrine*; it is, in a special way, taught and learned. As I said earlier, we do not, either as children or later in life, insist on finding out everything for ourselves, if this means investigating things quite independently of what others say. Most of the things that we believe we believe in the first instance because we have picked them up in conversation or from the television or radio or have read them or been taught them. Unless we are particularly interested in a certain subject or surprised by what somebody says, we do not usually bother to check it by going to see for ourselves. And if we do check, a standard way is not to go to see for ourselves, but to ask somebody else, or to look it up in a book. If I doubt my friend's assurances that

Pyong Yang is the capital of Australia, I do not check by going to Australia to see for myself, but by asking an Australian or looking in a geography book or atlas. That is, by consulting a source commonly regarded as authoritative. There may be circumstances in which such a procedure amounts to being lazy or unscientific. But the most obvious one is the quite rare one when the point of the investigation is to check the authoritative source itself. In most other situations it is standard and reliable to rely on what others say. There is sometimes no more that *can* be done, no such thing as 'going to see for oneself'. If, for example, I am not sure of the date of the battle of Hastings, I can only check by going to somebody with a better head for dates, or to a history textbook or other documents. There is no question of going back in history to find out 'directly'. (Which is only to say that the ways of checking that are open to me are not indirect, somehow second-class.)

That we rely on what we are told, on what others say, then, is as true of physics and geography and morals as it is of religion. This means that in all fields a large importance is given to *authority*. Our believing things because we are told them by our parents and schoolteachers or read them in books is equivalent to our seeing our parents and school-teachers and books as authorities. But the importance of authority in religion goes beyond its importance in, say, physics. In religion, what is said and done is not to be in conformity with what is established by impartial enquiry, by going and looking at how things are, by experimenting. Rather is it to be conformable to what is *authoritatively said*. What counts as an authoritative source of doctrine in a particular community of faith may be a set of scriptures, a class of experts such as priests or theologians, or perhaps the community as a whole. If you want what you say to be accepted, it does not have to be scientifically proved, but it does (if challenged) have to be shown to be compatible with or derived from what the accepted authoritative sources say. Or if that is not possible you have to persuade people away from existing authorities, get them to accept what you say instead of what they say. Again, changing your religious belief – coming to faith from atheism, abandoning it, leaving one faith and embracing another, modifying the content of your faith – all this typically involves some form of rejection of authorities or the adoption of new ones.

This *belongs* to religion. The voice of God – transmitted through holy books, particular people, the believing community as a whole, or even mysterious voices – is always authoritative, as a matter of logic. If you reject a religious voice (or any other, for that matter), you *ipso facto* do not see it as speaking with the voice of God. That is to say, it belongs to the concept of the voice of God that it speaks with authority. It makes perfect sense to say, "Pastor Charlie tells me that I will get to heaven if I forgive those who wrong me, but really it's all twaddle". This is to reject the authority of Pastor Charlie in this particular matter, to say that he does not speak with the voice of God. On the other hand, you would not be understood, in normal circumstances, if you said, "God tells me that I will get to heaven if I forgive those who wrong me, but I can't say I believe him". There is no question about whether to believe God or not; what God says is true, because God says it. (So neither can there be any question of carrying out an experiment to discover whether what he says is right.)

Something similar can be said about the commands of God. God is authoritative here, too; God is he who is to be obeyed. I can easily say, "Father Charlie tells me I have to go to Mass every week; but I really can't be bothered". That is, again, to say that Father Charlie has no authority over me in these matters. In particular, he does not speak with divine

29

authority; what he says does not stem from God. But I cannot, if I hope to be readily understood, say, "God tells me I have to love my neighbour as myself, but I don't fancy it". I cannot disregard the commands of God in such a casual way. I can casually ignore what are conventionally called the commandments of God, but that only shows that I do not seriously subscribe to the convention; if I describe them like that in conversation, it will be in an ironical tone of voice. If I really understand them as commands of God, then I take them seriously, regard them as authoritative. I may rebel against God, as I can rebel against any authority; but it is *only* against an authority that I can rebel.

But God is not just one more authority, along with my parents, my teachers, the police, and so on. God is *logically* different from human authorities. He is not just more authoritative than them. (He may not be more authoritative at all, for I may think of them as speaking with the voice of God.) He is not simply a bodiless Father Charlie. My parents, my teachers, church, and so on, can all cease to be authorities for me; I can come to ignore them, perhaps through a process that begins in rebellion. And if I ignore them, that of course does not commit me to saying they do not exist. But God cannot cease to be an authority for me, so long as I believe in God. If I no longer believe in what are called truths revealed by God, if what are called his laws are no longer important to me, that means that I no longer think of them as God's truths and God's laws. If I am not prepared to think of anything at all as a divinely revealed truth or a divinely imposed law – if I will count nothing at all as having the authority of God – then I do not believe in God. God is *essentially* authoritative; to believe in God is to believe in the authority of God. (Teenagers are supposed to be rebellious, to kick against the authority of parents, teachers, adult society. One form this often takes is the rejection of religion: "I don't believe all those silly fairy tales about God and Jesus". This is not surprising if religion is so linked with authority. On the other hand, we do not hear teenagers rebelliously proclaiming, "I don't believe all that Pythagoras rubbish".)

Third, and this again is a related point, it is a feature of religion that people *correct* each other in religious matters, or at least try to. Those with a more authoritative voice, the leaders, correct the followers (and a leader in one context may be a follower in another). This kind of correction differs from what we would ordinarily call the correction of a mistake. If a child who knows mathematics has made a blunder in solving a problem, the teacher can point out to him his mistake: "Look, you forgot to multiply this side of the equation by 2, like the other side". The child will, since he knows the subject, see his mistake. He knows what is the right thing to do, only he forgot to do it. Or again, a scientist may point out to a colleague that the results of his experiment are invalid because of a mistake in his procedure. And they both know what counts as correct procedure. This kind of thing, pointing out a mistake, can happen in religion, too. For example, one Christian may speak to another Christian of the three inspired gospels, Matthew, Luke and John. He can have his mistake pointed out to him, and then perhaps he will say, "Oh, yes, four. Of course. I forgot about Mark". But something different may happen. He may say instead, "Well, I read Mark, and it didn't seem very inspired to me. I think it must have got into the Bible by mistake". Here he is no longer making a mistake. The orthodox Christian will indeed say he has got things wrong, but something quite different is going on from the first case, and its treatment will also be quite different. Now he has a wrong *opinion*. He has to be corrected, not in the sense of having his mistake pointed out to him (that has already been tried, and shown to be inappropriate to the situation), but in the sense of being persuaded to orthodoxy, won from his error. He has to be taught what is the right thing to say. To take another example, a parishioner may say proudly to his priest, "I really hate my neighbour, just like Jesus says". The shocked priest will point out that Jesus said we have to love our neighbour, and perhaps produce the relevant texts. Here the parishioner may be terribly embarrassed: "How could I have got it so stupidly wrong all these years?" He has made a mistake and been shown it. But he might react differently to what the priest says: "I know that is what Jesus says to most people, but he speaks to me sometimes in visions and tells me different". This is no mistake, but a dangerously erroneous opinion which the priest will have to try to correct. (Whether he has success or not will depend on how much of an authority the other regards him as.)

There are many such cases in religion, where it is a matter not of reminding somebody of what he knows or pointing out a slip, but of correcting them, correcting their opinions, teaching them what is the right thing to say and the right thing to do. There will of course be all kinds of arguments deployed but, notoriously, arguments in the field of religion are not conclusive; despite all arguments it is possible for people to have widely differing religious beliefs. In the end the argument of the orthodox may have to come down to saying, "This just is what the Christian faith is. This is what is said. This is what is believed and is to be believed. Believe this, not that". It is not that no other position is reasonably tenable, but that no other opinion *is to be held*. However, it is always possible to refuse to be corrected, to stick to one's own opinion, in spite of what another says; that is to reject the authority of that other.

These cases are somewhat like the case of the child who does not know mathematics, who has to be taught the right way to handle equations. Here it may in the end have to be said, "This is how it is done. This is the right way to do it. Do it this way". But the child may still not do it this way. An important difference, though, is that we do not say that such a child has another way of doing mathematics, which produces different results; it is simply that it is impossible to teach him mathematics. Nor would we say of a scientist who insisted on following unscientific procedures that he had a different way of doing science; he is simply incompetent. Science and mathematics depend on a wide measure of agreement to get going at all. But religion tolerates great diversity and fundamental disagreement. The man who has private revelations and thinks it wonderful to hate his neighbour may have bizarre and intolerable opinions, but they are religious beliefs for all that.

CHAPTER 2

THE EQUATOR, CHARLIE AND PAIN

The Equator
Confronted with the logical oddity of "God", it may be tempting to say that this is connected with God's being an *invisible* thing, as if the problem were that there is some difficulty about the notion of an invisible thing. But that cannot be right. We quite easily talk about the existence of invisible things (here I begin to use "invisible" as shorthand for invisible, intangible, tasteless, and so on – altogether undetectable). Take, for example, the equator. The equator is a line that runs round the middle of the earth. It is important in geography and navigation; there are ceremonies for crossing it at sea; generally it gets warmer as you approach it; the seasons are arranged differently on either side of it; some people believe that water starts going down the plughole in the opposite direction as you cross it; and so on.

Otto finds it a difficulty that people talk of and even to God when there is nobody there to talk about or to talk to. But, as he was by some oversight taught no geography, he might have somewhat the same difficulty if he is taken to the equator. He knows what a line is, and that several different sorts of things can count as lines: things drawn on paper, things dangling from fishing rods, rows of men, and suchlike. But now when he is taken to the equator, having been told that the equator is a line running round the middle of the earth, he can see that there is just no line there; there is only jungle or water or mountains. And he is not going to be helped much by being told that the equator is an *invisible* line. It would simply shift the difficulty: What is the difference between this line's existing and its not existing? What problems would be solved by the truth of the hypothesis that it exists? People relate various phenomena, like changes in temperature and the seasons, to it, but would not everything be exactly the same if it did not exist? As far as he can see, everything is indeed the same: Nigeria is warmer than Finland, and when it's winter in Minsk it's summer in Adelaide, even though there seems to be no such line.

And yet of course the equator does exist, and it is invisible. And it is not an accident that it is invisible; it is part of our concept of the equator, belongs to our use of the word "equator". If you did see something when you went there, that would not be the equator; it would only *mark* the equator (though you could point to such a thing, e.g. a length of red tape or a stake in the ground, and say, "See, that's the equator"). So it is possible to say that the equator exists and that the equator is invisible. It might even be possible to say that, though the equator is invisible, we *believe* it exists. It would certainly be a very odd thing to say; we would never say it unless Otto said something like this: "You tell me there is a line called the equator here. But how can you believe such a thing? You can see for yourself, as well as I can, that there's nothing there". In such circumstances, if he were so ignorant of the way we use the word "equator", we *might* say that we believe that the equator is there, since Otto has himself introduced the word "believe". But it would definitely be misleading to say, "We believe that the equator is there, despite its being invisible", as if we regretted our inability to see it but coped with this by adducing evidence about the variation of the seasons, etc., so feeling justified in inferring the existence of the equator. That would be to misrepresent entirely the way the word "equator" fits into our language. The existence of the equator is not a hypothesis that might or might not be justified. Though it is associated with certain phenomena, it is not inferred, on the basis of evidence, as a causal factor by means of which they can be explained. The correct thing to do in the face of Otto's scepticism would not be to re-assert our belief and then attempt to justify it by adducing evidence, but to explain the way our talk about the equator actually functions in our language and in our lives: how it is part of a system used for identifying positions on the surface of the earth, a system that is useful in navigation, in geography, when you want to make a note of where you are, etc.; that it is not itself a part of the earth, not even an invisible part; that it belongs to the system of measuring, not to the thing measured. What may possibly mislead then, if we say that we believe that the equator exists, and that the equator is invisible, is that we can give Otto and ourselves the impression that we believe that the equator is a hypothesised something extra, that apart from all the things that he and we can see on the earth – trees, mountains, rivers, cities, frogs – there also exists this one more thing that we cannot see. Then it is as if, if you made a list of all the things the earth contains, everything you can detect with the senses or with instruments, that list would be defective, incomplete; as if, in order to complete it, you would have to add on this one more, invisible thing. (I leave on one side any difficulties in the idea of making a complete list; e.g. if a rockpile is to go on the list, are also the rocks of which it is composed? For the rocks could exist and the pile not; would we want to say that if the pile is knocked over there is now one less thing than there used to be?)

A symptom that we had misled ourselves here would be if, when Otto said he doubted the existence of the equator, we affirmed our belief in it and tried to justify it with evidence or argument. Of course, we are not likely to make such a mistake. Why not? Perhaps for this reason: the rules for the use of the word "equator", and the part it plays in language and life, are laid bare, made explicit to us, as we are taught about the equator. We are taught it as a technical term, and its use explained to us, so that we could, if pressed, probably give at least a rudimentary account of its use. Since it is, unlike most of our words, a technical term, the way it is used is relatively simple. We can easily get an overall view of its use, so that we are not misled when we concentrate on one small part of it – that we call the equator a line, just as we do one of the white marks on a football pitch.

There is within the technical system that makes use of talk of the equator no talk of the existence or the non-existence of the equator, as far as I know. (But it is conceivable that there might be a place for such talk. There might, for instance, be some point in speaking of the disappearance of the equator at certain times of the year and its reappearance at others.) However, it might be possible for somebody to reject *any* talk of the equator, and so simply deny that the equator exists. The equator is supposed to be a line running round the middle of the earth; but somebody might claim that the earth has no middle in that sense, that it is not round but flat, and extends infinitely in all directions. This would not necessarily be to say that the line popularly called "the equator" does not exist, or that it cannot be used as part of a reference system in the way it is now used, but would only be to claim that the picture of the earth that led us to pick on this line as particularly significant is a false one; the equator does not divide the earth into two equal halves, as we had all thought.

A denial that the equator exists, then, might go together with a view of the earth quite different from the one we are commonly brought up to accept. It might be very difficult for us to know what to make of anybody at all well educated who said there is no equator. Part of our difficulty would be to understand why anybody should want to reject our commonly held picture and propose an alternative. What difference does this person's holding this alternative view make to the way he runs his life? Is it perhaps the rejection of the way *we* think that is the most significant thing here? How do his opinions on the equator hang together with the rest of his beliefs? – We might well expect him to have other ideas which are equally strange to the rest of us.

God & the Equator

The question of the existence of God resembles to a certain extent the question of the existence of the equator. It is perfectly in order to say, when faced with Otto's scepticism about the existence of God, that God is invisible, intangible, etc., and so of course undetectable. But it would be a mistake to think that this means that, apart from everything we can see, feel, and otherwise sense around us or detect with our instruments, we are affirming that there exists *in addition* an invisible being whom we call God. If we made a list of everything that exists in the universe, that list would not be defective if it omitted God, just as a list of everything on earth would not be defective if it omitted the equator. Nevertheless, Christians want to affirm the existence of God, even the *obvious* existence of God, just as most of us want to affirm the obvious existence of the equator. Only to say that is not to want to add one more item to a list of things existing. God is not something *extra*, any more than the equator is. And it is a symptom of our misunderstanding of our assertion of the existence of the invisible God if, in response to a denial of the existence of God, we re-affirm our belief and offer what we claim to be evidence in support of it, just as it would be a mistake to offer evidence in support of the existence of the equator. What we have to do, rather, is to explain, describe, the use of the word "God", to show the part it plays in our language and in our lives. Then it would also be possible to give some account of the *rejection* of God, that is, an account of the use of the sentence "God does not exist" or of refusal to use language about God. This too, if not based on a mistaken idea of belief in the existence of God as the adoption of a hypothesis on insufficient evidence or against strong counter-evidence, will hang together with other things atheists say and with things they do and refuse to do.

If we want to give somebody an explanation of certain phenomena, such that the seasons are arranged differently in the north and south hemispheres, that the water starts going down the plughole the other way, and so on, we might make reference to the equator. But that does not mean it is an *assumption* that the equator exists, an assumption made partly to account for these phenomena.

I want to suggest that, in the same way, it is not an assumption that God exists, even if the word "God" is used in sentences explaining why certain things are as they are (e.g. that Jesus rose from the dead, that I have these spiritual experiences, that the townspeople prayed and the town was saved from destruction, that the world exists, etc.). Though we make use of the word "God" in our explanations, the existence of God is not a hypothesis, mistaken or otherwise. The question whether God exists is not a factual question, a question about what we might find. It is a question whether to adopt the concept "God" (the word and its use) into the language, or to retain it. For me, the question of the existence of God is the question whether I can find a use for the word "God" in my talk, whether I find it useful or natural, or feel impelled, to accept some sentences containing the word "God" as true (be prepared to agree to them, repeat them in particular contexts, etc.) and reject others as false. And by no means all of those sentences, or even a large proportion of them, will be explanatory ones, for the explanatory use of the word "God" is by no means the only one, nor the most important; it hangs together with the use of the word in worship, prayer, the reading of scripture, talk about the meaning of life, what one must do, and so on. There is no reason why we should give the explanatory uses a privileged status, as is so often done in the philosophy of religion.

God and the world cannot be summed, just as the equator and the earth cannot be summed. In using sentences that make reference to the equator, even sentences asserting the existence of the equator, I am not trying to add to the contents of the earth. So, in using sentences referring to God, even sentences asserting the existence of God, I am not trying to add to the contents of the universe. If I say that the universe is the sum of all things, I do not make the universe larger by asserting the existence of God. This could be expressed by saying: God is not a thing. God is outside the world, not part of the sum of everything that there is. And a corollary to this is that whatever there is or might be, whatever you might want to put into a list of the contents of the universe, of the sum of existing things, of nothing on that list will it be true that it is God; anything on the list that is called God will be wrongly so called. That is to say, there is nothing, exists nothing, that can be called God. We might say, if we have a taste for the paradoxical, that God is nothing, does not exist. But this only means that there is nothing to which the word "God" corresponds as a name corresponds to an object. So while we may want to call God an invisible thing, that does not make him part of the world. An invisible thing is not like everything else, except that you cannot see it or touch it or smell it. An invisible thing, like a spirit, is not a kind of thing.

Just as you cannot, except as a joke, sum the equator and the earth, so you cannot, except as a joke, sum God and the world. In the former case, it would be misleading to say: This mark on the football pitch is a line, the equator is a line; that makes two lines. So too you cannot say: This chair exists, God exists; that makes two existents, two things. It is right then, in the sense that it is grammatically correct, to say that God exists. And it is also right to say that God does not exist, if by that is meant that God is nothing, in the sense I have outlined. There is nothing to be found which is God, and of whatever is found it must be said that it is not God. God is neither this nor that.

God & Absence

What value is there in this approach, in seeing God as nothing, not a thing, not a part of the universe? To begin with, it avoids all the difficulties and obscurities of the traditional 'arguments for the existence of God', and it avoids putting Christianity on such shaky foundations as might be established by these arguments. Secondly, it gives us an opportunity to characterise Christian belief in God as other than a conclusion that is based, or ideally ought to be based, on a particular kind of philosophising; it may be possible to do better justice to the observation that Christian belief is not surmise, that it occupies a quite different place in people's lives. Thirdly, and most importantly for my purposes (though this will turn out to be related to the second point), it enables us to give a much more positive role to the absence in the visible world around us of anything that might be called "God", an absence that is not accidental, a failed presence, but essential, insistence on it being a feature of the Christian aversion to idolatry; and it was this absence that caused Otto's original puzzlement. We do not have to pretend that it is really a presence in disguise, or apologise for it and try to make do with 'evidence'. Rather can we take it for what it is and use it to throw light on the way "God" functions, see it not as something to be got round but as typical of those situations that mystify Otto, situations in which God is talked about, talked to, reverenced, and so on. We will find that this approach is truer to the way language about God is actually used by Christians.

This will mean that Otto will after all have to learn to use words in new ways. He does not simply need more information, about beings that happen to be – unfortunately for apologetic purposes – invisible. He will have to learn new uses of language, since we do not ordinarily make absence a central feature of situations in which we talk about or to people or things. However, talk of God is far from unique in this respect. There are other occasions in which reference to absence is important in illuminating the way our words work. I will later go on to talk about some of these.

God & Charlie

A mark on a football pitch is a line, and the equator is also a line. Some of the things we say about them are the same: both are straight, both divide one area from another, both might appear on a sufficiently detailed map; and there may be other important similarities. But there are also significant differences between them: the one can occur anywhere you choose to mark out a football pitch, the other has a determined position, or it *is* a position. The one might fail to be straight if it is badly drawn; the other is straight by definition. The appearance of the one on a map has a different significance from the appearance of the other: if the line on a football pitch appears on a map, the line on the map represents the line on the pitch, and seeing the line on the map we expect to see a corresponding line on the ground, whereas if the equator appears on a map we do not expect to find a corresponding line on the ground; etc. We are well aware of these differences, and we are not blinded to them by the similarities.

Charlie is a person, and God also, we might want to say, is a person. Actually, things are a good deal more complicated than that in Christianity. We sometimes want to say that God is three persons. Still, there are also times when our talk makes a single person of God. When we speak of God we can use a masculine personal pronoun, just as we can when we speak of Charlie. Because he is a person, we talk to Charlie; we also talk to God. Because Charlie is a person, we can say of him the things that we say of persons; many of these things we can say also of God. Charlie gets angry sometimes, and so does God. (I know God gets angry, because I read so in the Bible or in other authoritative texts, or I am told so by parents, priests and theologians; and in these and other ways I learn many other things about God. And that means that it is from the Bible and from other people that I learn many of the things that *we say* about God.) Charlie loves his children, and so does God. Charlie likes to sit in an old armchair at his home in Wimbledon; God sits on a throne in heaven. Charlie once sent his son to France; God once sent his son to Palestine. Harry tells me that Charlie sometimes ventures forth from Wimbledon, and Habakkuk tells me that God once came from Paran, from Mount Teman (3:3. Habakkuk is an authority in Christianity). When he gets annoyed, Charlie sometimes stamps his foot; and so, according to Habakkuk, does God:

> In rage you trod the earth; in anger you trod down the peoples. (3:12)

Charlie likes to give people gifts, and so does God. People thank Charlie, and they also thank God. Charlie is very important, and so is God, so people ask them both for things and are careful to be respectful of both, careful to do what Charlie says and careful to do what God says. Some people are afraid of Charlie and some people are afraid of God. Some go to Charlie to ask his protection; some ask God for his protection. If you do what Charlie says he rewards you; if you do what God says, he rewards you.

We are familiar with all these ways, and many more, in which God is like Charlie. Because of these similarities, there is nothing wrong with calling God a person, just as we call Charlie a person. God and Charlie are quite alike, grammatically speaking; they have something of a family resemblance, just as the equator and a line marked on a football pitch do. But there are differences too in the former case, just as in the latter. And God and Charlie do not just differ as one individual differs from another. It is not just that God is very much bigger, more important, stronger, more tolerant, etc., than Charlie (not forgetting the detail that he is also invisible, bodiless). The differences between them are logical; the way we use the word "Charlie" is in many instances quite different and opposed to the way we use the word "God". The most striking difference between God and Charlie is that, while Charlie is somebody, God isn't anybody, he is nobody. "Charlie" is the name of a person, whereas "God" is not the name of a person, because it is not the name of anything. (Nevertheless, God is, of course, a person: "God is a person" is a sentence we have a use for. We might, for example, use it as a way of summarising all the undoubted similarities between God and Charlie. And we might do this without prejudice to our right to speak of God as three persons.)

It is principally the differences – the logical differences – between God and Charlie that I want to talk about, the differences between the ways we use "Charlie" and the ways we use "God". The point is to establish that you cannot, without producing confusion, add God and Charlie together to get two persons, just as you cannot, without producing confusion, add the equator and a line on a football pitch together to get two lines. As I have mentioned some of the logical differences between the equator and a line on a football pitch, so I want to point out a whole range of logical differences between God and Charlie; and all (or at any rate, most) of the differences I want to talk about stem from or are related to the observation that God is not a thing, that "God" is not the name of anything, or any person. That is to say, they are related to the fact that when Otto sees somebody doing what is called "talking to God", he does not see or otherwise detect somebody called God who is being talked to; to the fact that when he sees somebody doing what is called "obeying God", he does not see anybody called God who is being obeyed; to the fact that when somebody says that he has been helped by God, Otto has not been able to detect anybody who has been helping him; and so on.

God & Pain

The problem of the existence of God is related to the way the function of the word "God" is characterised in general. There is a parallel, I have suggested, with the (actually probably non-existent) problem of the existence of the equator. But there is also a parallel with the better known, because more interesting, case of the problem of the existence of other minds, which includes the problem whether other people really have sensations. The problem is that it seems I cannot know whether other people have sensations as I know that I do, for though I associate certain kinds of behaviour with the occurrence of particular sensations (I have learned to associate the two from my own case), I can only see other people's behaviour. I cannot observe their actual sensations, so for all I know they may all behave in ways that I associate with, say, pain yet not be having the actual sensation of pain. The actual pain of others, if they ever have pains, is not part of my observable world; it leaves everything that I can see just as it is. So I can never actually *know* that somebody else is in pain. On the other hand, I always know when I am in pain; "pain" is the name that I give to a particular kind of sensation I have, which I can always recognise when I have it (though of course nobody else can know what I call pain, since nobody else can observe my pain).

There is a similar problem about the existence of God. If we say that "God" is the name of a thing, then it looks as if the existence of that thing is actually irrelevant to religion. Since God is invisible, intangible, and the rest, he makes no difference to the observable world; everything carries on just as it does whether God really exists or not, just as other people's pain makes no difference to the observable world, but everything goes on just the same. People are in fact taught how to use sentences with "God" in them and do in fact use them, and they do perform all the various ritual actionns associated with religion. The use of "true" and "false" in relation to sentences containing the word "God" is also in fact taught. People claim that God has answered their prayers; others say that there is no God at all. All this talk and behaviour concerning God goes on, regardless of the fact that it cannot be established that God exists, just as I and others may talk about the pain of others, and others carry on behaving in the way I associate with my own pain, regardless of the fact that I cannot establish that others are ever really in pain. The real existence of God, like the real existence of other people's pain, seems to be irrelevant to what actually goes on, observably, in the world. Everything goes on, just the same, whether God exists or not, just as everything goes on the same, whether other people are in pain or not.

46

The situation with God and other people's pain, it might be said, is quite unlike that with, say, chairs. The question of the real existence of chairs does make a difference to the observable world, and it also makes a difference to what people do and say. Normally, if there is a chair in front of me, I can see that there is, and if there isn't, I can see that, too. Even if I am blind or suffering some optical illusion or hallucination, I am not at a loss, for I can settle the question whether there is really a chair there by feeling for it, or by trying to sit down on it. And then whether there is a chair there or not makes an observable difference to me and to my behaviour. And so it is useful to have the word "chair" in the language: now people can invite or command, "Sit down on that chair"; warn, "Mind you don't bump into that chair"; they can ask, "Where has that chair gone?"; chat about the chair they have just bought; write books on the history of chair design. But there are no such reasons for talking about pain (other people's pain) or God. If I had another word for my own pain, so that I only used the word "pain" to refer to other people's pain, then I could, if I wished, do without the word "pain" altogether; for it is only their behaviour that I need talk about, it is only that that makes a difference to the world. (But in fact I probably would need the word "pain" after all, since part of other people's behaviour that I might want to record is what they say; and some of their sentences use the word; they say, for example, "I am in pain".) I cannot see other people's pain; and that is not just an unfortunate accident, or due to my defective senses. It is a matter of logic. Other people's pains, if they really have them, are, like all their sensations, logically inaccessible, invisible, to me. It makes no sense to say "I see his pain" or "I feel his pain", since anything that I could see or feel would, for that very reason, not be his pain. Sensations are, we might want to say, in some sense *private*. In the same way we could do without the word "God" altogether, since God, if he exists, makes no difference to the observable world; and that not as an accident, but as a matter of logic. God, like pain, cannot be discovered, because anything whose existence might be discovered would by the same token be disqualified from being called God. If sensations are private, God is a *spirit*.

But all this is off beam. We *can* know that other people are in pain; we have a use for the sentence "He is in pain", or "I know he is in pain". (And the description of the use of those sentences also contributes towards elucidating the use of the word "know" in this context; or, if you like, it helps explain what we mean by the word "know" here). Similarly, we *can* say "I see his pain" or "I feel his pain", though these sentences are used differently and work differently from a sentence such as "I can see his chair"; e.g. the sentences or gestures we would continue with (perhaps 'explain our meaning with') if asked would be of a different kind in each case.

The strategy of somebody who says that we cannot know that others are in pain is to treat "pain" and "chair" as if they were alike, to treat "pain" as the name of something, just as "chair" is the name of something, and then proceed to show that "pain" does not do the job of naming that it ought, since pain is inaccessible, a private something. Whereas we have the word "chair" and we have access to chairs, we only have the word "pain", not to the pain itself that the word names. But this is only to say that it was a mistake to construe the working of the word "pain" on the model of that of the word "chair" in the first place. Once we abandon that model it is easier to see why we can say those things the model forbids us to say, use sentences the model forbids us to use.

In the *Philosophical Investigations* Wittgenstein has a long discussion (beginning at 243) on the way words for sensations, particularly "pain", function. At one point in the discussion he says:

> If I say of myself that it is only from my own case that I know what the word "pain" means – must I not say the same of other people too? And how can I generalise the one case so irresponsibly? Now someone tells me that he knows what pain is only from his own case! – Suppose everyone had a box with something in it: we call it a "beetle". No one can look into anyone else's box, and everyone says he knows what a beetle is only by looking at *his* beetle. – Here it would be quite possible for everyone to have something different in his box. One might even imagine such a thing constantly changing. – But suppose the word "beetle" had a use in these people's language? – If so it would not be used as the name of a thing. The thing in the box has no place in the language-game at all; not even as a *something*: for the box might even be empty. – No, one can 'divide through' by the thing in the box; it cancels out, whatever it is. That is to say: if we construe the grammar of the expression of sensation on the model of 'object and designation' the object drops out of consideration as irrelevant. (293)

But pain is not irrelevant; it makes a great deal of difference to people and the way they behave; and they talk about it. So it cannot be a private 'object' of which the word "pain" is the designation. And it is only construing it as such that appears to make it a problem whether other people are really in pain at any time. In the same way, we can say many things about this invisible God (we *do*). We can say, for instance, "I was helped by God"; "I *know* God hears me"; "God tells me what to do"; though these sentences work differently from, are used differently from, sentences like "I was helped by Charlie", "I know Charlie hears me",

"Charlie tells me what to do". We would expand these sentences, explain what we mean by them, in different ways. God is invisible, etc., so he is like a beetle in a box, only this time one that is inaccessible to everybody. And that means that if the word "God" has a use in our language, as it does, it is not used as the name of a thing; it does not function in the same way as "Charlie"; *we do not use* the word "God" in the same way as we use the word "Charlie". God, like pain, only begins to look irrelevant if his relation to "God" is construed on the model 'object and designation'; then this 'invisible object' "drops out of consideration as irrelevant". Like pain, God is not a *something*; the use of the word "God", like the use of the word "pain", has to be explained otherwise, or rather the description of its use will show that it is not the name of a something.

We sometimes want to say that sensations are private, and one way we are tempted to put this is to say that the beetle really is hidden from us in the box – inside somebody's head. And then "we should really like to see into his head" (*Philosophical Investigations* 427, where, however, the subject is thought-processes, not sensations). At the same time we know that this would be fruitless; sensations are not private in the sense of being hidden away from our sight in a box; they are *logically* private. Nothing counts as discovering a sensation, unless it is what we all mean when we say that we have discovered that somebody is, e.g., in pain, that they have a sensation. We could never stumble across a sensation in the street, so that we might say, "Look, there's a pain". We have no use for such a sentence. Whatever we can stumble across, point out, is *therefore* not a pain. We would not, then, try to teach somebody what "pain" means by showing him a pain, as we might teach the word "chair" by pointing out a chair. We would teach him it by explaining what it is for somebody to *have* a pain, or to be *in* pain; and that we would do perhaps by giving him a pain, but also by showing how people who are in pain behave. Pains can only appear to be intrinsically and mysteriously hidden from us if we are tempted to look for them in the wrong way, to look for one lying around on the pavement or in somebody's brain rather than looking at somebody who is in pain. So, too, God is hidden from us logically, which is to say he is not *hidden* from us at all; God only appears hidden because we are tempted to look for him. But just as we might be tempted to say that sensations are hidden in somebody else's head, so there is a temptation to say that God is hidden *in heaven*. And we really would like to take a peep into the heavens to see what God is like. But at the same time we recognise that any such attempt would be a waste of time. The heavens are not heaven, the 'place' of God, just as the head is not the 'place' of our sensations. Nothing counts as looking into heaven, nothing counts as seeing God (or otherwise perceiving him with the senses), except the sense, if any, that we give to the words "seeing God" or "experiencing God", and that is not the same kind of sense that we give to the words "seeing Charlie" or "seeing a chair". So we would not teach somebody the word "God" by showing him God, but by explaining what it is to believe in God, what we mean when we say that God does things, and so on.

Or again, we really would like to see the anger of God, for example, just as we want to see people's sensations. But we can see people's sensations, in a perfectly ordinary sense; we find a use for the phrase "seeing somebody's pain", though it is a different kind of use from that we have for, say, "seeing somebody's bicycle"; it is equivalent to seeing *that* somebody is in pain. And in the same way, just as we can see somebody else's pain, we can see or experience the anger of God. That is to say, we find a use for the phrase "experience the anger of God" or "see the anger of God", which amounts to "see that God is angry". In this sense God's anger can be revealed for all to see. So St. Paul writes:

> From heaven has been revealed the wrath of God upon all the impiety and injustice of men who unjustly suppress the truth... They claimed to be wise but became stupid, and exchanged the glory of the immortal God for the likeness and image of a mortal man and of birds and beasts and reptiles. So through the desires of their hearts God gave them over to the uncleanness of dishonouring their bodies with each other – those who exchanged the truth about God for a lie... And as they did not see fit to know God, God gave them over to an unfit mind, to do improper things, full of injustice.... (Romans 1:18, 22–25, 28)

Pictures of God

We can easily form pictures of God in heaven (just as we might picture to ourselves what is going on in somebody else's mind). And when we do that we picture God in a *place* (just as we picture what is going on in somebody else's mind as going on in a place). But we also want to say that God is not localised, not in a place, that heaven is not a place. But still, to picture God in heaven and to call heaven a place need not mislead so long as it is remembered that heaven is not a place as Wimbledon is a place. Though it is possible to get to Wimbledon from Esher, it is not possible to get to heaven from Esher. (Of course it is, but "getting to heaven" has a quite different use from "getting to Wimbledon"; for example, you cannot ask, except as a joke, what number bus you need to get to heaven from Esher. It is differences such as these that bring out the difference between what is meant by calling heaven a place and calling Wimbledon a place.) Heaven is not a place that has a spatial relationship to all other places, as Wimbledon has. If we want to call heaven a place, that does not mean that it is a place like any other, a member of the class of all places. It is discontinuous with all places; it is not part of but outside all space, outside the totality of places. And that does not make it a *strange* kind of place, one we find it hard to understand; heaven is not a kind of place at all, just as God, who is in heaven, is not a kind of thing. In calling heaven a place we are doing something strange with the word "place". Wimbledon is a place, and heaven is a place, but you cannot without causing confusion add them together to get two places. Heaven is outside the world, just as he who is in heaven is outside the world. This is shown by the fact that, though we can make for ourselves pictures of God in heaven, either literal pictures – paintings or drawings – or verbal pictures, we say of them that they are 'only' pictures. We do not claim that they are accurate representations of what is actually so. We do not claim that a picture of God is an accurate representation of God, in the same way that we might claim that a picture of Charlie is an accurate representation of Charlie. A picture of God does not correspond to God as a picture of Charlie corresponds to Charlie, and so neither does it *fail* to correspond to God in the same way that a picture of Charlie might fail to correspond to Charlie. You cannot get the colour of God's eyes wrong in the same way as you can get the colour of Charlie's eyes wrong; and that is because you cannot get it right, either. You can misrepresent God in a picture; but this is not to make a mistake, it is to have a wrong vision. The point of some icons is to give us a right vision of God, as is the point of much theology, which is one reason why icons can be important; both icons and theology teach what is to be held as a right view, and seek to correct inadmissible views.

We only have pictures of God, no original to compare them with. If there were an original, it could not be God, so anybody who called it a picture of God would be an idolater. It is essential to understanding them properly that we do not think of them as corresponding to an original (even an original that we can never see). A picture of God is not a picture of something (or of somebody). We show that we understand this, understand the right use of pictures of God, by, among other things, our willingness to accept and use several different, even contradictory pictures for different purposes or according to circumstance; by moving on from one to another without rejecting the former as false; by distinguishing between relevant and irrelevant details in pictures – the curve of the lips, the expression of the face, will be important, the colour of the eyes, not; by saying, "Of course, these are only pictures"; by being willing on occasion and for particular purposes to reject all pictures. (Which may be the same as proposing a *blank* as a picture of God. It is important that such a picture has no privileged status; it does not correspond to the original any more than the more imaginative pictures, since there is no original for it to correspond to.) And so on. We treat pictures of God in a very special way, quite unlike the way we treat pictures of Charlie; and that goes for verbal as well visual pictures, such as the descriptions of God in scripture (see, for example, Isaiah 6 and Daniel 7). All pictures of God are, though perhaps useful for some purposes, in the end dispensable. There is no definitive one, no divine passport photo, that shows us exactly what God is like (even though we cannot see him), so that all alternative pictures are inaccurate.If we are willing to entertain several different pictures of God, or none at all, this is not because they are all inaccurate, because 'no picture can show what God is really like'. How would we know? And what is the point of the 'really' here? Pictures of God do not show us a thing; they are not copies of an original, or descriptions of an original. If they were, it would be possible for us to get an accurate one in the end. And that would mean that we would also have to have some criterion of accuracy – we would have to *count* something as being accurate, if we are to count other things as inaccurate. The reason we treat pictures of God in this way is rather that nothing counts for us as showing what God is really like; if it did, we would not allow ourselves the freedom we do in our use of pictures of God. And so such pictures do not *fail* to show us what God is really like, either. Here again, this might be said of a particular picture. But that would be to say, not that it contains a mistake ("The colour of the eyes is wrong"), but that it expresses a wrong vision, conception, of God ("You present God as vindictive and selfish, whereas he is generous and forgiving"). There is no success or failure here. And if we do not count anything as showing what he is really like, that means that God is not like anything.

Sometimes we say that human language is inadequate to describe God. How do we know? Nobody ever discovered it; what, in any case, would such a discovery look like? And if our present language is inadequate, why not invent a language that is adequate? If we know beforehand that we cannot, that is because we have *determined* it beforehand. The determination is enshrined in the way we use language about God; and *we* have determined it, since the language in which we talk about God is, like the rest of our language, *our* language. If nothing counts for us as an adequate description of God, that is not because the task is so terribly difficult; it is because there is no such task. We place God beyond the boundaries of what can be described. But *everything* can be described: God is not part of the totality of things, a member of the universe. God is not a thing, so he is not an ineffable thing, either. The 'impossibility of describing God' comes from there being nothing there to describe.

55

But on the other hand, it is very easy to describe God: God is merciful, compassionate, omnipotent, omniscient, just, watchful, faithful; and God is everything that Jesus Christ shows him to be. But such a description of God is not a description of a something we know not what: what we call "a description of God" is not the same as what we normally call "a description of something"; the two phrases function in different ways. If I describe something to you, you can form a picture of what I am describing. If that picture corresponds to my description, if I accept it as corresponding to it, still it may be either correct or incorrect; it may or may not be what the thing is really like. But if I describe God to you, the picture you form is neither correct nor incorrect, for there is no question of its being or failing to be what God is really like. The description has a different relation to God from that which a description of something has to that thing.

All this is complicated by the doctrine that Jesus, who could be adequately represented pictorially, is, as the epistle to the Colossians says (1:15), himself "the image of the invisible God". But even if we say that he is the perfect image of God, still the fact that Jesus has long brown hair and soulful blue eyes does not show that God has long brown hair and soulful blue eyes; the invisible God does not have hair or eyes of any colour. Details like this are irrelevant in any picture of God – even his living image – in a way that they are not in pictures of things or people. In the latter case, any detail can be relevant or irrelevant, according to the kind of interest we happen to have in the thing pictured, what we are looking for in the picture. But in the case of God, we do not *happen* to have some interest or other. The kind of interest we can have in any picture of God is already narrowly circumscribed. We cannot go to a picture of God because we are interested in finding out the colour of God's eyes. There are in any case difficulties about the notion of adequately representing Jesus in a picture; we have no idea what Jesus looked like. Yet we do make pictures of Jesus. Such pictures, then, never have the point of presenting us with a likeness of Jesus, in the way that somebody might make a picture of Charlie so as to present us with a likeness of Charlie. If we talk about the adequacy or inadequacy of, say, an icon of Jesus, our concern is somewhat similar to the concern we have when we see an icon of the invisible God: not whether he really looked like that, but how it presents Jesus to us, what *picture* it gives us of him.

We can of course be concerned with a picture of Charlie in the same way. It can be for us a good picture or a bad one, an adequate one or an inadequate one, not according to whether it shows what he looks like but according to whether it gives a good picture of him. It can be a bad picture not only if it gets the colour of the eyes wrong, but also if it makes him look forbidding when really he is very approachable, or because it gives no hint of the permanent depression behind his smile.

But once again we can make sense of a comparison between the picture and what Charlie is really like; only here the comparison is between the impression the picture gives us of his character and his actual character as we can see it in his behaviour. There is no such comparison that we can make in the case of God. (Neither is there in the case of Jesus, unless we mean a comparison with an *authoritative account* of his behaviour, such as one of the gospels.)

A picture, verbal or pictorial, of God is not one that we hope corresponds to some inaccessible reality, an invisible thing (leaving aside the question of what would count as correspondence in such a case). Nothing corresponds to the description, the picture. And the frequently met idea that

God cannot be described actually points in the same direction: it says that God is not a thing, that God lies, logically, outside the world. It is like saying that a description of God is not a description in the way that a description of Charlie or of an economic crisis is, but functions in a different way. It is a grammatical reminder, like saying that the equator is not a line, which is not to say that it is impermissible to call it a line (it is our language, we do not need permission), but to remind us that when we call it a line we are doing something different from when we apply the same word to a line on a football pitch or a fishing line. And the point of the reminder is that forgetfulness can produce confusion.

The God Next Door

But to say "God is not a thing, God is nothing, there is nothing that is God" and the like, is not this to leave Christianity without foundation, built upon nothing, an insubstantial structure of baseless and pointless words and actions? Is it not to say that there is in reality no God? For when we say that God exists we surely mean that there really is something or somebody there, and it seems to be mere deception to take away that meaning while retaining the words.

But, first, it adds nothing to the discussion to insist that when we say God exists we mean that God *really* exists, that there is *really* somebody there, that God is real, and the like. The function of the words "real" and "really" here, if they have any, itself stands in need of elucidation. We cannot say, as if there were nothing further to be said, "You know what reality is. You know what it is for a chair to be real. Well, with God it's just the same; God is real too." Second, it is not obvious how "God exists" is to be understood, even though it may be obvious *that* it is understood, that many people use it quite competently. But to be able to use words

58

competently is not the same as to be able to give an accurate account of the use of those words. That is a specialised task, and none too easy. And it does not particularly help towards such an account to say that when we say God exists we mean there is somebody there.

For it is not clear in this case what we mean by that, not yet obvious with what sentences we might want to expand this one, what expectations it might arouse, and so on. That is so, even though it may be clear in all sorts of other cases what we mean when we say that somebody is there. For example, if we say there is somebody there, in the next room, we know what it is like for that to be true. If we went next door, we would expect to *find* somebody, unless they are well concealed (and we know what counts as finding somebody, and also what counts as being concealed). But this is just what we do *not* expect when we say that God is there, if we do say that. We might perhaps find occasion to say that God is in the next room, but we would not expect to *find* him there, and anything we did find would not be God.

In what circumstances might we say that God is next door? Perhaps most of us never would say that. But religious language is a fluid thing, and there might be situations where somebody wanted to. Here is a possible case: We believe that God is present with anybody who retires to a room alone to pray. We might come to such a belief, not through discovering it to be a regular law, since necessarily we never discover God in rooms with people who are praying, but through reading some theologian or pondering the words of Jesus in Matthew: "When you pray, go into your room and shut the door and pray to your Father who is in secret; and your Father who sees in secret will reward you" (6:6). A few moments ago we saw Sebastian slip into his room next door and close the door, to pray as is his wont. So we can now say with confidence that

59

God is with him in that room. But we say God is there not because we find or expect to find him there, but because we know that Sebastian is there, praying. If we suddenly burst in next door, and saw him praying, that would confirm us in our belief that God was there, and we would need no other confirmation. In particular, we would not expect to find God there. We might see some apparition there before the kneeling Sebastian, and that would surprise us very much. But we would not identify the apparition as God. (We might say it is a saint or an angel.) The fact that we already know that God is with Sebastian but are surprised to see the apparition suggests in itself that the two are not to be identified. Our criteria for the presence of God are the solitude and activity of Sebastian, nothing more. That does not mean that God is really not there at all, any more than the fact that our criteria for a man's suffering unbearable pain relate to his visible behaviour – that we say somebody is in agony because of how we see him acting – means that there is only the behaviour, that a man who behaves in the appropriate way is not suffering pain at all. (Though of course it is possible to simulate pain-behaviour, and anybody who does that is not in pain; and in the same way it is possible for Sebastian to be pretending to pray, in which case God is not there with him.) The point is that in this case we have visible criteria for determining the presence of God – and since our language about God and its application have to be learned empirically, what other kind of criteria might there be? The criteria do not involve the detection of an invisible (undetectable) presence. That is to say, we can establish empirically the presence of God in the absence of anything that we might call God. And this absence is something that we ourselves guarantee, since we would refuse the name "God" to anything or anybody that we did discover there.

We might note here that since the absence of anything we might call God is not established empirically, it is pointless to urge the sceptical argument that we can never conclusively establish the absence of something empirically, because of the possibility of camouflage, defective senses, etc. Not only is it false that we can never empirically establish something's absence, but even if it were true it would not be to the point, for the most it could establish, if God were a thing whose presence might be tested for empirically in this way, would be that *just possibly* God is there despite all appearances to the contrary.

The presence of God is not the presence of a *something*; we do not use the phrase "presence of God" in that way. "God" is not the name of a something we know not what, which is present when God is present. There is nothing that is God, but it is very easy to establish empirically the presence of God next door. So if Otto is with us when we burst into Sebastian's room, and we say to him, "God is present in this room with this man", we shall not be disconcerted if he points out that there is nothing and nobody there with him. We can see that as well as he can. We shall not claim that there is somebody there whom he cannot detect, for we see no sign of him, either – and we know that there *could* be no sign of him. We shall rather explain to him why we say what we do, explain to him that Sebastian is praying, refer him to the gospel of Matthew or to our favourite theologian, and so on.

It could be objected that the conclusion can only be that there is nothing earthly or material that is God. And that everybody admits: God is a heavenly, spiritual being. Yes, but what do these two adjectives "heavenly" and "spiritual" mean? They mean only: not earthly, not material. They certainly do not mean that God is in another place, heaven, for heaven is not another place; and in any case we want to say that he is next door. Nor that he is made of some undetectable stuff called "spirit". Stuffs are detectable; that is what makes them stuffs. And whence suddenly this extra purported sphere of existence, whence this contrast between two categories of being, the earthly and material and the heavenly and spiritual? There is nothing wrong with using these words to make a contrast we are interested in; only we must be careful not to be confused about the nature of the contrast we are making. The words "heavenly" and "spiritual" are part of an earthly, material language, spoken by earthly, material people, taught and learned by them in an earthly, material environment. If they are to have any meaning, that is to say any established use, then it must be possible to establish such a use, to say when and where they are appropriately used. And that means that they must be taught and learned like any other word; their use must be governed by earthly, material criteria. We can establish the presence of the heavenly, spiritual God, but not by detecting, *per impossibile*, the presence of something that is heavenly and spiritual; we do it by seeing an earthly, material man saying his prayers, *and nothing else*. I repeat: we establish the presence of God in the absence of, or without trying to establish the presence of, anything that we might call God. That is part of the way the phrase "presence of God" works. And because we establish the presence of God in *this* way, because we say "God is there" in *these* circumstances (rather than, say, when we see or feel or smell something), we say that God is a spiritual, heavenly being. These adjectives do not pick out a class of being; God is not a something, so he is not a spiritual something, either. The words "heavenly" and "spiritual" serve as logical markers to remind us that we do not use the word "God" as the name of something, so that, among other things, we establish the presence of God in quite a different way from how we establish the presence of Charlie.

There is another connexion here between talk of God and talk of sensations. If we think of pains, for instance, as things people have internally, just as they have warts externally, then they can come to seem peculiar and strangely inaccessible things. All we can get at to establish that somebody is in pain is his behaviour, not the pain itself. But this is an illusory difficulty, a logical one. We do not count anything as getting at the pain itself. It is part of the logic of the word "pain" that the way we establish when people have a pain is very different from the way we establish they have a wart – mostly by looking at their behaviour (not *only* by looking at their behaviour. See *Philosophical Investigations* 245). It is only misconstruing the logic of the word that makes pains and other sensations seem such strange things. The things that Wittgenstein has to say about pains are not designed to show that there are really no sensations, but to banish the illusion that they are strange and elusive things. This is also part of the point of my talking about God as nothing, or as not a thing, of stressing the importance of the notion of absence in connexion with out talk about God. I do not aim to deny the existence of God, but to point up aspects of the logic of "God". If it seems a bit bald and misleading to say simply that God is nothing, still, he isn't a something, either. Compare here another of Wittgenstein's remarks on the way language about sensation works:

"But you will surely admit that there is a difference between pain-behaviour accompanied by pain and pain-behaviour without any pain?" – Admit it? What greater difference could there be? – "And yet you again and again reach the conclusion that the sensation itself is a *nothing*." – Not at all. It is not a *something*, but not a *nothing* either! The conclusion was only that a nothing would serve just as well as a something about which nothing could be said. We have only rejected the grammar which tries to force itself on us here... "Are you not really a behaviourist in disguise? Aren't you at bottom really saying that everything except human behaviour is a fiction?" – If I do speak of a fiction, then it is of a *grammatical* fiction. (*Philosophical Investigations* 304, 307)

Absence and the Presence of God

But this still, we might think, looks very much like inventing something out of nothing, conjuring God up out of thin air, making talk of God a mere verbal trick. And if the presence of a spiritual being is defined simply as the absence of a material being, i.e. any being at all, then "the presence of God" is a grossly misleading phrase. In any case that surely cannot be what we are doing when we talk about the presence of God. When anybody talks about the presence of God, they mean not an absence but a real presence, and a very important one at that. And it is not just a theoretical presence, in which we believe just because we are told to. Many people have had very forceful experiences of the presence of God, e.g. when praying or in great danger, and this has sometimes had an enormous influence on their lives. How could a mere absence be the source of such experiences, how could it have such an effect?

I am not saying that when people talk about the presence of God they are really talking about an absence. But for God to be present is not what it is for, say, a chair to be present. The presence of a chair is established primarily by seeing it, bumping into it, etc.; that is, by detecting what we call a chair, and regardless of whatever else may or may not be present. The presence of God is not so established, but by, for instance, seeing a man saying his prayers. The presence of God is established without detecting anything called God, and indeed without attempting to detect it. It is established without reference to anything other than the praying man. It is established in the absence of anything called God; for if anything is present apart from the praying man, it is irrelevant to establishing the presence of God. So what people may feel when they (for example) pray may be an important, even an overwhelming experience, but it is not the presence of a thing called God, since there is no such thing present, nor could there be.

This does not mean that such experiences are all delusive, as an atheist would claim. That claim rests on the same mistaken view of how the word "God" works, that it is to be construed as the name of something, like the word "Charlie". An experience of the presence of Charlie is delusive if Charlie is not in fact present; and there are ways of determining whether he is present. I may suddenly wake up one night in terror, with an overpowering sense that Charlie is standing there in my room. Now I can check whether he really is there by turning on the light and looking around the room, checking in cupboards, and maybe in the corridor outside in case he slipped out of the room quietly just as I woke up. If I find nothing, then I conclude I was wrong. Charlie was never there, and my sense of his presence was delusive. Calling it delusive, then, is bound up with there being methods of checking, of *establishing* that it is delusive. And those methods include looking for Charlie. Similarly with a true or veridical sense of Charlie's presence. If I turn on the light, look to the middle of the room and there he is, then I was right; and my being able to say I am right depends on there being a way of establishing that I am right, a way that includes looking for him. And it is essential to the notion of looking for Charlie that the search can turn out either way; if one result or the other was assured *a priori*, then it could not be the result of a search.

But the case is quite other with God. If I suddenly have an overpowering sense of the presence of God, I precisely do not look round to see whether he is really there. It is not that I carry out such a test, as I would test for the presence of Charlie, with negative results, as the atheist might think; not that there might have been a thing called God there and in fact there is not. I cannot search, for what I would find is already established *a priori*; it would not be a finding. I already know that I will not find God by looking; if I do find something when I look, it will not be God, since there is nothing that I will be prepared to call God.

Perhaps people do sometimes feel the presence of God (we may sometimes want to say that of ourselves or others – and we may also want to distinguish between true and false feelings of the presence of God); but if they do, they feel that presence in the absence of anything called God. And here 'absence' is not a contingent, discovered absence, a failed presence, but a logical one, like the absence of square circles; we prescribe it *a priori* by refusing to give the name "God" to anything whose presence we might discover. Just as we have no use for the sentence, "Look! There's a square circle", so we have no use for the sentence, "See, there is God!" (No use, that is, for it as marking the discovery of God, the conclusion of a search. We could not use it, in orthodox Christianity, while pointing to an object we wanted to call God, or while indicating the sudden activity of a meter on a presence-detecting machine. It is of course easy to think of a use for it in the context of a *picture* – for instance, while pointing out to somebody the characters on the ceiling of the Sistine chapel.)

If there is a feeling of the presence of God, it is a feeling that people have been taught to call "the feeling of the presence of God". They have learned what is to count as a feeling of the presence of God, the kind of situation in which it makes sense to claim to feel the presence of God, etc. And the circumstances in which that sort of thing is learned do not include the presence of an invisible, intangible thing called God. If they did include it, it could never be established that the correct circumstances held, so the phrase could never be properly taught or learned; but it *can* be taught and learned.

But still, is it plausible to say that when people experience, and are struck by, the presence of God, they are really experiencing, are really struck by, an absence? No, that is not plausible, but I do not say they experience an absence; on the contrary, they experience the presence of God. (Though there might also be circumstances in which we want to say that people do experience the absence of God; but those are different circumstances.) But if people feel this presence, it is not the presence of a thing called God that they feel, for they feel it in the absence of anything called God. (And when they feel the absence of God, they do not feel the absence of a thing called God.) And in feeling the presence of God they are not struck by an absence; it is not a case of: "That's odd – I have the peculiar feeling that something's missing". The sense is of a presence, not an absence. They are struck, not *by* an absence, but *in* an absence – in the absence of anything called God.

CHAPTER 3

THE IMPORTANCE OF NOT BEING SOMETHING

Déjà Vu

Far from making talk of the presence of God empty, even making all talk about God empty, this element of absence I have been talking about can be exactly what gives it its significance and its importance. Think of the case of *déjà vu*. You say, or want to say, "I have been here before", or "This has happened to me before", or "I have done this before", or "I have seen this before". There are many kinds of circumstance in which we might want to say that sort of thing, but what characterises *déjà vu* is that you want to say it even when you know that you have not been there before, that this has not happened to you before. Indeed, it is precisely *because* you have not been there before that you want to say, "I have been here before", and say it with a particular tone of voice, a particular expression, as something uncanny, weird, significant. In the other circumstances where you might want to say this, it is with a different tone of voice, a different expression: "Don't worry. I've been here before; I know what to do"; "I don't care what you say; I *have* been here before, I *know* I have. I'm not going mad"; "Oh, I have been here before, after all. I'd forgotten all about it"; and so on. But all these are situations where you believe you have been there before.

When the man who experiences *déjà vu* says, "I've been here before", it is not because he believes he has been there before; he feels impelled to say it, despite the fact that he knows he has not been there before. So he is not using these words to convey any belief or information. So neither is he

68

giving a false account of his beliefs or false information. He is neither lying nor mistaken. So it would be inappropriate to try to correct him, to say, "No, you were in the cathedral at Cologne; it's very similar to this one", or "No, I know for certain that this is the first time you have ever been to Ulan Bator". He is not making a mistake and would not see himself as corrected. He would not say, "Oh, I see; I must be wrong, then". His reply would be different, if he had the concept of *déjà vu*; he would say something like, "No, I don't mean that; It's *déjà vu*". And that is the end of the matter. (Though it might be through such 'correction' that a person first learns the concept of *déjà vu*, learns in what circumstances it is appropriate to say of himself or somebody else that he is experiencing *déjà vu*.)

Here a comment of Wittgenstein is relevant:

> The way music speaks. Do not forget that a poem, even though it is composed in the language of information, is not used in the language-game of giving information. (*Zettel* 160)

In an analogous way, expressions of *déjà vu* use sentences that in other – perhaps most other – circumstances are used to give information, but they are not used in that way here; here they are not used "in the language-game of giving information". When "I've been here before" is said as an expression of *déjà vu*, it does not pretend to give information. So neither is it based on any evidence or otherwise grounded; it is not an inference from evidence or from anything else. Nor is it a matter of belief or knowledge not based on evidence. Belief is not in question here. The sentence is more akin to an exclamation.

Nevertheless, though it does not convey information, or even attempt to, what is said is not idle; it has a use as the expression of *déjà vu*. And though it is not an information-bearing experience, *déjà vu* is still widely regarded as a significant experience (even if it might be difficult to say in what way it is supposed to be significant). It is just *because* in this case, in these circumstances, the words "I've been here before" – words which everybody knows are normally used to give information – do not convey (true or false) information that it is significant that you want to say them. It is not a matter of ignorance of the normal uses of such a sentence. And it strikes you as significant that you want to say it; you perhaps interrupt the flow of conversation to say it, draw particular attention to what you want to say, say it in a particular tone of voice, accompany it with certain gestures, adopt a particular bodily attitude, or remember it, recount it to others afterwards. It would not be surprising to find people connecting the experience with the supernatural.

It is possible to imagine a society in which what in our society is called *déjà vu* is a recognised form of religious experience, where it is understood as, say, a memory of an event in a previous life, a memory of an extrabodily experience, a glimpse into somebody else's soul, a warning from the gods that what is about to happen will be invested with significance and stand in need of interpretation, or a sign that he who has the experience has a priestly vocation or other supernatural powers. In such a society the experience would not be regarded as we regard it – as an admittedly curious experience, slightly weird, but to which no determinate meaning is attached. It might rather be regarded with awe, reacted to by the reciting of certain words, the performance of certain rites, by taking off the one who had the experience for training as a priest, or by shunning him or drowning him.

But this is not quite right. I am assuming here that we can speak of our having the *same* experience as they do, only we react to it differently. This is a false assumption. The typical situation in which we learn the concept of *déjà vu* would be something like this: I say, "I've been here before", in a struck sort of way, and somebody who knows my history well says, "No you haven't; that's what's called '*déjà vu*'". Or I go to a friend and say, "I had this funny experience this morning. I went to such and such a place and it seemed to me I recognised the street, the buildings, even the people; it all seemed so familiar. Yet I know for a fact I have never been anywhere near there before in my life". And I am told, "Yes, I get that too sometimes; it's called '*déjà vu*'. Peculiar, isn't it?" We then learn to recognise *déjà vu* in ourselves and in others. We learn how to apply the words "*déjà vu*", and part of that learning will be to distinguish the circumstances in which it is appropriate to call a sentence like "I've been here before" an expression of *déjà vu* from those in which it is appropriate to call it a true (correct) memory, and from those in which it is appropriate to call it a false memory. And it will be appropriate to call it an expression of *déjà vu* if I or others want to use it in circumstances roughly like those in which I first learned the phrase *déjà vu*. But now suppose that in another society people also sometimes say, "I've been here before", etc., in a struck sort of way, and are told, not "No, that's *déjà vu*", but "That is a memory from a previous life", or "This is a visit to you from one of the gods, who has come to choose you for his priest". Then what people learn in that society is not the concept of *déjà vu* but the concept of a memory from a previous life, or of a visit from one of the gods. It is not that they learn the concept of *déjà vu*, but then go on to invest it with a greater or more determinate significance than we do, perhaps making inferences from it about former lives or the gods. There is no reason to suppose that any inferences are being made on the basis of the experience. It is not that people form hypotheses about the existence of previous lives when they hear others say, "I've been here before", in circumstances where they

71

know they have not. They simply react differently to what is said from the way we do. They therefore end up with a different concept. That concept may be expressed in a form that we would normally understand as an information-bearing sentence, such as "That is a memory from a previous life", or "That was a visit from a god", etc.; but it no more seeks to convey information than the initial "I've been here before" to which it is part of the response. What is going on here is the teaching and learning of the use of words, of concepts, not the instilling of beliefs. But it is important that their reacting to the initial utterance in this way would probably only make sense to us if the experience was thereby given a place in some wider network of religious beliefs and practices. (Though part of what I want to show by this example is that, at least in some instances, holding a religious belief is as well or better described as having acquired, and using, a particular concept.) The things people do and say become intelligible by being related to other things they say and do, so that we can see their behaviour, their way of life, as a whole.

Which is not to say the things they say and do then appear perfectly reasonable. If we were actually to come across a society like that we should probably dismiss its members' talk of spiritual experiences and say, "It's only *déjà vu*". But that would only be to insist on the language *we* speak, the language *we* have learned (or a language directly translatable into it), and not the language they have learned. It would be to insist on describing what is going on in the concepts familiar to us, and rejecting theirs. And that means also to be determined to stick to the *way of life* that we know, and to reject theirs, to refuse to entertain it as a possibility. For it is part of the way of life that we lead that we sometimes react to what we and others say by saying, "It's *déjà vu*". We do not try to fit certain utterances of the type "I've been here before" into our system of memories, into our scheme of the world. And neither would we relish risking being taken off to a seminary to be trained as a priest, or something of the sort, every time we had *déjà vu*. Not only would we not like it, we would not see the point of it. For it would have point only within the wider context of this people's way of life, and that context is one we reject, one in which we would not like to find ourselves. We do not attach any practical consequences to *déjà vu*; we have not been trained to do so, and we are happy with the way of life in which that is so. Calling certain experiences "*déjà vu*" and certain utterances "expressions of *déjà vu*" is part of our way of shunting them into a siding, so that they play no further part in the way we manage our lives, do not affect what we do or how we see ourselves.

There is a temptation to say, "What we call *déjà vu* really is just *déjà vu*, and not any kind of spiritual experience". But that is only to say that what we call "*déjà vu*" we call "*déjà vu*" and not "a memory from a previous existence", " a visit from a god", or suchlike. That is, it is not that in saying this we give anybody any information about what *déjà vu* really is. In that sense, it is to say nothing except that we use the concepts we use and not the concepts other societies use. But this can be a significant thing to say, significant in terms of our lives. It means that we are *determined* to treat certain utterances in the way we do treat them, and not in the way the other society treats them. It is a rejection of their way of life. For most of us, it is not even a matter of a decision to reject it, to cling to our own way of life. The way the others carry on seems absurd; it would be impossible for us, in our right minds, even to think of adopting it. We do not even get as far as forming a judgement on it.

But we can imagine that some of us might react differently. For some of us the reaction which treats such utterances as visits from gods, or memories of former lives, might seem a possible one, or even an illuminating one, a satisfying one. And that would mean that they saw the corresponding way of life, or something like it, as possible for themselves. Think of the way religious converts, particularly converts to alien religions, are often prepared, if not eager, to abandon the way of life we regard as normal to adopt strange ways of behaving – cutting their hair in peculiar ways, wearing funny clothes, walking through shopping centres banging drums and chanting unintelligibly, refusing to eat beans, etc. But to see another way of life as possible, another way of talking about the world as illuminating, is not to be so closely wed to our way of life as perhaps most of us are. To people who reacted in this way, our way of life would by no means appear obviously the 'right' one, the 'rational' one. And perhaps that would manifest itself in the way they live our way of life. They might be people on the fringes, people we should regard as a little odd, who do not take part in mainstream activities, who are restless, perhaps always flirting with oriental religions, or take themselves off to join monasteries, in whose eyes we may sometimes fancy we detect strange looks. Think here of: "What kind of person could believe that?" or: "He must be really odd to be able to believe that sort of thing". The kind of thing you can believe, that is the kind of concepts you can find it illuminating or satisfying to use in describing and reacting to your world, depends on and shows the kind of person you are – the way you live, or the ways you are prepared to live.

Neither do we have any warrant for saying that the experience that in this other society is called, say, "a memory of a former existence" is the *same* as the one we call "*déjà vu*", except that they interpret it differently (or perhaps that they interpret it in their way, whereas we do not interpret it at all). It is not that there is some basic phenomenon that we interpret in one way and they in another, unless it be that in both kinds of experience people say, "I have been here before" etc. But then that is also what people say when they have true memories, and when they have false memories (and no doubt in many other cases too). But these three – true memories, false memories and *déjà vu* – we do distinguish from one another; and so we must also distinguish them all from the experience that these other people have. All these are distinguished from each other by the way we react to them and by the part we allow them to play in our lives.

So is it right to say that when these people say they have spiritual experiences on certain occasions when they utter words like "I've been here before" they really are having spiritual experiences, and not just *déjà vu*? On similar occasions in our society we should treat such utterances as cases of *déjà vu*. And that is what we mean when we say that of course what these people experience is only *déjà vu* and has no spiritual significance at all. But it *is* neither the one thing nor the other before it is *treated* as the one or the other. So neither is it *really* the one or the other before it is treated as the one or the other. It is not that in treating it as *déjà vu* we have somehow got it right, reacted to it in accordance with 'its essential nature' or 'how it is in itself'. Its essence is how it is treated. So neither have these other people made a mistake about its essential nature, apprehended it wrong. When we reject what they say it is not because we think they have made a mistake, but because we do not or cannot *react* in the same way as they do, because we have already established or been trained into our own patterns of reaction, which fit in with the whole of our way of life.

Mistakes occur *within* conceptual systems, within patterns of reaction. For example, if somebody says, "I've been

75

here before", I might react by saying, "No you haven't. You must have made a mistake, your memory is playing tricks on you". And then I may correct myself, or be brought to correct myself: "Oh, yes, I remember now; you did come here once, years ago". And in the same way this other people might want to distinguish true memories of former lives from false ones. For example, a true one might only be able to come after the person concerned has gone through a particular kind of preparation (i.e. what is said will only be *called* a true memory from a former life if such preparation has been gone through); or perhaps such memories only come on wednesdays; etc. Then a reaction to "I've been here before" might be, "This isn't what you think it is. It is no memory from a former life, for you have not been prepared for it"; or, "This is an illusion, for it's the wrong day for such memories. – Oh, no it isn't. Sorry, I thought it was tuesday today".

Suppose one of these people had the experience that people in his society call a memory from a former life, and we wanted to give a report of it to people in our own society. It would be quite wrong, a misleading report, to say that he had *déjà vu*, for what we call *déjà vu* has quite a different place in our society from that occupied by what they call a memory from a former life or a visit from one of the gods. It would be wrong to say, for instance, "He had an experience of *déjà vu*, and everybody round him fell on their knees and said ritual prayers". To say that they did all that just because he had *déjà vu* is to make them look stupid or mad. There might just possibly be independent reason for thinking that they are all stupid or mad, but there might also be evidence that they are neither: they are all able to manage their lives perfectly competently, perhaps they all have good degrees in a variety of disciplines, are capable of holding an intelligent conversation on all sorts of topics, have a good sense of what is and what is not done in polite society; and so on. To say that he experienced *déjà vu* is to presuppose all the ways that we react that *make* the experience one of *déjà vu*. And if you do that, then of course the way they react is bound to seem stupid, since it is behaviour that is quite inappropriate as a reaction to *déjà vu*. On the other hand, it might be behaviour completely appropriate as a reaction to what they know as a kind of spiritual experience. Here compare Wittgenstein's criticism of Frazer:

> Even the idea of trying to explain the practice – say the killing of the priest-king – seems to me wrong-headed. All that Frazer does is to make this practice plausible to people who think as he does. It is very queer that all these practices are finally presented, so to speak, as stupid actions. But it never does become plausible that people do all this out of sheer stupidity. When he explains to us, for example, that the king must be killed in his prime because, according to the notions of the savages, his soul would not be kept fresh otherwise, we can only say: where that practice and these views go together, the practice does not spring from the view, but both of them are there. It may happen, as it often does today, that someone will give up a practice when he has seen that something on which it depended is an error. But this happens only in cases where you can make a man change his way of doing things simply by calling his attention to his error. This is not how it is in connexion with the religious practices of a people; and what we have here is *not* an error.(*Remarks on Frazer's Golden Bough* p.1f.)

But would it be correct then for us to say, "He had a memory from a former life, a visit from a god, was temporarily possessed by the spirit of the place, and so everybody fell on their knees, and said prayers"? Most of us would say obviously not, for we just don't believe in that kind of thing – we do not live like that. Perhaps there is nothing that counts as an accurate description, just like that, of what happened. In order to make sense of it (and that would include not having to think that all these people are stupid), it would be necessary first of all to explain the context in the life of the people into which certain experiences, which they think of as spiritual, are fitted. – And the kind of way they are fitted into the life of the people would also make clear what is meant by calling such experiences spiritual. We can say broadly, in this context, that what makes an experience a spiritual one is the way it is reacted to. To call an experience spiritual is to react to it in one or more of a range of ways. To the atheist or anti-religious person there may be no such thing as a spiritual experience, just as there is no realm of the spiritual; but what this means is that he is not prepared to *do* certain things, which may strike him as absurd. It is to get things the wrong way round to say a reaction like falling on one's knees or undertaking a fast has to be licensed by an independent proof that the experience is spiritual.

Only once we have seen the way such experiences fit into their lives could we be said to understand the report of a particular occurrence involving one of those experiences. In the same way, one of them might well require such an account of the context of *our* way of life in order to make sense of actions of ours which to us are obviously reasonable. To insist on describing the experience as one of *déjà vu* would be to make a judgment on these people, to dismiss them as stupid. On the other hand, to describe it straightforwardly as some kind of spiritual experience would be to express a sympathy with that description, to see it as a possible one, even a natural one. And that means being sympathetic to that people's way of reacting to it that makes it a spiritual experience, seeing a point to that reaction, perhaps feeling an inclination to react in a similar way. And since that reaction is not isolated but forms part of a pattern of life, that means seeing the possibility of living in a similar way. And so anthropologists and others who go to share in the way of life of foreign societies also sometimes find themselves becoming more sympathetic to the beliefs of those societies. They come to see how people can believe that sort of thing by coming to see how they can live like that; and they come to understand how people can live like that by themselves living like that. That way of life now seems genuinely human, instead of being some grotesque aberration. They understand one more possibility of the human animal that they are.

For example, Evans-Pritchard lived and worked among the Azande, a people of the southern Sudan. One of the most important ways the Azande have of managing affairs is apparently by reference to the *benge* oracle: the answer to somebody's question is determined by whether or not a bird survives a dose of *benge*, a specially prepared poison. (Though they do not see it as poison; they have no concept "poison", according to Evans-Pritchard.) This may a seem to us a ludicrous way to run a life, quite without rational foundation; we could never see ourselves allowing the course of our life and our major decisions to be determined in such a way. Yet the Azande, who show no signs of all being mad, do not find it ludicrous and do run their lives like that (or did in the late 1920's, the date of Evans-Pritchard's studies). Evans-Pritchard is very much a westerner, but his stay among the Azande makes it impossible for him to have a dismissive attitude to their practices and the beliefs accompanying them. Towards the conclusion of his book *Witchcraft, Oracles and Magic among the Azande* he writes of the Zande magical beliefs and attitudes to oracles:

When a writer brings them together in a book and presents them as a conceptual system their insufficiencies and contradictions are at once apparent.

Yet:

They only appear inconsistent when ranged like lifeless museum objects. When we see how an individual uses them we may say that they are mystical but we cannot say that his use of them is illogical or even that it is uncritical. I had no difficulty in using Zande notions as Azande themselves use them. Once the idiom is learnt the rest is easy, for in Zandeland one mystical idea follows on another as reasonably as one common-sense idea follows on another in our own society. (p.540f.)

But this is only to say that for the Azande these 'mystical' ideas just are commonsensical, and are rendered such by the place in their lives they give to them and to the activities in which they are embedded. To get his information, Evans-Pritchard had to give them a place in his own life, so he too came to find them reasonable:

I never found great difficulty in observing oracle consultations. I found that in such matters the best way of gaining confidence was to enact the same procedure as Azande and to take oracular verdicts as seriously as they take them. I always kept a supply of poison for the use of my household and neighbours and we regulated our affairs in accordance with the oracles' decisions. I may remark that I found this as satisfactory a way of running my home and affairs as any other I know of. (p.270f.)

Ghosts
When we experience *déjà vu* we say we have been there

before when we know we have not. We are not mistaken, and we do not lie, for we are not trying to convey information. Yet we may speak with absolute seriousness and conviction, and be impressed and want to impress others with the importance of the experience, just *because* we feel impelled to use these words outside their normal context, not for their normal use in giving information. Though the circumstances make our use of these words a little unusual, we are not merely playing with words here. Though somebody from a society where people never used these words in such a context might find it difficult to understand what we are doing with them, this is no light-hearted attempt to baffle, no joke. We are *impelled* to say this, perhaps against our will, perhaps fearing that we will sound stupid, even though we know that in terms of the normal use of the words the circumstances are inappropriate: that is the reaction of this linguistic animal. And because this impulsion is to something unusual, apart from the run of our normal behaviour, it is natural to see it as significant; it impresses.

Take also the case of ghosts and spirits; think of the language we use in connexion with them and the circumstances in which we might use it. We go into a dark library late at night in an old, rambling, unfamiliar house. We sense a presence; we want to say that there is somebody or something there, and this despite overwhelming evidence that there is nobody there: all the lights are out, nobody has been seen in the vicinity, and in any case this is an isolated, seldom visited part of the house; we have had to struggle with an old key in a rusty lock before we could get into it. Despite all that evidence, it might actually turn out that there is somebody or something there after all. Perhaps we turn on the light suddenly to reveal an intruder crouching in the corner, or a rat scurrying across the floor. So we were right in our suspicions. But on the other hand we might make a thorough search and establish positively that the place is quite empty, that there is nobody there, that our suspicions were wrong – and *still* want to say that there is somebody there, or something, some – *thing*. Once again we want to say what we *know* is not the case, for we know that there is nobody there – we have just established it. And it is just *because* we know that there is nobody there that our inclination to say that there is is significant, important for us, and frightening in a special way; so we speak in a particular tone of voice, hold our body in a particular way, speak with frightened, staring eyes, let our mouth hang open. There may be all kinds of things that make us want to say this – noises like the creaking of floorboards, heavy breathing, the clanking of chains, shadows that seem to move, what seems to be a momentary glimpse of somebody or even a prolonged sighting of them; or there may be just a feeling of unease, oppression, a peculiar chill in the air, sudden terror. What we feel, hear or see would have been explained by the discovery of somebody there. Indeed, we might at first think we have discovered somebody there, precisely because of what we feel or hear or, particularly, see. But when we check, what we discover is that actually there is nobody there; the phenomena remain without explanation. We react to the phenomena in the absence of anything that might explain them, and it is that very absence that makes the whole thing so weirdly frightening. (If our searches had revealed that there was indeed somebody there, that might have been frightening, depending on who we found. But this would be a different kind of fear; we would not be frightened by things being so *weird*.) So it would be no good anybody going to have a look round and then assuring us that he has made quite certain that there is absolutely nothing there. We already knew that, and it is what makes it so awful; we would be relieved if something were discovered there. So when we insist, terrified, "There *is* somebody there", we are not mistaken; we are not trying to convey information that may turn out to be false. Neither are we lying. We are perfectly well aware of the situations in which that sentence might be used to convey information, and this isn't one of them. Our use of language is odd here, and that is part of what makes the situation odd for us.

The move we are taught here – the move that our language makes available to us – is to speak of ghosts or spirits. They are introduced as if they were another class of beings. Now, when we want to say in a particular tone of voice that there is somebody there, and we know that there is nobody there, we can say that there is nobody *physical* there; there is a *spiritual* presence. Now when we want to say, "There's somebody there" when we know there isn't, we can say, "There's a ghost here". But this does not alter the situation. "There's a ghost here" isn't suddenly an information-bearing sentence where "There's somebody there" was not. When we learn the word "ghost" we do not gain new information; we learn a new linguistic move that we can make in certain circumstances. This use of the word "ghost" is taught as applicable in situations where you want to say that there is somebody or something, there, and you have established, or believe, that there isn't. And using it goes together typically with not being reassured when you have established there is nobody there, and with a particular kind of fear.

But surely there is new information, if it really is a ghost? For now we have an explanation for the phenomena that we did not have before. – But this is not an explanation in any normal sense. It is not an explanation in the sense that, say, a leaking pipe overhead might be explanation of the puddle on my floor. Say, if you like, that the noises and the sudden chill are explained by the presence of a ghost, but the ghost is introduced to be an explanation *by definition*. It is not as if there were the noises and the rest, and then the ghost were discovered, and then a causal connexion were established between the two. So it could not be, for example, that there was indeed really a ghost present, but that it was nevertheless not responsible for the noises – that it just happened, by coincidence, to be hanging around the place at the time, but was not doing anything – so that the noises remained without explanation. Neither could this happen: that we sense a presence, turn on the light to reveal that there is indeed somebody there, and then be faced with the problem whether our sense of presence was caused by the person we have discovered or by a ghost. Ghosts do not stand on the same explanatory level as people, as alternative ways of explaining things. If we have discovered somebody there, then the question of ghosts simply does not arise. We explain phenomena in terms of ghosts only when we have ruled out explanation in other, 'natural' terms. And if somebody says, "There's a ghost here", he is not forming a hypothesis on the basis of evidence, as he might be if he says, "There's a man here somewhere". If that were the case, it would turn the situation back into something ordinary: we would have phenomena and their cause. But to say, "There's a ghost here" is to say that it is an *extraordinary* situation. His attitude to what he says is not like the attitude to a hypothesis; he is not inclined to test, but to run.

And what would count as testing here? What would establish the presence of the ghost, so that "There's a ghost here" really did give us new, true information? Nothing could count as the discovery of the ghost, except the failure to discover any cause for the noises and the other phenomena. This is no less true when there are visual phenomena, when we say we have seen a ghost. If we actually see somebody in our spooky library – a bearded man in fashionable mid-seventeenth-century costume – then what is there might be just that: an actor in a costume drama being filmed nearby is making explorations between shots, or somebody has wandered in from a fancy-dress party, or a friend has been lying in wait to give us a fright. But now the figure fades into air before our eyes or walks slowly and silently through a book-lined stone wall. Since flesh and blood cannot do that we know that what we have just seen is not a human being, that there was nobody there to see. It is at this point, when we are persuaded of the absence of human beings, that we are finally convinced we have seen a ghost. In general, to discover a ghost is not to discover the presence of something that might be called a ghost. It is to establish the *absence* of any cause for the noises and the chill, or for what we see. We say that a ghost causes the noises when we have discovered *no* cause, and when we predict that we won't discover any. We say we have seen a ghost when we believe there was *nobody* there to see. A ghost is what causes the phenomena when *nothing* causes them.

To that extent it is misleading to speak of ghosts as another class of being, spiritual as opposed to material. For "ghost" is not related to a ghost as "book" is related to a book; they are not related as name and thing named. "Ghost" is not the name of a thing. So, if we want to call a ghost a spiritual being, as opposed to a book which is a material being, that is not, as its appearance might suggest, to divide beings into two classes, as books might be divided into red ones and blue ones. It is to point to logical differences between ghosts and books, differences between the uses of the words "ghost" and "book", to say that in some important instances they function in quite dissimilar ways.

To say that "ghost" is not the name of a thing, that we talk about ghosts not because we find something in certain circumstances but because we do not, is not to say that there are no ghosts. It simply describes part of the working of sentences about ghosts. And to give such a description, to say that this is how ghost-language works, is not to prove that there are ghosts, to spirit them up out of thin air by some linguistic trick. What our linguistic training does is to make language about ghosts available to us. But not everybody is prepared actually to use that language at all seriously. To say that ghosts really exist is to express readiness to use it seriously; to say that they do not is to express a disinclination. I might say, "Actually there are no ghosts". And that is to say: If I were in a dark, lonely library late at night, heard all sorts of noises, etc., and then looked around and established there was nothing there, I would think of explanations for the phenomena that did not involve anybody's presence – of course, for I have just established that there is indeed nobody there. I would be curious, but not frightened, or at any rate not in terror as of something weird.

But I might be wrong about that, wrong in my prediction of what I would do, how I would react. I might, in spite of what I now say, whisper to myself, trembling, "There really is somebody, something, a ghost there". I might then describe myself as having been compelled to believe in ghosts by what I had seen, heard and felt. Not that I would then have made an inference from what I had seen, heard or felt. I simply had this experience and reacted in this way. And I already knew that that reaction was among the range of possible ones in this kind of situation; that knowledge was given to me when I learned the language. Though there are no ghosts, still I would know one if I met one. I would not mistake an encounter with a ghost for, say, an experience of *déjà vu*. I already know how to use ghost-language, even if I do not feel inclined to. If, in the library, I do after all say, "There really is something there" – meaning a ghost – that would mark a kind of *conversion*, from one kind of language to another; and that means from one kind of reaction to another. Henceforth I will be readier to take certain kinds of occurrence as evidence of the presence of a ghost, rather than as, say, tricks of the light, or evidence of faulty plumbing. And then they will have an importance for me that they never had before, when I looked for discoverable causes.

Whether I believe in ghosts or not is a matter of my *reaction* in particular situations, what the organism *does* – what happens to my body, my temperature, my posture, what I say or feel compelled to say, whether I gaze full of dread or full of curiosity, whether I am tempted to take a closer look or to run. And the situation I react to is an empirical one – sights, sounds and feelings. There is nothing hidden about it. If I run, or shriek "A ghost!", that is not because I make an inference to something unseen, behind the phenomena. I simply react to the phenomena in the absence – presumed or established – of anything that might explain them, and without looking for anything that might explain them. And it is important that what is said is only part of a total reaction, and that it gets its sense from the reaction it is embedded in: A man is seen half running, trying not to, from a dark library. He says later, "I know it's silly, but for some obscure reason I was terrified; I couldn't help it. But of course I don't believe in ghosts or anything stupid like that". – Yes he does.

Part of what I am getting here is that although absence plays a central role in the teaching and use of this language about ghosts, that does not make talk about ghosts any the less significant, less important. In fact it is just this absence that makes it important, extraordinary. How can anybody doubt that something important is going on if somebody (perhaps you yourself) is impelled to say, even reluctantly, at the risk of appearing stupid, "There's somebody there", even when he *knows* there isn't? For the way people use language – the words they use, the circumstances they use them in, the other things they do in that context – is important. Since we are linguistic animals, since language does form such a central part of our lives, we do not readily, except in very special situations, play with it. So here it might be possible to describe those who talk of ghosts as playing a strange language-game, but that is not the same as to say they are merely playing games with words, making a game of language. It is a disadvantage of the "language-game" terminology used by Wittgenstein and some of his followers that it can seem to make uses of language quite arbitrary, even frivolous. (Not that this remotely reflects Wittgenstein's thought, but it is easy for unsympathetic critics to misrepresent it in this way.) But clearly there is nothing like that here, when people speak of ghosts. It is not a question of playing with words, of arbitrarily choosing to talk about ghosts instead of looking for faulty plumbing. We all know the game; we all picked up the rules governing the use of the word "ghost" when we learned English. Some of us may have been gripped by it from the beginning; of these we may say that they have always believed in ghosts. To many of us it may have seemed an idle game, even a stupid one; we saw no point in it. We use the sentence "I do not believe in ghosts" as an expression of our rejection of this way of talking. If it now happens that some of us feel impelled to take it up, to use the word, that is not a light matter, or something arbitrary. It means we have come to see the point of it; perhaps because of what has happened to us, the way we have reacted in certain situations, we can no longer dismiss this game as idle, mere wordplay.

Poltergeists

So too some people are impelled to use language about poltergeists. When things move because people or other things move them, that is normal and excites no particular comment. But when things move in a way that they might move when somebody moves them – and yet nobody moves them – *that* impresses, *that* is significant. We want to say, "Somebody moved it", but we know that nobody did. The cup just suddenly took off from the table, flew past us and smashed into the wall. It is true that Peter sometimes smashes cups against the wall when he is in one of his moods, but he was nowhere near it at the time, and neither was anybody else. Now we can talk about poltergeists: a poltergeist is what moves something – in certain circumstances – when *nobody* does. In this case, too, no inference is made. I am not frightened by the presence of an invisible being which I infer. I am scared when I see the thing moving though nobody moves it. I do not wait until I have completed any inference before I feel fear. It is what I *see* that scares me, not what I don't. Everything about the situation is in the open; nothing lies hidden. It is the absence of any visible agent here – the visible absence of any agent – that is important, not the inferred presence of an invisible one. And it is that absence that makes me think in terms of the weird, the supernatural, that makes me talk of the presence of a poltergeist. We talk of the presence of a poltergeist, if we do, not because we detect an invisible agent, but because we detect no agent at all. The presence of a poltergeist is not the presence of a thing, albeit an invisible one, called a poltergeist. "Poltergeist" is not related to poltergeist as name is to object; it is not the name of a thing. So we do not infer a causal relationship between one object, a flying cup, and another invisible one whose presence could be established independently. If nobody threw it, and there are no other discernable causes for its movement, like a sudden earth tremor or hurricane, then it was a poltergeist, by definition.

So again it could not be that by coincidence a poltergeist did happen to be around at the time, but was just standing about peacefully minding its own business, and was not responsible for throwing the cup across the room. It is its business to throw cups across rooms. Poltergeists are active; we only speak of them as doing things – visible things. Neither are natural causes and poltergeists same-level competing explanations. If we can account for the flight of the cup perfectly adequately by reference to an earth tremor, then we do not have two possible alternative explanations – earth tremor and poltergeist – which we then have to choose between. Poltergeists only enter the picture when we have already ruled out 'natural' causes (that is, *all* causes), when we can think of *no* explanation for what happened, or will accept none. A poltergeist is what explains an event when *nothing* explains it.

Ghosts, Hypotheses and Reactions
Nothing would count as a proof of the existence of a ghost to somebody who did not believe in ghosts. No new evidence or chain of inferences could lead to the establishment of a being called a ghost. The phenomena that lead people to believe in ghosts do not stand to that belief in the relation of evidence to hypothesis or conclusion, and the belief is not the result of a process of inference from what is seen, heard, etc., to what is unseen, or some thing that lies behind, is responsible for, the phenomena. For the one who believes in ghosts everything is already there, on the surface; there is no need for any inferences. It is what he sees or hears or feels that makes him scared or amazed. (I always speak,

for simplicity, of being scared or amazed in the presence of ghosts. Is this necessary? Maybe not. Perhaps there is a variety of possible reactions to ghosts. But can you be simply indifferent to one when you meet it? I would guess not: a ghost is not just encountered as something there, as you might pass somebody in the street (otherwise, how do I know that all the people I pass in the street are not ghosts?) but as present *to* the one who meets it – as a threat, perhaps even as a comfort (one's dear departed), but not just there. When you say, "There's a ghost there", the force of the *there* is quite different from what it is in "There's a book there". It marks a presence for or to the one who encounters the ghost.)

What scares one who is scared by a ghost is not the result of an inference that he makes from what he sees or hears or feels. On the contrary, it is precisely those who do not believe in ghosts who make inferences to hidden causes, who suggest what might be responsible for the phenomena: the faulty plumbing, the mouse just disappeared into its hole, the concealed projector or loudspeaker or practical joker. And the hypotheses may be multiplied as each in turn proves false when checked out. The making of hypotheses is the nonbeliever's alternative to fear, the fear that rests with what is perceived and says, "It's a ghost". And even if all the hypotheses that the nonbeliever can think of are proved false, he still has two alternatives. He might say to the believer, "You win; it must be a ghost. So there are ghosts after all". Or he might say, "Well, I can't think what might be causing these phenomena, but I'm sure that *something* must be causing them, whatever it is; there must be an answer somewhere. There's no need to go talking about ghosts".

Now, if all he knows about what is causing all this is that it is a *something*, how does he know that that something is not a ghost? – Because a ghost does not count as a something; it cannot be hypothesis, an entity postulated to explain the phenomena. A ghost is not a thing, and the difference between the one who does not believe in ghosts and the one who does is not that they make different inferences, but that the one does make inferences and the other does not. Belief in ghosts is not an inclination to make mistaken inferences, come to conclusions that might be shown to be false. It is simply a disposition to react in a particular way or number of ways to particular kinds of phenomenon that arise in various circumstances. In any individual instance somebody who said "It's a ghost" may be led afterwards to say, "No it wasn't, after all". He might say this when, say, it is discovered that there is a hidden projector, or that the blood-curdling sounds came from a horror film showing on the television next door. But that does not mean that he has made a false inference in the first place.

It is here as in general wrong to speak of changes of mind or the withdrawal of statements or changes of behaviour in terms of admitting that we have made a wrong inference or have acted on a false hypothesis. Sometimes we make inferences from what we see, and sometimes our inferences turn out to be wrong, and we have to abandon them. But it is a mistake to generalise this to all our activities. We do not spend our lives making inferences. If I smile and call out when I see a friend, it is not because I make any inferences from what I see: I smile at what I see, and my call is a reaction to what I see. I may smile and call out immediately, and that is not because I can make inferences very quickly. I do not hypothesise that what I can see is my friend, and act on that basis. That is true, even though it may turn that it was not my friend after all. Then I may be embarrassed, apologise, and say that I had made a mistake. But what that amounts to here is not that I now discard a mistaken hypothesis (for I formed no hypothesis), but that I reject my former reaction as inappropriate. In the same way, if the man who thought it was a ghost now says he was mistaken, he is rejecting his former reaction, not a hypothesis. And if he admits that it wasn't a ghost, this need not weaken his belief in ghosts in general, though we would think him odd if he maintained his belief just as strongly if he often claimed there was a ghost there, and every time was brought to say that he had made a mistake.

The fundamental difference between the believer in ghosts and the nonbeliever is that they are disposed to react to certain kinds of phenomenon in different ways. The one would be disposed to say, "It's a ghost", while the other would say, "There must be a cause, a natural explanation, even if we can't find one". (Here "natural explanation" might be replaced by "explanation" *tout court*, without any loss of meaning.) And this difference in their verbal behaviour only has significance if it is related to other aspects of the way they act. The two are disposed to react in different ways to the phenomena; the one is inclined to fear, amazement, etc., while the other is inclined to stifle any fear he may feel initially and react instead with puzzlement or curiosity. (This difference we might expect to be related to other differences in the ways they live their lives in general, in their reactions to things.) There is no disagreement about the existence of something, in any normal sense. What is called "a dispute over the existence of ghosts" is not like, say, a dispute over the existence of a tenth planet in our solar system. There is no disagreement over the existence of things called ghosts, weird, spiritual things. A dispute over the existence of a tenth planet would be settled by looking for and finding, or failing to find, a planet (and there are accepted criteria for what is to count as finding a planet). A dispute over the existence of ghosts is not settled by looking for and finding a strange kind of being, but by looking for perfectly ordinary things: people, hidden loudspeakers, scuttling mice, and so on. If there is disagreement over the existence of ghosts, it is over the existence, in each individual case, of perfectly natural, empirically ascertainable causes for what is seen and heard.

For the one who is disposed to seek causes, the phenomena, though perhaps unusual, are thereby rendered ordinary, natural, able to fit perfectly into the ordinary scheme of things; what has happened will turn out to be quite explicable, if only the cause can be found. And even if it cannot, there must be one: there must be a place for the phenomena in the ordinary scheme of things, even if we cannot say where. And if there *must* be a place, that is because it has been determined beforehand that there is; he will not contemplate there being no place. For the one who believes in ghosts, on the other hand, there need be no place. Though he lives in the same ordinary world as the non-believer, he is prepared that things might happen outside the normal scheme of things. In some cases he is content to say, even compelled to say, "Here there are no material causes – it's a ghost". And because he lives in the same ordinary world, the occasions on which he says this are to him extraordinary, weird, uncanny or spiritual, having a quite peculiar importance.

Déjà Vu, Ghosts and God

God is not a ghost or a poltergeist, and neither is experience of God, if we are prepared to allow such talk, a case of *déjà vu*. (If we are prepared to allow it: It is a feature of religious language that it is sometimes not settled what may and what may not be said; some may recommend one way of talking and want to rule out another way followed by others. Others again may be unsure what is to be said. Talk of experience of God is a case in point. For some, concern with what they call experience of God comes close to the centre of their religion, while others find they can do little or nothing with the idea – and here I do not mean only adherents of different religions.) But there are several points of contact between what I have just been saying and talk about God, which help to illuminate Christian language.

First, looking at talk about ghosts and *déjà vu* shows that not all language that looks as if it is giving (true or false) information about how things are or about what exists is in fact doing that. In these cases, as in Wittgenstein's poem (*Zettel* 160), though the "language of information", i.e. forms of words that would normally or often be used when giving information, is being used, it is not used in the language-game of giving information. Here as elsewhere, to understand the language properly we have to look and see how it is in fact being used; preconceptions as to how it ought to be being used only stop us seeing.

Second, an important part of the context of these utterances – talk about ghosts and expressions of *déjà vu* – is a perceived, even a claimed absence of any evidence that might be offered in support of them. In the case of *déjà vu* there is nothing to make the speaker believe that what he says is true; indeed, he is sure it isn't. In the case of ghosts, the speaker says there is somebody or something there in the absence of anybody or anything.

Third, it is just that absence that makes the experiences special and important in their peculiar way, extraordinary, so that they may be described as spiritual or supernatural. The analogy with such talk shows that taking absence as central to talk about God does not show it to be empty and devoid of significance, a mere playing with words. On the contrary, it is precisely this absence that can make it important, that makes it talk of the extraordinary, the spiritual, the supernatural. And it is the absence of anybody or anything that makes the experience of the presence of God extraordinary, or spiritual. (Though of course we would not want to accept every extraordinary experience, even those claimed to be of God, as in fact experiences of the presence of God, even if we did not want to avoid such language altogether. But it is not a sheer accident that people link together experiences of ghosts and experiences of God by applying the same adjectives to them, or sometimes run to a priest when they have seen a ghost.) People sometimes talk of experiences of God in terms of awe or intimate union. To have a feeling of intimate or ecstatic union when making love to somebody may be a marvelous experience, but it is quite normal in the circumstances; to feel awe when standing before the vastness of the sea or an erupting volcano, this again is natural enough. To have such feelings when praying alone in your room, this is something else, this is extraordinary. Though there is nobody there to be intimate with (you know there is nobody, you have taken pains to be alone), you want to talk of intimacy or ecstasy; though there is nothing before you for you to be in awe of, you want – and very seriously – to talk of being in awe before something. Here one may speak of God.

Fourth, *déjà vu* and talk of seeing ghosts suggest the importance to religion too of the ways phenomena are reacted to, rather than the formation of hypotheses. Both "I've been here before", when you haven't, and "There's somebody (something) there", when there isn't, can play an important role in people's lives, which we might describe as a religious role, and the people for whom they might play such a role are not for that reason stupid, nor are they making a mistake. In the case of *déjà vu* I have already sketched circumstances in which "I've been here before" when you haven't might be regarded as having religious importance. I have not done this for "There's somebody there", but it is easy to imagine such circumstances. For example, somebody says, "There's somebody there" when plainly there isn't, and this is taken as a visit from one of the ancestors, a god. It is possible too that the utterance actually name the one who is visiting and what he wants. Such things might even be prescribed, so that there would be no possibility of a mistake here; for it might all be part of ceremony to summon up a particular spirit, so that it is the ceremony itself that provides the criterion of identity for the spirit: it is *this* spirit that appears because it is *this* spirit that is summoned. And then the spirit speaks through the one it appears to. It might only be possible at particular times of the year, and special ritual dances have to be performed and ritual incantations sung in order to make it work. Perhaps the whole thing is prepared for by undertaking a long fast, by eating certain kinds of mushroom, or by the telling of creepy stories about visits from the gods. Only under these circumstances might the utterance "There's somebody there" count as the announcement of the presence of a god. We could even imagine that a similar utterance made outside the correct ritual context is treated as an insignificant hallucination. There is no reason why they should have our concept of seeing a ghost.

As with the example of *déjà vu*, a people who did all this would not be making a mistake in treating the utterance in this way, surrounding it with all these rituals. It would, on the contrary, be a mistake on our part to say that what they think is a visit from one of the ancestral gods is *really* only a ghost, or perhaps only faulty plumbing, or a hallucination brought on by mushrooms. For the visit from a god in this society would play a quite different role from seeing a ghost or having a hallucination in ours. It is not that they wrongly attach to a hallucination a special religious significance it does not in fact possess. For there is no 'in fact' about it. It has not been discovered that hallucinations have no such significance. "Hallucination" is not a neutral term; it encapsulates our notion that certain kinds of experience have no significance; which is to say it reflects our custom of *treating* them as insignificant. Hallucinations are always mere; their importance ends when they do. We give them no further place in our lives. An inclination to give an experience, however produced, some further place is an inclination not to call it a hallucination at all. It is not a disposition to treat a hallucination in a mistaken way.

It is perhaps worth remarking here that we commonly make distinctions between experiences, whose verbal and other expressions might be similar, on the basis of their context or their causes, and we vary our reaction to them accordingly. If somebody sees somebody who isn't there after he has been told creepy stories – stories to do with the one he claims to see – then we might talk about an over-excited imagination. If he has the experience as a result of taking drugs, then we are more likely to speak of it as a hallucination. In this second case, we should probably be reluctant to say that he has seen a ghost, even if we ourselves believe in ghosts. If the experience is set in a religious context, say prepared for by prayer and fasting, then we might be inclined to speak of it as a *vision*.

Some years ago there was something of a vogue for taking drugs like mescaline and LSD and seeing religious significance in the experience produced. Such drugs are normally described as hallucinogenic; normally, if you take them you get the kind of experience we call a hallucination, seeing things that are not there, or seeing real things distorted or altered in some way. But it was claimed by some that it could produce states of consciousness akin to or even the same as those experienced by great mystics and other religious devotees. There was some woolly thinking in all this. One part of that woolliness was the failure to recognise that states of consciousness often depend for being what they are on their contexts and their causes. Having a hallucination of Charlie after taking LSD may *seem* exactly the same experience as actually seeing Charlie; indeed, its seeming similar is part of what is implied in its being described as a hallucination of *Charlie*. But it is not the same experience. You can only see Charlie when Charlie is there to be seen, but you can have a hallucination of him whether he is there or not. Seeing Charlie involves light waves bouncing off Charlie and getting into your eye, but the hallucination requires LSD. So with religious states of consciousness. An experience you get from taking LSD may seem the same as one you get after a life of great virtue, practising years of austerities, saying prayers and going on a prolonged fast, but it by no means follows that it is the same. Many religious people in fact took the view that the difference in causal antecedents was sufficient to render it different, a counterfeit. – And this amounted to a decision to *treat* it differently, in particular not to accord it the same significance, not to build religious rituals around it. But this is not to say that those who did and do treat it as a genuine and important religious experience made a mistake in doing so. The mistake is not in thinking it important but in thinking it the same as other kinds of religious experience which arise in different ways. Conversely those who pooh-poohed the whole idea, while right in pointing out that the LSD experience was not the same as what some traditional mystics had had, however much it might *seem* the same, were not right if they thought that its merely being different entailed its being insignificant.

So, as in the case of "I've been here before", these people who have visions of people who are not there, would not be getting it all wrong, making a mistake. And *we* don't get it *right*, react to such experiences as they *really* are. They are not really hallucinations or anything similar. They are not really anything in abstraction from the way we react to them and the place we give them in our lives. All we can say is that that society gives them a different place to ours, assigns them an important religious role where we assign them none, and that the people of that society react to them differently from the way we react to similar utterances and behaviour; and we can expect that this will tie in with other differences between the ways life is lived in their society and in ours. We cannot accept their institution of visits from the gods because we cannot or will not bring ourselves to *do* the things they do as part of that institution, or to live in such a way that the institution will be at home in our society.

Our religious behaviour too, if we behave religiously, and our religious utterances (verbal behaviour), as in these simpler cases, are rooted in our reaction to what we experience and how we live among the things we can see and touch, rather than beliefs about or reactions to something invisible, intangible, etc., whose existence we infer from what we can see and touch. We react to visible situations, not to what we think we can infer from them. This approach enables us to appreciate another of the ways in which religious believing is different from scientific believing. It would be to give a wrong account of the nature of religious belief to say, "You know what it is to have beliefs about the internal structure of volcanoes; well, this is belief, just the same, except about God". Religious beliefs are related to reactions to things and to the way life is lived in a different way from scientific beliefs. That is why we speak of *empty* belief in religion, when religious utterances are made by an individual without his providing the proper context for them by his way of life; we would not similarly speak of an empty scientific belief. – We could certainly give the phrase "empty belief" a use in connexion with science, but it would not be a use similar to that given it in connexion with religion.

God as Real

But this objection can be made to all that I have said: God is an agent. He creates, and he acts in his creatures. And what we do we sometimes do so that God will act in certain ways. We give alms, pray and fast in secret so that God will reward us (or at least we are urged to: see Matthew 6:1ff.); we confess our sins so that he may forgive us; we forgive each other that he may forgive us; we ask for peace in the world that he may give peace, for rain that he may send the rain; we ask him for wisdom that he may make us wise, for generosity of spirit that he may make us generous. When we are in difficulties over what to do we may ask him to give us a sign to tell us what to do. Perhaps we fear that he may punish us when we have done something terrible. And so on. Surely, if God does things, and if we expect him to, then he must be something; he must, we believe, actually be there. And so also when we talk about God in general we must be talking about something positive, some *thing*. So that it is not enough to say that we talk about God in the absence of anything called God. When we talk about, for example, the presence of God, we must, if our faith is not empty, be talking about the presence of something real.

I do not want to deny the reality of God, that God really exists. But it is not yet settled what the reality of God consists in. In the same way, it is not yet settled what it is for God to create and to act, to give rewards, to punish, to forgive, to give rain, to inspire virtue, and to do all the other things that God does. We know what it is for Charlie to reward and punish, to forgive, and to give things, but we do not therefore know at once what it is for God to do these things. We may know what it is for Charlie to be an agent, but we do not thereby automatically know what it is for God to be an agent. It is not enough to say, "You know what it is like for Charlie to give rewards; well, here the same thing is going on, only now it is God who is doing the giving". It is tempting to say this because of the great similarities between Charlie and God, because we call both of them persons. And now, if you like, we can call both of them agents. But still there are differences between the two, though the complexity of our language, both about Charlie and about God, makes these differences less than obvious, especially when we are so impressed by the similarities. Here things are much more difficult than in the simpler case of the equator and the line on a football pitch. But the procedure must be the same. We actually have to *look* at how language about God works, how it is used, if we are to get any real understanding of what it is for God to be a person, an agent. If we look, then we find that absence does indeed play a central role – not of course the absence of God, but the absence of quite ordinary things, parts of our ordinary, material world (just as the absence of these things plays a central role in talk about ghosts, for those who speak of them).

CHAPTER 4

TRUST, LOVE AND FEAR

Trusting in God

If I fear Charlie, I may also fear Bill and David. (These three are the local school bullies; or I am a timid man, and fear most of the people around me.) If I work for Charlie, I may also work for George and Harry. (They are all partners of the firm I work for; or I manage to hold down several jobs at once.) If I trust Charlie, I may also trust Carol, Christopher or Christine, or all three of them. If I hope for a reward from Charlie, I may also hope to get one from Harry. (They have both put up a reward in return for information leading to the arrest of ....) For many of the things I do, I can spread my activity around a number of different people. There is not just one person my action is confined to at any one time; I can make a list of people my actions are concerned with, a list that can have more than one member. And the same is true of my mental states. My fear, trust, love, hope, and so on, can have more than one person as object. I can make a list of objects that can have more than one member. God cannot appear on such a list. For many of my activities, God can only appear on the list if *nobody* (i.e. nobody in the world) does; God and the world cannot be listed together. Take the following examples from scripture:

> Nobody can serve two masters... You cannot serve God and mammon. (Matthew 6:24)
> Do not fear those who kill the body but cannot kill the soul. Fear rather him who can destroy both soul and body in Gehenna. (Matthew 10:28)
> Do not trust in princes, in the son of man who has no

power to save... Blessed is he whose help is the God of Jacob, whose hope is in the Lord his God. (Psalm 146:3,5)

How can you believe, when you take glory from each other and do not seek the glory that is from the only God? (John 5:44)

You cannot drink the cup of the Lord and the cup of demons. You cannot share the table of the Lord and the table of demons. (1 Corinthians 10:21)

When you fast, anoint your head and wash your face, so that you may appear as fasting not to men but to your Father who is in secret. (Matthew 6:17f.)

The king is not saved by the size of his army; a warrior is not delivered by his great strength. The horse is not to be relied on for victory; for all its strength it cannot save. Behold, the eye of the Lord is on those who fear him, on those who wait for his love, to rescue their soul from death, and to preserve their life in famine. (Psalm 33:16–19)

These examples, all from texts of fundamental authority for Christians, separate God from the world, logically. If I do something to God, I don't do it to anybody else; if God does something to me, nobody else does; if others do something to me, God does not; if I do something to others, I do not do it to God. God does not belong to any list of agents or persons or things. I can trust Charlie and Mary, but not Charlie and God, or God and horses; I can seek praise from Charlie and from Peter, but not from Charlie and from God. I can locate objects of trust, fear, hope, etc., in the world, but not in the world *and* in heaven. So also we find:

Do not lay up treasures for yourselves on earth, where moth and rust disfigure and where thieves break in and steal. But lay up treasures for yourselves in heaven, where neither moth nor rust disfigure, and where thieves do not break in or steal. (Matthew 6:19f.)

You can lay up treasure in London *and* in Zürich, but not in London *and* in heaven; with George *and* with Hermann, but not with George *and* with God. Men and God, the world and heaven, are logically discontinuous; you cannot share out things between them. It is not that it is very difficult to share between them, but that it is impossible, logically impossible: the way language about God is used, *nothing counts* as serving both God and mammon, or as putting your trust in men and God. If you seek a reward on earth, then *ipso facto* you do not seek a reward in heaven, and *vice versa*. To seek glory from God is *eo ipso* not to seek glory from men, and *vice versa*. And so on.

How does this manifest itself 'on earth'? That is, if Otto is engaged in a project of trying to understand our language about God, how does he learn what it means to trust in God or to lay up treasure in heaven? What does he actually *see*, that enables him to learn the use of the words, when he sees people trusting in God, laying up treasure in heaven? If he sees Alvin trusting in Mary, he sees somebody (Alvin) trusting and somebody else (Mary), somebody trusted, between whom he sees a bond of trust being manifested in various ways. He will see Alvin behaving towards Mary in a complex of ways that we would describe as trusting. He will, say, go to see Mary and share confidences with her, have recourse to her when he gets into trouble, say things like, "It's all right. I know Mary will help me out". This is not what Otto sees if he sees Alvin trusting in God. If Alvin trusts in God, Otto does not see Alvin and see God and see Alvin putting his trust in God. What he sees is Alvin *not* putting his trust in anybody, refusing to put his trust in men.

105

If Otto is to understand the notion of trust in God he will also have to learn that this is a special kind of trust, one whose scope is fairly limited. It is not that Otto will never see Alvin trusting in anybody in any way at all. He may be for the most part what Otto recognises as a very trusting person. To trust in somebody in the sense that you might trust in God is to trust in them for your salvation, to look to them for final safety, be committed to them as completely reliable, see your life in terms of them. Otto sees Alvin trusting, for example remaining confident when things go wrong for him, and uttering expressions of trust of a kind Otto is already familiar with, like: "However bad things get, I know God will help me out". But he sees him behaving in this trusting way in the *visible absence* of anybody in whom he puts his trust. This may strike him as odd, but his failure to find anybody called God in whom Alvin may be said to trust is not an objection to talk of trust in God. On the contrary, registering such an absence is part of learning what such talk means, how it functions. Otto has to take on board that "Alvin trusts in God" works differently from "Alvin trusts in Mary". And only when he has learnt how the language works will he be in a position even to begin to raise objections to it, or indeed to approve of it. Only when he *can* use the language can he reasonably decide whether there is any point in doing so, or whether on the contrary the whole business is ludicrous. He may find it strange that, look around as he might, he cannot find this one in whom Alvin trusts, but the fault does not lie with Alvin or with the language he is using. Rather, because it works differently from other uses of the word "trust", it is a mistake in the first place for him to look to find the object of Alvin's trust. If he points out to Alvin that he cannot find the one he claims to be trusting in, and that therefore he must be suffering some delusion, this would not show how hardheaded and sensible Otto is; it would simply show he had failed to grasp the working of this part of our language about God. If on the contrary he understands it properly, then he knows that if Alvin puts his trust in God, then there is *nobody* in whom he puts his trust. "Alvin trusts in God" tells him not what he should expect to find, but what he should expect *not* to find. And so if he does find that there is somebody in whom Alvin puts his trust – if he puts his trust in Mary or in princes or in horses – then he does not put his trust in God.

So the evidence that would confirm "Alvin puts his trust in God" is different in kind from that which would confirm "Alvin puts his trust in Mary". We can see whether Alvin trusts in Mary by his attitude towards her, how he behaves towards her, and so on. An important presupposition of our ability to do this is that we can distinguish Mary from Peter and from Sebastian; we can identify Alvin's attitude and behaviour towards *her* as opposed to others. So if we want to find out Alvin's attitude and behaviour towards her, we study his relationship with her, and not his relationship with Peter or Sebastian (except in so far as they may be relevant to his relationship with Mary). We do not set about things this way if we want to find whether Alvin puts his trust in God, for there is no God whom we can identify as a being separate from Peter and Sebastian, and whose relationship with Alvin we can study. If Mary lives in Bayswater, then we do look partly to Bayswater to find whether Alvin puts his trust in Mary. But though God is in heaven we do not look to heaven (how would we do that?) as part of our study of Charlie's relationship with God. Rather, we look around us, at beings who are *not* God. In any case, you can only identify who is *not* God, not who is. You can only identify who God is *not*, not who he is. If it is true of anybody whom we can identify that Alvin puts his trust in him, then "Alvin puts his trust in God" is false. If, on the other hand, we find that there is nobody in whom Alvin puts his trust, then given certain circumstances we are entitled to say that Alvin puts his trust in God.

Given certain circumstances: It is not enough to show only that he puts his trust in nobody, that there is nobody in whom he trusts; if that were all, we would rather describe him as totally mistrustful, a misanthrope, or despairing. There must, to repeat, be something else about his behaviour that makes us want to describe him rather as trusting in God. There have to be other circumstances, a context, certain kinds of behaviour, characteristic attitudes. We want to say that the one who trusts in God does have something about him that distinguishes him from the merely misanthropic or despairing. We want to say that in some sense he trusts, even though there is nobody in whom he has this kind of trust. There is something about the way he lives, acts and speaks that makes the word "trust" a natural one to apply to him. Perhaps it is that in certain situations, of a kind in which we normally have to depend on or trust in somebody, he too behaves in a trusting way. He will be quiet and confident in adversity, even though he himself is weak, and though there is nobody he looks to to get him out of trouble. He does not, as most people might, go to pieces or act and speak as one beset by insecurity when he has nobody to trust in. And we will expect him to speak as one who trusts, to say in difficult or apparently hopeless moments, things like, "Whatever happens, I trust in God"; or, "I know it will be OK in the end. God will see me through all this". So he will be prepared to make serious use of language about God; he will be a believer of some sort. His trusting behaviour will probably go together with other kinds of religious activities, like prayer, worship and trying to do the will of God. (This is not to say that we would never say of non-believers that they trust in God. If somebody did not go in for religious activities and never spoke of God, still the rest of the pattern of his life might make us think it appropriate to say he trusts in God. But the primary application of the words will be to those who believe in God.) Circumstances such as these will make his trusting behaviour and words intelligible, and make us want to say of him that he trusts in God. *This* is how the concept of trusting in God works, this is the kind of thing Otto must see if he is to understand that concept. But whatever these other circumstances, which will make us want to say that Alvin trusts in God, they will not include the identification of anybody called God and establishing that Alvin trusts him; for of everybody that we can identify we have established that Alvin does *not* put his trust in him.

In these circumstances we are then entitled to say that Alvin puts his trust in God. But the fact is not established conclusively, so that we cannot later revise what we say. For we might at some later stage discover that there is after all somebody (or something) in whom Alvin puts his trust. That Alvin does *not* put his trust in God can be demonstrated by a single piece of empirical evidence, by finding somebody in whom Alvin puts his trust. But establishing that Alvin does put his trust in God is a matter of establishing a negative universal proposition, that there is nobody in whom Alvin trusts. Though such propositions can be and are established, yet what we call "establishing a negative universal proposition" does not exclude the later abandonment of that proposition if evidence incompatible with it is discovered. Compare here what I said earlier about ghosts. In the particular instance, that it was a ghost can be disproved by a single piece of empirical evidence: a hidden projector, a tree brushing against the window. Those who believe in ghosts feel entitled to say that it was a ghost if no cause for the phenomena can be discovered. But what the nonbeliever clings to is that there *must* be a cause, whether we can discover it or not; he will say therefore that it cannot be conclusively established that there was no cause and therefore that it was a ghost. To admit otherwise would be to break his view of the world, to throw his life out of joint.

Perhaps there is a parallel here too with the case of God. The atheist might claim that there is no God, so nobody puts his trust in God. Everybody who trusts, he might say, trusts in *somebody* or *something*, whether it be money, another person, himself, or some fictional projection of a father-figure that he calls God. The only alternative to that is despair. So if we see somebody living with confidence, quietly maintaining his balance in times of adversity, so that we would describe him as trusting, then there must be something he trusts in, whether we can discover it or not. The atheist refuses to contemplate the possibility of living like that, with that kind of confidence, without there being some object of trust, real or illusory, to cling on to. For him, the possibilities of the human animal are too circumscribed for that, and to admit the possibility of the way of life we call "putting your trust in God" would wreck his view of what it is to be human. So part of the difference between the Christian and the atheist lies in the difference between their attitudes as to what is possible in human life.

It can be objected here: Of course when we say that somebody trusts in God we do not mean only that he does not trust in people and things. We mean also that he does positively trust in God, that is, in somebody, some being, that we call God; only God is invisible, and that is why he cannot be identified in the same way as everybody else. Yes, of course it is true that we don't just mean that he trusts in nobody; that would mean that he was despairing. We mean that he does trust in God. But the question is what that means, how we use those words. It is not enough to say, "It is not true that Alvin trusts in nobody if he trusts in God; he just trusts nobody visible. He trusts in one who is invisible". If the language is to be used, as indeed it is used, we need visible criteria for when it is correctly applied, and which those learning the language can learn to apply. This means that anything invisible, undetectable, is *eo ipso* irrelevant to the use of the language: if we construe the relation between God and "God" on the model of 'object and designation', the object drops out as irrelevant (cf. *Philosophical Investigations* 293). What is invisible is not like what is visible, with the slight difference that it cannot be seen or otherwise detected. To call God invisible is to give him an altogether different logical status from what is visible. "God is invisible" is, like "Sensations are private", a grammatical remark; it is a guide as to how we use the word "God". Among other things, it warns us not to treat the word "God" as if it were the name of something: the criteria for its use are going to be quite different. It does not mean that criteria for its use are going to be invisible, for they must be visible, like any other criteria for the use of language. Only, they are going to be different, and I have just been pointing out some of the ways in which they are different. Among those is that God cannot be listed with Mary or Sebastian as one whom Alvin trusts in. "Alvin trusts in God" excludes "Alvin trusts in Mary", and *vice versa*. Here "Alvin trusts in God" is shown to have a different use, a different kind of meaning, from "Alvin trusts in Sebastian", in that the former does, while the latter does not, exclude "Alvin trusts in Mary".

Here another possible objection is: It may well be true that trusting in God excludes trusting in others, but that is only because God's demands are absolute. He demands the total trust that excludes putting any trust in anybody else.

And that is also why you cannot serve God and mammon, seek rewards from both God and man, and so on. But this objection misses the mark because it treats a conceptual, philosophical point as if it were a moral or theological one. God may make absolute demands, but men need not comply with them. Indeed it is one of the major complaints of much of scripture that men in fact do not comply with them. It is not that we *ought* not to seek rewards both on earth and in heaven, but that we *cannot*. It is not just very difficult to seek both the glory that comes from men *and* the glory that is from God: it is *impossible*. And it is not, either, that God will simply not give us a reward if we seek rewards from men as well as from him. That would only be to say that, God being awkward, if we seek both we are bound to fail. But the point is rather that we cannot seek both in the first place: there is no such task or activity.

Loving God

In general, then, this holds true: If you do something to God, you do not do something to anybody or anything called God (God is not a thing), and you don't do it to anybody or anything else, either. This is true in general, but there is one famous apparent exception: we are commanded to love God *and* to love our neighbour. Replying to a question about the greatest commandment of the law, Jesus says:

> You shall love the Lord your God with all your heart and with all your soul and with all your understanding: this is the great and first commandment. And there is another like it: You shall love your neighbour as yourself. From these two hangs the whole law, and the prophets. (Matthew 22:37–40)

I do not want to go into this in any detail, but immediately a link can be seen with what I have said. If we are asked to love

112

God with all our heart, all our mind and all our understanding, and if we are also asked to love our neighbour, then, plainly, loving our neighbour does not conflict with loving God with all our heart. Loving God and loving our neighbour does not divide us as serving two masters or loving two people might. (Neither, evidently, does our loving ourself as well as God and our neighbour, since we are asked to love our neighbour as ourself.) So this in no way conflicts with the general thrust of what I have been saying: that we can divide ourselves and our attention (make lists) only on earth, not between earth and heaven. If we love God, God is not somebody we love *in addition to* Charlie, David and Sebastian.

Christian tradition in fact goes further than seeing the commandment to love God and the commandment to love our neighbour as two distinct and parallel requirements. They are to be understood rather in the light of each other. In particular, loving our neighbour is a condition of loving God, or is even what loving God consists in. So the first epistle of John says:

> If anybody says "I love God", and hates his brother, he is a liar; for one who does not love his brother whom he has seen cannot love the God whom he has not seen. (4:20)

While Jesus, in Matthew 22, speaks of the two great commandments of love as those on which the law and the prophets depend, he also, earlier in the same gospel, gives this same fundamental role to just one rule of conduct:

> Everything you would like people to do you, do likewise to them; for this is the law and the prophets. (Matthew 7:12)

In the same vein, Paul says:

113

He who loves the other has fulfilled the law. For "Do not commit adultery, Do not murder, Do not steal, Do not covet", and whatever other law, are summed up in this word: "Love your neighbour as yourself". Love does not work evil against a neighbour; therefore love is the fulness of the law. (Romans 13:8–10)

This makes the love of God quite different – logically – from the love of Charlie. It is perfectly possible for Alvin to love Charlie without loving Charlotte, indeed while hating Charlotte; but it is not possible for him to love God while hating Charlotte. This difference stems from the fact that while Charlie and Charlotte are logically distinct individuals, who may therefore be listed separately as possible objects of Alvin's love (this possibility is part of what is meant by calling them *logically* distinct), God and Charlotte are not logically distinct individuals, may not be listed separately. Because Charlie and Charlotte are logically distinct individuals, if Otto wants to find out whether Alvin loves Charlie, he will first of all have to identify Charlie and then watch to see how Alvin behaves in relation to him, not to Charlotte. Otto knows what sort of behaviour counts as loving, and will watch to see whether Alvin behaves like this towards Charlie. Whether he behaves lovingly towards Charlotte will (unless the story is somewhat complicated) show how he feels about her, not about Charlie. But if Otto wants to know whether Alvin loves God, he will go about it the wrong way if he searches for an individual called God to see whether Alvin is behaving lovingly towards him. And that is not because God, being invisible, is hard to spot, but because the *concept* of the love of God requires no such search. It is not that Alvin loves God, as he might love Charlie, except that God is invisibly present; but that Alvin may be said to love God in the visible absence of anybody called God. The concept of the love of God works in this way: Alvin can be said to love God, not if he can be shown to love one invisible person, but if (perhaps among other things) he is seen loving perfectly visible people, like Charlotte, and perhaps a whole number of them. And conversely what would demonstrate that he does not love God is not his being discovered behaving spitefully or vengefully or neglectfully towards some poor invisible individual, but his acting like that towards poor Charlotte.

Fearing God

If we say that somebody trusts in God, this may be partly because the word "trust" seems a natural one to apply to him, because he acts and talks in a way we would normally describe as trusting or confident. But in a number of significant cases things work differently: to do some things with God as object is, given a certain context of behaviour and circumstances, just not to do them at all.

Take the case of the fear of God:

> Do not fear those who kill the body but cannot kill the soul. Fear rather him who can destroy both soul and body in Gehenna. Are not two sparrows sold for a penny? – And not one of them will fall to the ground without your Father's will. As for you, even the hairs of your head have all been counted. Therefore do not fear; you are worth more than many sparrows. (Matthew 10:28–31)

Here we have again the opposition between men (those who kill the body) and God (who can destroy both soul and body). And we are told: do not fear the one, but fear the other. The reasoning seems at first sight to be that men can hurt you, but God can hurt you a lot more, so fear God. But if we think of God as somebody who is to be feared, if we think that when you fear God there is somebody whom you fear, and who is called God, then what Jesus says here seems not to work. If Charlie threatens me, and is in a position to hurt me, then I fear Charlie; and one of the consequences of that fear is that I am likely to do what Charlie tells me. But now suppose Harry comes along, who can hurt me more (he can not only beat me up, but also drive me out of my home and make sure, through his contacts, that I will never be safe wherever I go). So I will fear Harry even more than I fear Charlie, and so be likely to do what he tells me to do. But now, unfortunately for me, Charlie and Harry tell me to do different, contradictory things (they are members of rival gangs). In fact, because Harry can do worse things to me than Charlie can, I will be inclined to do what Harry tells me, rather than what Charlie tells me. But that does not mean that I will fear Harry *rather than* Charlie. My fear of Harry does not banish my fear of Charlie; it is simply that I will fear him more. And so whatever I do now I will do in fear, knowing that whatever I do I will get hurt. Fear will come to dominate me.

But this, of course, is not what is going on in the words of Jesus. It is not that God is a kind of superlative and invisible Harry, a being more powerful than all men, who threatens me more harm than they do. It is not the object of Jesus to paralyse us with fear. It is true perhaps that God is here pictured as an extremely powerful thug, but that it is *only* a picture is shown by the consequences that are and are not drawn from it. Jesus does not draw the conclusion that we should fear God *in addition to* and more than men. As we have already seen, you cannot fear both God and man: God and people cannot be listed together as objects of somebody's fear. God is not a potential object of fear in the same way Charlie is. "Fear God" does not function in the same way as "fear Charlie", since the former excludes "fear Harry" while the latter does not. "Fear God" functions rather to exclude Harry, Charlie and all others as objects of fear. And it does not say: fear somebody *else*. "Fear God" says: fear *nobody*.

The man who trusts in God does not trust in somebody called God. He trusts in God when there is nobody in whom he puts his trust. And yet we may still want to describe him as in some way trusting. So too when a man fears God, there is nobody whom he fears; he is not frightened of men, nor is he frightened of some other invisible being called God. But is he still in some sense fearing, frightened? Is fearing God in this respect like trusting God? Is the attitude or the behaviour of somebody who fears God in some way similar to what it would be if he feared Charlie? Not if he is a Christian: "As for you, even the hairs of your head have all been counted. Therefore *do not fear*; you are worth more than many sparrows". To fear God is not to fear one being instead of another, nor to fear one as well as another, and neither is it to fear without any object of fear; it is *not to fear at all*. If you fear God, that does not mean that you have transferred your fear from one object to another; it means that you have ceased to fear. (This is not to say that there are not many Christians who do fear God as they might fear Charlie, who are terrified of what God might do to them. But such an attitude is not the orthodox Christian one. It is part of the job of pastors and theologians, those who speak as authorities, to correct the terrified, to free them from their fear.)

So "fear God", in contrast to "trust in God", functions something like a pure negative. But once again, as in the case of trust, not fearing anybody only counts as fearing God given other circumstances, a particular kind of context. There are numerous circumstances in which you might not fear at all. You may be alone on a desert island, where there is nobody to fear; you may be in a coma with little hope of recovery, and so incapable of any emotions at all; you may be so exceedingly powerful and protected that you need fear nobody. These are not circumstances in which it would be appropriate to say that you fear God. One set of appropriate circumstances is adumbrated in the section of Matthew's gospel we have been looking at. The context is one in which there is cause for fear, where there is somebody or something you might ordinarily be expected to fear – and yet you do not fear. The fear of God is a form of bravery. Here the situation is that of disciples who face persecution for acknowledging Jesus:

> They will hand you over to councils and they will beat you in their synagogues. And you will be brought before governors and kings on my account... Brother will hand over brother to death, and the father his child, and children will rise against parents and kill them. And you will be hated by everybody because of my name. (Matthew 10:17f., 21f.)

It is the *Christian*, the good disciple, who is said to fear God; it makes sense, in the first instance, to say that somebody fears God only in the context of a life devoted to God as a follower of Jesus. It is not atheistic communists who primarily fear God, however fearless and virtuous they may be. There might indeed be communists of whom we want to say that they fear God, but if we say that it marks an extension of the concept of fearing God; we would not begin to teach Otto what it means to fear God by telling him to watch the behaviour of atheistic communists. It is a concept that is at home in Christianity. (It is tempting to add here "and related religions, like Judaism and Islam", for these two also speak much of fearing God. However, use of the same phrase does not necessarily imply use of the same concept. It would be surprising if the Jewish and Muslim concepts of fearing God were quite unrelated to the Christian one, but how close the relationship is can only be

118

settled by actually looking to see how the phrase, as well as related ones, is used in all three religions. I have not done that.) Within the general context of a Christian life, it is in situations that would normally occasion fear that the fear of God is manifested as fearlessness: fearlessness, the fate of the sparrows suggests, even in the face of death.

There is a parallel here with the concept of trusting in God. Trusting in God may be described as a general feature of the life of the believer, but it is manifested in situations which would normally call for trusting in somebody or something – for your salvation – for that, remember, is the kind of trust in question here. The believer exhibits trust in God when he trusts, yet there is nobody he trusts in. You have the kind of confidence that comes from looking to somebody trustworthy to save you from a situation of peril; you trust in God when you are imperilled yet look to nobody (not even yourself) for your salvation. This is the kind of situation that is met with in chapters 30 and 31 of Isaiah, which refer to a time when Jerusalem is in peril, under threat from Assyria. The plan of the powers that be is to look to Egypt and its military strength for salvation, and therefore, in the eyes of the prophet, not to God (you cannot trust in Egypt *and* in God). The leaders of the nation should instead trust in God. *Instead*, not as well; so there is no question, for example, of making an alliance with Egypt but relying on God for a bit of extra help, praying to God for salvation in case Egypt can't do the trick, taking out a kind of divine insurance policy; God cannot be an *extra* help to Judah. If they put their trust in God, that means seeking salvation in *nobody*, not even their own strength:

> Woe to rebellious children, says the Lord, who follow counsel which is not from me and who weave plots not of my spirit, adding sin to sin; who are going down to Egypt without asking me to take refuge with Pharaoh

and to shelter in the shadow of Egypt. The protection of Pharaoh will turn to shame for you, and the shelter in the shadow of Egypt to humiliation... For thus has said the Lord, the Holy One of Israel: In returning and resting you will be saved; in quietness and trust will be your strength, But you will not. You said, "No, but we will fly on horses": therefore you shall flee; "On swift horses": therefore your pursuers will be swift. (Isaiah 30:1–5, 15f.)

And there is a similar message a few verses later:

Woe to those who go down to Egypt for help, who rely on horses and trust in chariots because they are many, and in warhorses because they are so strong, but do not look to the Holy One of Israel and do not seek the Lord... Egypt is man, not God; and their horses are flesh and not spirit... Like birds hovering the Lord of hosts will shield Jerusalem. (31: 1, 3, 5)

To trust in God, then, is not to seek salvation, security, in situations of peril, situations in which it would be normal to seek salvation; that is, in situations in which worldly men, those who do not believe, would seek salvation from somebody or something. Believers do not think and act like that; their ways are different from the ways of the world. To be a believer is manifested in this context by not seeking security at all. One way you might explain this is to say you believe you are *already* secure, secure with the protection of God. In Isaiah's case, that means trusting that Jerusalem will not fall, that in the end no harm will come to the city and its people, if and only if they do not seek help, salvation, from others, or from themselves.

The notion of fearing God in Matthew is somewhat similar, but goes further. Here too the believers are under the protection of God. As with the sparrows, so with the disciples: nothing will happen to them apart from the knowledge and will of their heavenly Father, and they are worth more than many sparrows. But here the implication does not seem to be that the believers will be safe in Isaiah's sense; it is not that those who kill the body will not succeed in killing the disciples' bodies. For though not one sparrow falls to the ground without the will of God, yet it still falls to the ground. The point is not that the disciples will be saved from any particular fate. (So the reason why the disciples are not to fear men is not that God offers protection against men, so that men cannot harm them, as Harry might offer protection from Charlie.) Their security lies rather in their being safe, *whatever* fate befalls them; they are secure, *whatever* happens to them. Their protection is that God knows what happens to them, not that certain things will not happen to them. This, incidentally, also shows something about the knowledge of God. It is not always a consolation for us when we suffer, or any protection for us, that somebody knows what is happening to us. In fact, that somebody knows we are suffering can make things a lot worse; e.g. if we love him and he loves us, our suffering hurts him, and that can increase our suffering; or if we know that somebody is in a position to stop our suffering but will not, perhaps because he delights in our harm, that can be an additional burden to us. That God's knowledge of our suffering can, on the contrary, be a consolation and a protection is an indication that God's knowing something is not a matter of *somebody's* knowing it.

The way God protects the disciples here is what might be called a *spiritual* protection: God is the one who protects them when *nobody* protects them, and there is *nothing* that he protects them from, for anything can still happen to them. For the disciples, because they enjoy the protection of God, everything is all right, even when *nothing* is all right, when everything has gone wrong. Even when they lose everything, even life itself, they are unharmed.

One way this could be expressed is to say that the *souls* of the disciples are under the protection of God. (For men cannot kill the soul – a 'grammatical remark': the soul's immunity here does not come from its being so tough, but is part of the way we talk about souls; whatever it is, if men can kill it, it is not a soul. This is obviously relevant to Christian talk of the immortality of the soul.) Of course, a man's soul is not something *else*, another constituent of him apart from his head, arms, heart. A man's soul is what is safe when he has *no* safety. And conversely, given the right circumstances, a man's soul can be in peril even when he is *totally* secure. He may lose his soul, though he gain the whole world (cf. Matthew 16:26). (This is related to a feature of the Last Day, that it will irrupt suddenly into an apparently secure world; then men will be lost, even though they dwelt in complete security:

> As were the days of Noah, so will be the appearing of the Son of Man. For just as in those days, before the flood, they were eating and drinking and marrying right up to the day when Noah went into the ark, and they didn't know what was happening until the flood came and killed them all – so will be the appearing of the Son of Man. (Matthew 24:37ff.)

There are many other passages in the same vein.)

If God protects a man, if his soul is safe, then it is *he*, the whole man, who is safe, not just part of him. So there is no need to seek protection. To attempt to achieve safety, in conditions of persecution, by denying Christ, to rely on yourself and what you can do to become safe, shows that you fear men and not God; and it is not to have the protection of God, it is to lose yourself, your soul. So the passage in Matthew continues:

Everybody who acknowledges me before men I too will acknowledge before my Father in heaven. But whoever denies me before men, I too will deny him before my Father in heaven... Whoever does not take his cross and follow after me is not worthy of me. Whoever has found his soul will lose it, and he who has lost it for my sake will find it. (Matthew 10:32f., 38f.)

To trust in God is not to trust in somebody, and to fear God is not to fear somebody. To trust in God is not to trust that some particular fate will not befall you, and to fear God is not, at least in the Matthean conception, to fear that some particular fate will befall you. To trust in God and to fear God are both to have a kind of confidence about your life, to know that you are safe, that you are all right, whatever happens to you, however unsafe you may be, however much things may go wrong. The one who fears God or trusts in God is the one who lives in this way, who is not overcome by events, lost, however wrong things go for him. He may well recognise that things have gone wrong for him – he has lost his job, his wife has left him, his house has burned down, or he is dying in pain, young, lonely and unfulfilled thousands of miles away from home, or suffering in life in any of a thousand possible ways. Yet, though all is lost, he does not see himself as lost; in a sense, he is all right. All his suffering, which matters very deeply, does not matter finally. Even though he may have lost everything, *he* is not lost. And that will be shown by what he says, but also by how he lives, in the face of the catastrophes he has suffered. Though he may certainly speak and act as one who has suffered great misfortune, he will not kill himself, go round despairing, take to drink, or spend all day in bed. He continues to do his best to live through all his adversity according to the same Christian values (for once again, the context of a Christian life is presupposed if sense is to be given to the notion of trusting God). He takes what happens to him seriously, but not with final seriousness.

One way this might be given verbal expression is to talk of 'levels of sense'; we, or he, might say that, though in an obvious sense he may be ruined or afflicted, yet in a deeper sense he is all right. Wittgenstein gives an example of this kind of usage in the *Remarks on Colour*:

> When someone who believes in God looks around him and asks "Where did everything that I see come from?" "Where did everything come from?" he is not asking for a (causal) explanation; and the point of his question is that it is the expression of such a request. Thus, he is expressing an attitude toward all explanations. – But how is this shown in his life? It is the attitude that takes a particular matter seriously, but then at a particular point doesn't take it seriously after all, and declares that something else is even more serious. In this way a person can say it is very serious that so-and-so died before he could finish a certain work; and in another sense it doesn't matter at all. Here we use the words "in a profounder sense". What I actually want to say is that here too it is not a matter of the words one uses or of what one is thinking when using them, but rather of the difference they make at various points in life. How do I know that two people mean the same when both say they believe in God?... *Practices* give words their meaning. (p.58f.; also in *Culture and Value* p.85)

The man who has lost everything but is, in a deeper sense, all right, might say, "I trust in God", and his life gives his words their meaning. (So if somebody did lose everything, and did despair and make repeated but genuine suicide attempts, did take to drink, become bitter, and yet said that he trusted in God, we should not know what to make of his words, or would say they are empty.) Or he might, as an expression of that trust, of his confidence that, in spite of appearances and in a deeper sense, God protects him, say, "God loves me". And now his life gives sense to that remark as well.

The Love of God

In a contribution to the symposium *Theology and Falsification* in *New Essays in Philosophical Theology*, Antony Flew says this about the love of God:

> Now it often seems to people who are not religious as if there was no conceivable event or series of events the occurrence of which would be admitted by sophisticated religious people to be a sufficient reason for conceding 'There wasn't a God after all' or 'God does not really love us then'. Someone tells us that God loves us as a father loves his children. We are reassured. But then we see a child dying of inoperable cancer of the throat. His earthly father is driven frantic in his efforts to help, but his Heavenly Father reveals no obvious sign of concern. Some qualification is made – God's love is 'not a merely human love' or it is 'an inscrutable love', perhaps – and we realise that such sufferings are quite compatible with the truth of the assertion that 'God loves us as a father (but, of course,....)'. We are reassured again. But then perhaps we ask: what is this assurance of God's (appropriately qualified) love worth, what is this apparent guarantee really a guarantee against? Just what would have to happen not merely (morally and wrongly) to tempt us but also (logically and rightly) to entitle us to say 'God does not love us' or even 'God does not exist'? I therefore put ... the simple central questions, 'What would have to occur or to have occurred to constitute for you a disproof of the love of, or of the existence of, God?' (p.98f.)

This challenge, which seems so reasonable, actually misses the point of what Christians say about the love of God. Flew asks, "What is this assurance of God's (appropriately qualified) love worth, what is this apparent guarantee really a guarantee against?" But why should it be thought that "God loves me" is intended to express belief in a guarantee against anything, to rule anything out? If I say that Charlie loves me, perhaps that is supposed to be a guarantee against something. If he stabbed me, refused to speak to me except to hurl abuse at me, ran off with all my money, poisoned my pet parrot, that would certainly constitute strong evidence that he did not after all love me, and it would be irrational of me not to entertain the possibility that he did not like me very much. (My irrationality might be born of a desperate need to believe that Charlie loves me, the feeling that all would be finished if he did not love me.) That is the way our talk of the love of human beings works. But that does not automatically mean that our talk of the love of God works like that; we have already seen a number of ways in which God is logically different from Charlie. And in fact it is *not* how our talk of the love of God works. To one who trusts in God, one who says things like "God loves me", what actually happens to him is irrelevant to the love of God for him. He has confidence in God, but that is not because he has learned by experience that God is loving, trustworthy and solicitous for his welfare. To say that God is loving is an expression of confidence in God, and so of a disposition to live in a certain way – not to despair, take to drink or commit suicide, in the face of adversity. While he has that confidence, nothing is going to count as evidence of God's not loving him (though not everything may count as evidence that God does love him; there may be many events in his life he does not understand). And to say that is not to convict

126

him of irrationality; it is to make a comment on the meaning, that is the use, of the phrase "the love of God". Flew's question cannot be answered, as he obviously suspects; but that is not because it is such a good and penetrating question. It is because it is misplaced. It construes the love of God as the love of Charlie. His challenge cannot be met, but that is only because it is a challenge against his own false conception of the love of God. The man who says "God loves me" does not believe that certain events are ruled out, that there are certain things that cannot happen to him; for he may say it when every conceivable misfortune *has* afflicted him. And in the same way, if he says "God loves you" or "God loves him", that does not mean that he thinks certain things just will not happen to those other people. Indeed, he may say such things precisely when they *have* happened to them, and *because* they have happened to them, not in spite of their having happened. He may say it to the boy with inoperable cancer of the throat, and he may say it to the boy's father. Most importantly, the father, as well as doing all he can to help, may say to his dying son, seriously and lovingly, "God loves you". (Though it is probably true to say that if he is capable of this then, though passionately concerned, he will not be driven *frantic*.) On Flew's understanding of the love of God, it would be a bizarre, even nonsensical thing to say in such a situation, but that only goes to show how wide of the mark his understanding is. Rather than looking to see how talk of the love of God is used, in what situations it is at home, and so coming to understand it, he has assumed he knows how it is used without having to look, because he understands how talk of the love of Charlie is used and thinks God is logically the same as Charlie. Hence he wants to say that one of the central and typical situations in which talk of the love of God is used – comforting people in great anguish – is one where it is not to be used at all. But this is

127

like saying that it is illegitimate to use a hammer to bang nails; and that God cannot be thought of as an invisible Charlie is shown by the absurdity of such a conclusion.

If, on the other hand, we take "God loves me" more nearly for what it is, an expression of confidence in God, then it is possible to understand that somebody might use it or similar sentences in such a distressing circumstance as Flew imagines. To say "God loves you" in time of adversity is to try to give the one spoken to that confidence in God, the ability to carry on, not to despair in spite of everything, to get him to say that though everything may have gone terribly wrong, yet in a deeper sense he is all right. And to say "God loves him" to the boy's father is to express the attitude that though everything may be all up with the boy, though – as he can see perfectly well – his situation is hopeless, yet in a deeper sense he is all right, he is not lost, he has hope.

This may, by the way, be put in terms of life beyond the grave. But that does not mean that he will not really die, that his certain imminent death will only be a charade. If it is said that he will live beyond the grave, that will be *despite* his being dead; he will live 'in a deeper sense', with God. So it would also be possible to say seriously to one who is dying, or of one who is dead or dying, that he will never die. This is in fact what is said by Jesus to Martha in John's gospel, just before he raises Lazarus:

> I am the resurrection and the life. He who believes in me will live – even if he dies; and everybody who lives and believes in me will never die. (11:25f.)

This might be a starting point for an investigation of what Christians mean when they say there is life beyond the grave, or life after death.

People do sometimes lose faith entirely in the love of God, and so lose faith in God. (For you cannot, in

Christianity that is not deviant, have a God who is not loving. Charlie may or may not love me, but if I am a Christian I cannot doubt that God loves me: God's love belongs to his essence.) But if they do lose faith, that is not because they have discovered that God is unloving, in the same way that they might discover that Charlie does not love them. It is because they no longer have it in them to carry on as they have been living, or even to try to carry on in the same way; events have proved too much for them. They can no longer see events either as expressions of God's love for them or as something they do not understand. Things appear to be against them. A father whose son dies of some horrible disease may react like this, and lose his faith in God. But that will not be a theoretical change; it will mean a change in his attitude towards his life, and a change in how he lives it: he will feel cheated, become embittered, despairing. His life will change, because he has been hurt; he is like one who has had a limb torn off – he can no longer live, behave, in the way that he used to. To continue to believe in God means still to see a certain way of life as possible, and one who is that badly hurt may be unable to see it as possible. But if that is so, he has not been swayed by evidence; he has been affected, by what has happened in his life. A man may lose faith because of the death of his son; he is not likely to lose faith over the death of a stranger thousands of miles away, even if he hears of it, for it does not enter his life in the same way, does not affect him. (Though the vividly reported death of thousands of distant strangers may. Not that it might be evidence for something that the obscure death of one person would not be, but that it might have an effect on him.) Belief in the love of God is not based on evidence, and so neither is the loss of that belief.

Belief in the love of God, trust in God, is in a sense *a priori*. That God is loving is not something that anybody ever found out. Paul writes to the Romans:

> If God is for us, who is against us?... Who will separate us from the love of Christ: Anguish or distress or persecution or famine or nakedness or danger or sword?... But in all these things we are triumphant through him who loved us. I am certain that neither death, nor life, nor angels, nor authorities, nor things present or to come, nor powers, nor height, nor depth, nor any other created thing whatsoever will be able to separate us from the love of God in Christ Jesus our Lord. (Romans 8:31–39)

He also says:

> We know that for those who love God he works in all things for good. (Romans 8:28)

How can he *know* that? It is not because he has observed that good things (things which everybody would recognise as good) always happen to Christians, or that they are miraculously preserved from having bad things happen to them; he is fond of telling how he himself has suffered bad things (e.g. 2 Corinthians 11:23–33; 4:8–11), and he has just said how Christians face tribulation, persecution, famine and sword – just as Jesus predicts in the gospels. The fact of God's unremitting care for those who love him can be known, not by observation, but because it is written into the language of Christianity. Paul's use of such language (indeed his creation of much of it) reflects his determination to see things in a particular way, to live in a particular way, and the Christian acceptance of his language as canonical, authoritative, reflects Christian willingness to live similarly. This is how Christians are committed to seeing what happens to them, *whatever* happens to them. This is the language of those who are able to see things in that way and are disposed to see them in that way, who are able to be all right even when *everything* is wrong. (It is not that they cling to some element of their lives which is still all right, so that not quite everything has gone wrong. A man may say, "Even though I have lost everything, yet I still have God"; but not, "I still have God, so although most things have gone wrong, I haven't quite lost everything".)

Somebody like Flew might say, "If nothing could convince you that God does not exist, is not loving, if you cling to your belief regardless of what actually happens to you and those around you, that simply shows that you are determined to use a particular kind of linguistic expression; your 'belief' is empty". But if people are determined to use a particular kind of language, this can be a linguistic expression of a determination to live and to see their lives in a certain way, a determination to do certain things and not to do others, to adopt certain attitudes and avoid others. And that is how it gets its meaning; religious language, like all language, gets its meaning from being embedded in what people do. There is indeed such a thing as empty religious belief, but it is not a matter of a failure on the part of a believer to know what would convince him that his belief is false, but of its not being part of, an expression of, a determined way and view of life. It is of somebody who professes Christian faith with his lips, who says Christian words but whose language is not integrated with the rest of his behaviour, of one who uses the words of faith idly, that it might be said, "His belief is empty; he says these words, but they are not borne out in his life".

Getting Through

It should not be forgotten here that the same kind of suffering that can make people lose their faith in God can also give birth to it in others. This happens particularly, not just when people have a difficult time, but when everything around them, their whole life, collapses: they lose everything in a business failure, they suffer a heart-breaking bereavement, they are thrown into a concentration camp. To such people, there can seem nothing left, it can seem impossible to them to carry on living. And yet, in spite of it all, they stand firm, they manage to carry on, even though everything they had previously relied on for support is gone. It is here that language about God, which has before been available but unused (everybody knows what talk about God is like, even those who refuse to use it), may suddenly gain a hold. They might say, "I've no idea how I survived. God helped me through it all". And here of course it is not a question of discovering that there was somebody, called God, who they then in some way experienced helping them; that is not what makes the language appropriate here. God is not a somebody who helps. God cannot be a member of a list of people and things who helped out in this crisis. You cannot say, in Christianity, "I got through it all with the help of Mrs. Wilkins, and thanks to the self-discipline I got from my time in the army; and God also helped out a bit". If you can give an account of how you got through, that means you know how you got through: it was with these and these helps. But you come to use language about God because you *don't* know how you got through. But what 'not knowing' means in this context is that you cannot give an account of how you got through, how you were helped, because there is no account to give, because, quite visibly and obviously, *nobody* and *nothing* helped you; and yet you got through. In such a situation you might say, "God helped me", but here "God" is not the name of somebody who helped you, so that, after all, somebody did help you and you know who it was. God is the one who helps you when *nobody* helps you.

We might say that "God helped me" is not an explanation of how you got through; it is an expression of the *mystery* of how you, who needed help to get through, for whom it was even impossible to get through (that is how you see yourself), nevertheless did get through, *without* help. Of course you do not have to react this way when you get through. An alternative is to say, "I must be a lot stronger, a lot more capable, than I thought". It is possible to revise your attitude towards yourself in such a way that you do not think it a mystery how you got through. And then you need have no recourse to talk about God. Which option you take will probably depend on a number of things, among them your overall view of yourself and of the capabilities of human beings in general, your appreciation and understanding of talk about God, and perhaps whether you prayed God to help you. It is important though that if you talk about God coming to support you, then that God helped you through does not mean that it ceases to be mysterious how you got through; God does not banish mystery. But if you can give an explanation, an account of how you got through, then there is no mystery in the first place. If you can say it was all due to Mrs. Wilkins, then everything is made plain. But if you say it was all thanks to God, that does not make it plain; it is precisely because things are not plain, that there is a mystery, that God is talked about – not however as a hypothesis which, if true, would banish the mystery. If you say, "God helped me through", you are not making an inference. It means you have come to see the point of, even been gripped by, a particular type of language. Whereas before it meant nothing to you, now it does, since it now has its place in the way you live, a way which before seemed to you not a possibility; you were sure you could not carry on, and you have discovered you can; and this is to you a mysterious discovery. *This* might be spoken of as a "discovery of God". To speak of God is to articulate the mystery, not to solve it.

CHAPTER 5

HOW TO SUCCEED BY NOT TRYING

Serving God

Nobody can serve two masters.... You cannot serve God and mammon. So I say to you: do not worry about what you eat or drink, or what you will put on your body. Is not the soul more than food and the body more than clothing?... The gentiles pursue all these things. Your heavenly Father knows you need them all. But first seek the kingdom of God and his righteousness, and all these will be given to you as well. Therefore do not worry about tomorrow, for tomorrow will worry about itself. Content yourself with today's trouble. (Matthew 6:24–34)

Mammon is money. But even if we did not know that, we do already know that God cannot be listed with mammon to make a second; you may serve God, and you may serve mammon, but you cannot serve God *and* mammon. Nobody could ever be described as serving both God and mammon, for there is no such description. And this is not because in general you cannot serve two masters, for you can. I can serve Charlie faithfully from nine to five, and then serve Harry, for whom I work in the evenings. And I may serve them both at the same time if they are partners in the firm I work for.

What is it to serve God? You cannot serve God and mammon, and neither is there envisaged the possibility that you might serve neither. So you serve God if you do not serve mammon; to serve God is not to serve mammon. So we can find out what it is to serve God by finding out what it is to serve mammon and negating it. To serve mammon is, basically, to worry, to be anxious – about food, about clothing, about the morrow. So to serve God is not to be anxious about food, clothing, the morrow. These are the things the gentiles, those who do not believe in God, worry about. Naturally enough. The situations envisaged are the kind in which anybody would be anxious about those things: you don't know where the next meal is coming from, how you will survive the harshness of the winter, whether you will do well in tomorrow's crucial interview. If these were not situations in which it would be the normal, natural, human thing to worry, there would be no point in Jesus telling his disciples not to worry. So the one who serves God is the one who does not worry in situations that would normally call forth worry. Not to be anxious is to be secure, and once again, as in the case of the fear of God, the security of the disciples lies in the knowledge of God: "Your heavenly Father knows you need them all". (So it is not that the disciples are not to worry about these things because they do not really need food and clothing. They do need them, but nevertheless they are not to worry about them.)

But if to serve mammon is to be anxious about these things, is to serve God to be anxious instead about other things? The disciples are, to be sure, to seek first the kingdom of God, but they are not to be anxious; the whole tenor of the passage is against anxiety. Jesus is not encouraging his disciples to transfer their anxiety from one object to another. To serve God does not mean to be anxious about something *else*; it is not to be anxious at all, to be anxious about *nothing* (So Catholics pray at Mass to be freed from *all* anxiety.) So too, in so far as service is connected with anxiety – as Jesus does here connect them – we can say that serving God rather than mammon is not a matter of being anxious to please or serving somebody *else*; it is a matter of not serving at all. It is a matter of being free from service, of being subservient to *nobody* – not, for instance, of being subservient to somebody invisible): the service of God, as it is said, is perfect freedom.

This theme surfaces elsewhere in the New Testament. Paul urges the Philippians:

> Do not worry about anything, but in everything, by prayer and supplication with thanksgiving, let what you ask be made known to God. And the peace of God, which passes all understanding, will guard your hearts and your minds in Christ Jesus. (4:6f.)

More interestingly:

> I want you to be without worries. The unmarried man worries about the things of the Lord, how to please the Lord; but the married man worries about worldly things, how to please his wife, and he is divided. (1 Corinthians 7:32ff.)

Paul wants his readers to be anxious about the affairs of God, not about worldly affairs, and even speaks of division of interest, as if God and the world could after all be listed together as objects of anxiety. But he prefaces everything he has to say by: "I want you to be without worries". To "worry about the things of the Lord, how to please the Lord" is not, then, a way of being anxious about something. The expression does have a use, but its use is not like that of "worrying about the things of Charlie, how to please Charlie", for the latter implies having worries, while the former implies being free from worries. "Worry about the affairs of the Lord, how to please the Lord" is not used in connexion with what we would normally recognise as the expression of worry (just as "fear the Lord" has a use, but is not used in connexion with the expression of fear). If Otto wants to understand what it is to be anxious about the affairs of the Lord he can ask to be shown somebody who is. And if we point out Alvin, who is, as we say, anxious about the affairs of the Lord, he will not see Alvin behaving in a way that he would describe as anxious. He does not go around worrying all the time, unable to relax or take his mind off things. On the contrary, if Alvin is an anxious man, this will show that, whatever he is anxious about, it is not God. This will be true even if Alvin sincerely claims that all his anxiety, why he bites his fingernails and cannot sleep, is anxiety about the things of God. If he does say this, he will stand in need of correction; for God is what frees from worry, not yet another cause of ulcers. Alvin has misunderstood this part of Christian language, just as he would have misunderstood what it is to love God if he sincerely claimed that, though he is indifferent to most people, hates a few and spends his spare time devising new torments to inflict on his aged mother, yet he really loves God and indeed finds God is the only one he has ever been able to love. Remarks such as these mistakenly construe God as a kind of bodiless Charlie.

It may seem that, if I am right here, Paul is expressing himself in unduly paradoxical terms. But much Christian language is paradoxical, which is why it is so easy for Christians and non-believers alike to misconstrue. And this is not the only place where Paul uses language in this way. Think, for example, of Romans 6. In v.14 he says how in Christ believers are free from the dominion of sin. This idea of freedom from slavery to sin is a familiar one both in Paul and elsewhere (see e.g. John 8:31 -36). And the point of course is that through Christ the believer is *set free*; it is definitely not that he has simply exchanged one slavery for another. And yet Paul continues here:

> Do you not know that you are slaves of the one you obey – the one to whom offer yourselves as slaves to be obedient to – whether it is sin, which leads to death, or

obedience, which leads to righteousness?... But you, having been set free from sin have been made slaves of righteousness. (Romans 6:16– 18)

It is as a slave to righteousness that you are precisely *not* a slave.

So God is not somebody else, whom the Christian serves, somebody else, whom he is anxious to please. To serve God is to serve nobody, to be free, and to be anxious about the things of God is to be free from anxiety. Though here Wittgenstein's remark is again relevant. It is not that the Christian never works for anybody and is never worried about anything, but that this is of importance to him only up to a point. Food and clothing do matter, but they are not of final importance; while up to a point they matter very much, in a deeper sense they do not matter at all. And the freedom of Christians does not mean that they have to pretend that they are not in any way subject to human authority. It means that, whatever their condition in the world, they are ultimately free. This freedom is not a matter of their contingent social or political status, but of the way they see their lives. How does this freedom manifest itself in the lives of those whom God has freed? They consider themselves free, whatever their condition in the world. Whoever their earthly masters (that is, simply, their masters) may be, whoever they obey, they are not finally under authority. How people consider themselves comes out in how they act. So, while they may normally be respectful of authority and good law-abiding citizens (as they are urged to be in Romans 13:1–7 and in 1 Timothy 2:1f.), no state or other power has a final claim on their obedience. They are free to violate laws, to disobey masters. Hence the Christian tradition, dating from earliest times, of civil disobedience.

One other consequence of the freedom of Christians is that they do not have to seek liberty by changing their status

139

in the world; they are free to live in any social position
(which is not to say that actual freedom in the world does
not matter; of course it does – up to a point):

> He who was called in the Lord as a slave is a freedman
> of the Lord; and likewise the free man who is called is a
> slave of Christ. You were bought at a price; do not
> become the slaves of men. Each as he was called,
> brethren, so let him remain with God. (1 Corinthians
> 7:22–24)

Getting Rewards from God

> Be careful that you do not practise your piety before
> men to be seen by them; otherwise you get no reward
> from your Father in heaven. Therefore, when you give
> alms, do not sound a trumpet before you, as the
> hypocrites do in the synagogues and the streets, to be
> praised by men. Amen I say to you, they have had their
> reward. But when you give alms let not your left hand
> know what your right hand is doing, so that your
> almsgiving may be in secret; and your Father who sees
> in secret will reward you. (Matthew 6:1–4)

Here are instructions on how to go about getting a reward
from God. If you are seeking a reward from somebody, you
have to fulfil the conditions laid down by whoever is
offering it. But that is not enough: you must also *exhibit* the
fact that you fulfil the conditions, exhibit it to whoever is
offering the reward; you must show him you deserve the
reward. I may write the best book, and so qualify for the
literary prize, but that is no good to me unless I also submit
it, bring it to the attention of the judges. I may have all the
numbers on the card, but I will not win the jackpot on the
bingo unless I also show my card to the man who runs the
show. I may run a mile in three minutes, for which some
eccentric millionaire is offering a huge prize, but he will not

give the money if I make the run in private, with neither him nor his agents there, and without proof of what I have done. If I qualify for a reward, I must exhibit the fact, if I am actually to get it. So reward-seeking behaviour is in this sense necessarily exhibitionistic. This fact is central to understanding how to get a reward from God.

One way to get a reward from God is to do good deeds, for example to give alms. But such deeds also carry the promise of reward of some kind from men. People approve if you do good deeds, and the approval of others is one of the rewards normally most sought in human life. But if you want others to approve of your good deeds, you must see to it that they see them; you must exhibit them. When you give alms, you must sound a trumpet before you (but not too loudly; people do not approve if they think you are making an exhibition of yourself, too blatantly seeking their approval). So your almsgiving at once takes on a dual nature. On the one hand, and in the first instance, it is a response to the one who is before you, who is in need of what you can give him. But on the other hand, it is a piece of acting, designed to make you *appear* to be giving alms. You have one eye on the man before you, but also one eye on those standing by, who you hope will be watching (some slightly exaggerated gestures, words of compassion in a slightly raised voice – a muted trumpet – may do the trick, catch their attention while appearing to be indifferent to it). And if you succeed in your act, you win their approval and so get your reward from them. But if you do that, you cannot also get a reward from God for your almsgiving. You cannot get a reward from God *and* from men: God cannot be listed together with Charlie as giving you a reward for one and the same act. So in order to seek a reward from God in your almsgiving, you must *not* seek any reward from men.

So God is the one from whom you seek a reward when you seek a reward from *nobody*, and God is the one who rewards you when *nobody* rewards you. And nobody includes yourself. We may or may not promise ourselves identifiable rewards for our good deeds – an evening out, a drink. But we do like to approve of ourselves, just as we like others to approve of us. So we give performances to ourselves just as much as to others. So if it is a condition of getting a reward from God that we not exhibit ourselves to others, neither must we act out a performance for our own benefit. If we must not let others know that we are giving alms, we must not let ourselves know either. So there is a development in the words of Jesus; not only, "Sound no trumpet before you as the hypocrites do... that they may be praised by men"; but also, "When you give alms, do not let your left hand know what your right hand is doing". You yourself must be unaware of what you are doing, in the sense that you are not conscious of yourself as doing something meritorious, worthy of praise. For then, too, you have your reward, the reward of self-approval for doing something good.

In a way, acting to yourself is more basic than acting for others. If you are performing a good deed, you have to see yourself as doing so before you want to exhibit the fact to others; otherwise, from your point of view, you have nothing to exhibit. If you don't see your own action as praiseworthy you have no reason to think that you will win the praise of others by exhibiting it to them. So if you do not show yourself your good deeds, you don't show them to anybody. So, if you do not exhibit your good deeds to yourself, God cannot be somebody to whom you exhibit them. God is not somebody you hope will see what you are doing. When God sees you, it is not that somebody *else* sees you – not the men standing around, but somebody much more important (and, of course, invisible). If you are a hypocrite, you put on a public act, in the hope of being seen by men. When God sees what you do, it is not that you put on an act, and God is your public: God sees *in secret*. And the condition of your alms being in secret is that not even your left hand knows what your right hand is doing. You do not know what you are doing, so in doing what you do you do not put on any act, either for your own benefit or for anybody else; you have no audience at all.

But acting, self-exhibiting, is central to seeking a reward; reward-seeking activity is exhibitionistic. So the activity of the disciples in giving alms is not reward-seeking activity. So to seek a reward from God is not to seek a reward at all. What we call "seeking a reward from God" is not a kind of reward-seeking; we do not use those words in connexion with reward-seeking activity. Seeking a reward from God is not seeking a reward from somebody *else*, apart from yourself and other people. You and others are the sum total of what there is: there is nobody else to seek a reward from. To seek a reward from God for your good deeds is simply to give up the business of seeking rewards for what you do.

Seeking a reward divides your attention: you have one eye on what you are doing (say, on the beggar before you) and one eye glancing over your shoulder at your audience. (I do not mean this as a piece of psychology. You may be thoroughly engrossed in the reward-bearing activity, e.g. competition dancing, acting, or boxing. And if some of your attention is on the judges, that is a distraction, and may mean you perform less well than you might. My point is a logical one: your motives are split – and that, if you are not a disciplined performer, may lead to divided attention.) So seeking a reward makes a difference to what you do. In so far as you seek a reward for your almsgiving, you do not give alms if there is no audience about. The presence or absence of an audience makes a difference to what you do. Since seeking a reward from God is not a species of reward-seeking, to seek a reward from God means that the presence or absence of an audience makes *no* difference to what you do. You cannot say or think, "If it were not for the fact that God is watching I would not be giving you this money". If you seek a reward from God, your attention is not divided between the beggar and God; your eye is simple (cf. Matthew 6:22). (So here is another way in which God and people cannot be listed together: God and Charlie cannot *both* be objects of attention. Even if you are good at doing two things at once, even if you can talk to Peter while listening to Paul, you cannot perform the same feat with Charlie and God, for with them there is no such feat to perform). The beggar is the *sole* object of your concern. There is no motive for your action apart from the need of the man before you. It is not an act calculated to achieve something; it is a response to a visible human being, not a performance before an invisible, nonhuman being. In this context, to seek a reward from God you have to forget all about God. (Of course you don't: we are always to be mindful of God. What I mean is, if you fall prey to grammatical illusion, to the temptation to see "God" as the name of somebody, to think that God is somebody, then in order to get your reward from God you must get it out of your head that there might be this supposed somebody around watching, from whom you might expect a reward. Your mind is to be only on the one to whom you are giving.)

This can be put very simply by saying: If you are promised a reward by God, it is for being concerned with somebody else, another human being, for responding to their needs. It is not for being concerned for yourself and using particular acts, such as almsgiving, as an opportunity for furthering yourself or enriching yourself. It is for giving, not trying to get. Seeking reward from God is not a matter of hoping that your acquisitiveness will be satisfied from one quarter rather than another, as it is if you hope for a reward from Charlie instead of from Cecil; it is a matter of not being acquisitive at all, but generous.

Of course there is nothing new in this conclusion. It would be very odd if Christians were encouraged to engage in reward-seeking activity. They are not supposed to be self-seeking, but truly generous. *Truly* generous: Jesus reserves some of his sharpest criticisms for those who use apparently generous acts as a cover for self-seeking; these are exactly the hypocrites he is criticising in Matthew 6:1ff. If Christians differed from them only in seeking a larger reward (treasure in heaven, eternal life, etc.) from somebody much richer and more powerful than men (God), then they would be more self-seeking, more hypocritical, than the hypocrites. In fact, if we look at the way Jesus actually uses this language about seeking a reward from God, we see that it is not inconsistent with the rest of his teaching. Despite its appearance, its aim is to promote love of neighbour, not love of gain. The language of rewards is being used in order to encourage people to forget all about rewards. It is as if it were being said, "You want a reward? Then seek this one; it's much better than all other rewards. And the condition of getting this reward is that you don't seek any reward at all". So the approach of the Matthean Jesus, who is very fond of using the language of money and reward, is quite compatible with that of the Lucan Jesus, who is much more chary of it (think of his emphasis on poverty). While Matthew wants to encourage Christians to seek a reward from God, a heavenly reward, the attitude he wants to engender is no different from that which Luke wants to instil when he reports Jesus as comparing the disciples to servants:

Which of you who has a servant out ploughing or
minding the sheep would say to him when he comes in
from the field, "Come and sit down to supper straight
away"? Would you not rather say to him, "Make me
something to eat, gird yourself and wait on me until
I've eaten and drunk; then you can eat and drink too"?
Is he grateful to the servant for doing what he has been
told? So too, when you have done everything you have
been told, say, "We are useless servants; we have only
done what we ought". (Luke 17:7–10)

This is one of many instances of the great freedom of
terminology encountered in the New Testament and later;
different writers often use quite different, even apparently
opposed, ways of expressing their thought, as Matthew and
Luke do here. We should not be too impressed by such
purely verbal differences between writers. If we actually
want to get at their thought and the differences between
them, the important thing is to look at the way they actually
put their terms to work. Incidentally, there also emerges
here a connexion between Matthew's language of reward
and the traditional, more Pauline, doctrine of grace. If I seek
a reward from God, say through almsgiving, my concern is
wholly for the one in need; what I see in giving alms is him as
needy, not myself as generous. I do not consider myself as
generous, since I do not consider myself at all. Hence I do
not consider that I deserve any reward for generosity. So
what I receive from God I cannot conceive as reward, as
merited; it must appear to me, if I see it as from God, as gift,
as grace. And if I see what I receive as gift, that means that I
am disposed to be grateful for it.

Hence also the central place of gratitude in Christian life.
Part of the way that Christians (are taught to) see and live
their lives is that they are disposed to be grateful, even when
there is nobody to be grateful to, to see things as gift which

146

are obviously not given by anybody. Here notice another difference between God and Charlie. If something suddenly appears that I have long wanted, I might suspect it is a gift from somebody. I may then enquire whether anybody has in fact given it to me. If I find Charlie has given it to me, I will thank him. Here, giving thanks is dependent on establishing that it has been given, and it is important to identify the right one as the giver. If I discover no giver, there is nobody I can thank. But with God I give thanks without even looking for a giver, sometimes in the obvious absence of any giver. Though God gives, he is not somebody who gives: God is the one who gives when nobody gives, and the one who is thanked when nobody is thanked.

One of the things I want to show in these remarks and in many of those that follow is that Christian belief in and language about God is logically linked to the way Christians live and see their lives. It is through the attitudes and dispositions and activities of Christians that their language gets its meaning. It is not that belief in God, that he gives rewards, created the world, sees into the hearts of men, etc., is somehow given an independent, theoretical meaning, and that we are then exhorted to develop the attitudes appropriate to such a being. It is not that we should be grateful to him for having made us and given us life and everything we have, that we should be respectful of him, even (were he not so loving) frightened, because he is so exceedingly powerful, and so on. The attitudes, dispositions and activities are not just appropriate in the light of the beliefs we hold about some being called God; they are what give *sense* to our belief in God and what we believe about him. Our religious beliefs and language have their place within the context of a particular kind of human life, a life in which gratitude, generosity, lack of self-seeking, a sense of dependence and of mystery, among other things, play an important, even a defining part. If the language does not exist in that context, if it is not surrounded by that particular kind of life, then it is not just that the believer in question is 'failing to take his faith seriously', but that his belief is empty; the words are there, but they have no function, they no longer express any faith, any religious belief; here, language is idling. It is an advantage of the line I am taking – stressing the importance for the understanding of our language about God of the absence of anything called God – and an indication that it is somewhere near the truth, that it allows a much closer connexion between Christian belief and Christian attitudes and action than there is on the other, 'God-as-invisible-Charlie' model, and so that it enables us to make sense of the religious notion of empty belief. It also enables us to say here, as we do often in other areas of our language, that how you act is a good guide to what you believe.

Heavenly & Earthly Rewards

From the fact that seeking a reward from God is not seeking a reward there follow a number of other differences between, on the one hand, seeking a heavenly reward (a reward from God) and seeking an earthly one (a reward from men) and, on the other hand, seeking a reward from one quarter (Charlie) and seeking a reward from another quarter (Cecil).

You cannot seek *both* a heavenly reward and an earthly one – logically. It is not just that they are in a different place from one another, or that they are awarded for different, perhaps incompatible, activities. It is not a matter of my being unable to enter a dancing competition in Wimbledon and another one in Minsk. Nor is it like my inability to put on weight in preparation for a fat-man contest and at the same time take it off in preparation for a thin-man contest. If the competitions are open long enough, or if they are regular, repeated events, I can go to Wimbledon first and

Minsk afterwards, try to win the fat-man contest this year and go in for the thin-man prize next year. I can form a *plan*, a course of action that will enable me to get all the rewards I want. I can of course also seek a heavenly reward and an earthly one in succession. I may spend half my life seeking a heavenly reward, devoting myself to the things of God, then decide that the whole thing is a waste of time and go off and do my best to amass earthly rewards, to get rich and famous (perhaps, to increase my chances, I might pass myself off as a spiritual man, a guru, one indifferent to earthly rewards). Or I might, on the other hand, devote myself in my youth to acquiring everything the world can offer, then turn away disillusioned and dissatisfied to seek after higher things. But what I cannot do is to *plan* such a sequence. I cannot try to work it so that I get the heavenly prizes after I've got all the earthly ones. I cannot plan to spend ten years securing a reward in heaven and then the next ten getting rich. Heavenly and earthly rewards necessarily present me with a choice; I must, here and now, choose between them; I cannot place them in a sequence. And so also the choice I make now affects my view of my past. If I once pursued the one and now turn to pursue the other, this is not simply a further episode in my life; it means a turning away from my former life, coming to see my life in a different way, rejecting my former values; the rewards I formerly sought no longer appear to me as rewards. To seek the one and then the other is not a matter of sequence, but of *conversion*. So Paul writes to the Philippians:

> If anybody else has reason for confidence in the flesh, more so do I... But whatever advantage I had, I counted it as loss because of Christ. Indeed, I count all things as loss because of the greater worth of knowing Christ Jesus my Lord, through whom I have lost everything; and I think of it all as so much trash, so that I might gain

Christ and be found in him, not having any righteousness of my own from the law but that which is through
faith in Christ, the righteousness from God based on
faith. (3:4, 6–9)

The two kinds of reward represent two ways, and the ways
always part at the point where I am now. All this follows
immediately once it is recognised that seeking a heavenly
reward is not seeking a reward, that it is not a way of getting
but a way of giving. Of course if you are interested in
getting, you cannot plan to give, except as a way of getting –
and that is to be a hypocrite. And if what you want to do is to
give, you cannot plan to get. You have to cease being
interested in the one in order to become interested in the
other. To become interested in the one *is* to cease to be
interested in the other. Seeking the one and then the other
reward requires, not just different activities which you can
do in succession, but a change in the way you see your life,
metanoia.

Again, I can seek an earthly reward and fail. And that
means: I can fail to get what I am after. But when I seek a
heavenly reward, I am not after anything, not out to get
anything. There is no question of success in my venture,
because there is no venture. And so also I cannot fail. This
can be put, admittedly somewhat paradoxically, by saying
that I am bound to succeed:

Ask and it will be given to you, seek and you will find,
knock and it will be opened to you. For everybody
who asks receives, and he who seeks finds, and it will
be opened to him who knocks. (Matthew 7:7f.)

Yet this is really not so paradoxical if we understand it as a
kind of grammatical remark, as a comment on the way the
phrase "seek a heavenly reward" is used. It is like the
sentence "Sense-datum reports are incorrigible". A sense-

datum report simply says how things appear to you. All you have to do to get a sense-datum report right is to be able to speak the language, for it makes no claim about what is so; it only says how things seem – rightly or wrongly – to be to you. It is more akin to expression than to report; it does not 'point beyond itself' to some reality to which it claims to correspond. And so it is with "Seek and you shall find". To say that I am bound to succeed if I seek a heavenly reward is to say that seeking a heavenly reward is not a species of reward-seeking. My activity in seeking a heavenly reward does not aim beyond itself, at securing some end, so that it might fail to achieve that end. The activity I perform in seeking a heavenly reward I perform for its own sake; it is an end, not a means to something further. If I give my money, my time, my life, that is not with a view to getting something else. That is perhaps why giving your life, either through martyrdom or by some dedicatory gesture, is traditionally regarded as the surest way to get to heaven. Once you give your life (and you really give your life), there is nothing further; since you have given everything, there remains nothing you can be trying to get. If I really seek a heavenly reward by giving, my action is quite simply what it appears to be – a response to somebody else's need, a human reaction to another human being. This is also why simplicity has been seen as a mark of sanctity, and gives some insight into what is meant by being simple in this context. Christian simplicity is not a matter of deliberately acting unintelligently or of insisting on wearing drab clothes rather than colourful ones. It is a kind of logical simplicity. If you just respond, react, your action is *described* more simply than if you are also aiming at something with your action, or pretending to respond while in fact doing something else. What the hypocrites do is logically more complicated than what the disciples do. Because we can describe their actions more simply, we could say that the disciples have a simpler mental life than the others.

So if I seek a heavenly reward I am bound to succeed, not in the sense that my action inevitably leads on to what I value, as cause leads to effect, but because what I value is the action itself; I am happy *doing this*, not in thinking of what doing this will bring me. There is an analogy here with the saying "Virtue is its own reward". That says: virtue does not seek reward. That you seek rewards, if you do, shows something about what kind of man you are, how you view your life, what will make you happy (you think). The virtuous man, according to this saying, is not like that, not that kind of man. He is happy without rewards; his happiness lies in his doing what he does. We might think that anybody who was fond of saying that virtue is its own reward might rather find his reward in thinking himself virtuous. But there is no danger of that for those who do not think of themselves as virtuous, whose left hand does not know what their right hand is doing. Though somebody might think himself virtuous, nobody can ever think he deserves a heavenly reward; "merit a reward from God" has no first-person use in orthodox Christianity (anybody who tried to introduce such a use would be corrected by grammatical experts - priests, theologians, etc.), though one might use it of others.

This brings out another difference between talking about God and talking about *somebody*. You can say, "You merit a reward in heaven for what you have done", and that comes close to saying, "God approves of what you have done". But you can only say that if you yourself approve of what he has done. "God approves of what you have done" is something that men might say to each other as an expression of their own approval. You can't say (except ironically), "God approves of what you have done, but I think it's dreadful". Similarly, it would be very odd, have the air of a joke, to say, "God approves of your doing this – and I think it's quite a good thing, too". Compare this with "Charlie approves of what you have done". If I say this, it is a report on somebody else's attitude to an action, and says nothing at all about my attitude. You can perfectly sensibly say, "Charlie approves of what you have done, but I think it's dreadful". And you can also say quite seriously, "Charlie thinks it's good of you to do this; and what's more, so do I". Your attitude and Charlie's are logically distinct: you can list your attitude and Charlie's in a way you cannot list your attitude and God's. To say that God approves of something is not to report some (invisible) person's attitude; it is not to report a putative fact about somebody called God. (This consideration will be an important element in any clear discussion of what it means to do the will of God, to say that God has a will, and so on. It is connected the fact I mentioned earlier, that God is necessarily an authority for me, if I believe in God; it is important for me to do the will of God.) The close connexion between what I say about God's attitude and my own attitude shows again why I cannot think that I deserve a reward from God, whereas I can perfectly well think I deserve a reward from Charlie. Part of the conditions I have to fulfil to merit a reward from God is that I do not think of my action as meritorious; and if I do not think my action is meritorious, I cannot think that God thinks it is meritorious, either.

Again, Charlie might promise me a reward for every time I perform a particular task; the more often I do it, the more I get. He might, say, promise to give me £10 every time I give £1 to a beggar. (He has spies everywhere, who follow me round at a discreet distance.) I am on to a good thing here. But I might be in a bad mood one morning, and refuse a beggar when he asks me for money, before I have time to think. Afterwards I will naturally regret my refusal. And what I regret is that I have passed up a chance to get more reward from Charlie; I am suffering from frustrated avarice. But now suppose I am promised a heavenly reward, a reward from God, for giving alms. I wake up in a bad mood and, contrary to my normal Christian habit, refuse somebody who (for obviously good reasons) begs money from me. If I regret my refusal afterwards, my regret is of an entirely different kind from the first case. What I regret now is not that I have passed up the chance of a reward, but simply that I have not given him the money, that I have not responded to one in need but have been selfish. I regret, not being without a gain that would have been the consequence of the action, but not having performed the action itself. What I suffer from now is not frustrated avarice but remorse. Once again, my concern in seeking a heavenly reward is not with getting a reward, but with giving. If I hope to get a reward from God, the one I am concerned with in giving alms is not myself, or somebody called God, but the man before me.

This is not to say that I do not, after all, seek a reward from God. If I am a Christian, of course I do. But if I seek a reward from God, I do not seek a reward from somebody called God; that is not the way the language of reward is used in Christianity. (Though it is perfectly possible to imagine a deviant form of Christianity, or some other religion, in which some other account of seeking a reward from God would be appropriate.) So to say that you give money to a beggar in the hope of a reward from God is not to say that it is not your *sole* concern to help the one before you. We might even imagine that it was the practice, whenever a Christian gave alms, to say, "For the sake of my heavenly reward", or something similar. But those words would not, in this context, be the expression of a desire for reward, but of concern for the man. So we might imagine them spoken, not with glee at being presented with an opportunity to make such a profit, but with *compassion*.

Avoiding Punishment

It is possible to make exactly analogous comments on the Christian idea of punishment by God. By and large, the activities for which reward is promised if they are performed are also those whose neglect is threatened with punishment. You can do things in the hope of a reward from God, but that does not mean that you hope to get a reward from somebody called God. In the same way, you can do things from fear of being punished by God if you do not do them, but that is not to do them from fear that somebody called God might punish you. Just as a Christian cannot say to a beggar, "If it were not for the promised reward I would not be giving you this", so also he cannot say, "If it were not for the threatened punishment I would not be giving you this". Just as in almsgiving the Christian does not have one eye on the needy and one on the carrot, so neither does he have one eye on the needy and one eye on the stick. As the promised reward makes no difference to whether he gives or not, so neither does the threatened punishment. If you are a Christian, what matters is only the need before you. If you refuse to give, and regret it later, it is again remorse that you feel, not fear of what might be done to you; it stems from *what you did not do*, not from fear of the possible consequences to you of not doing it. Your concern is for the man before you, not for yourself, or for any invisible being called God.

Again, this might not be true in a deviant form of Christianity, or in some other religion. It is quite possible that some people might really only be concerned for themselves when they perform works of mercy, or do them to please God or avoid annoying him rather than to help the

155

one in need. It would be necessary to see how their words (if they are sincere) relate to their actions. To take a quick example, in the Koran reward is promised to those who perform acts of mercy:

> The just shall drink from a cup mixed with camphor; the servants of God shall drink from a fountain gushing forth – those who fulfil their oath and fear the day whose evil spreads wide. For love of him they feed the poor and the orphan and the prisoner: "We feed you for God's sake. We want from you neither reward or thanks, but we fear from our Lord a day of distress and anguish". (76: 4–9)

This might look as if the Muslim righteous do not really care about the needy at all. If they feed the poor for God's sake only, does that not mean that they do not do it out of concern for the poor? If they feed them because they fear from God a day of distress and anguish, does that mean that they feed them out of fear? But the presence of the words "for God's sake" and of the theme of fear are not sufficient to establish this; we have to see how they are actually used, what role they play in the text, what part they play in the lives of believers. One thing it seems can be said here straight away, without any great knowledge of Islam, is that the words "We feed you for God's sake" do not function to show that the righteous do not really care about the poor for their own sake; for they are followed not by "We don't really care about *you* at all", but by "We want from you neither reward nor thanks". They are not connected with disregard for the needy but with not seeking any reward. This begins to look like the Christian idea of seeking a reward from God.

To return to Christianity, the parable of the sheep and the goats is instructive here:

When the Son of Man comes in his glory, and all the angels with him, then he will sit on his glorious throne. And all the nations will be brought before him, and he will divide them up, as a shepherd separates the sheep from the goats; and he will put the sheep on his right and the goats on his left. Then the king will say to those on his right, "Come, blessed of my Father, inherit the kingdom prepared for you from the foundation of the world. For I was hungry and you gave me to eat, I was thirsty and you gave me drink, I was a stranger and you took me in, naked and you clothed me; I was ill and you visited me, in prison and you came to me". Then the righteous will answer, "Lord, when did we see you hungry and feed you, thirsty and give you drink...?" And the king will say to them, "Amen I say to you, in so far as you did it for one of the least of these my brethren, you did it for me". Then he will say to those on his left, "Go from me, you damned, into the eternal fire prepared for the devil and his angels. For I was hungry and you did not give me to anything to eat, thirsty and you gave me no drink..." Then they too will answer, "Lord, when did we see you hungry or thirsty... and did not minister to you?" Then he will answer them, "Amen, I say to you, in so far as you did not do it for one of the least of these my brethren, you did not do it for me". And they will go off to eternal punishment, but the righteous to eternal life. (Matthew 25:31–46)

Those who fed the hungry and clothed the naked are surprised to find that their actions had anything to do with God: "Lord, when did we see thee....?" What they did, they did solely out of concern for the hungry and the naked, not from any thought of God or of reward. So they are surprised, too, to find themselves in line for a reward.

Contrast this with those who are sent away to eternal punishment. It is the hungry and the rest of the needy they failed to show concern for; they are not accused of neglecting somebody *else*. When the king tells them they failed to feed him, etc., they are just as surprised as the righteous had been. But there is a hint of an important assymetry here. There is a suggestion that if the ungiving had known that they had been dealing with anybody as important as the king, or were threatened with punishment for any neglect, that would have made a *difference* to the way they acted, in a way it would not have made a difference to the righteous. They go off to punishment because their concern is not for those who needed their help, but for somebody else – the king – or for themselves in their desire to be pleasing to him and avoid his punishment. The righteous, the giving, are rewarded because of their concern for the needy, not for themselves or some third party. They simply responded to the need before them; in this sense they aimed at nothing in what they did. The punished did not respond to the need in front of them; but they would have acted, if they thought that their action would have led to something further, to some reward, or to saving them from trouble at some later date.

This difference between the righteous and the unrighteous is well brought out by Meister Eckhart in a sermon on the text *Justus in perpetuum vivet et apud Dominum est merces eius*:

> The just man does not seek for anything with his works, for those who seek something with their works are servants and hirelings, or those who work for a why or a wherefore. Therefore, if you would be conformed and transformed into justice do not aim at anything with your works and intend nothing in your mind in time or in eternity, neither reward nor blessedness,

neither this nor that; for such works are all really dead. Indeed I say that if you make God your aim, whatever works you do for this reason are all dead and you will spoil good works, and not only will you spoil good works, but you will commit sin, for you will be like a gardener who ought to have planted a garden, but uprooted the trees and then wanted to have a reward for it. In the same way you would spoil good works. Therefore, if you want to live and want your works to live, you must be dead to all things and you must have become nothing. It is characteristic of the creatures that they make something out of something, but it is characteristic of God that he makes something out of nothing. Therefore, if God is to make anything in you or with you, you must beforehand have become nothing. Therefore go into your own ground and work there, and the works that you work there will all be living. Therefore he says: 'The just shall live'. For because he is just he works and his works live. (Clark and Skinner, trans.: *Meister Eckhart. Selected Treatises and Sermons*, p.53f.)

"I say that if you make God your aim, whatever works you do for this reason are all dead and you will spoil good works, and not only will you spoil good works, but you will commit sin". That sounds like a very bold and paradoxical thing to say; like much else in this passage, it is the kind of thing that is typical of some 'mystical' writers. But if we bear in mind the whole thrust of this book, what he says here is quite comprehensible. Though we are all, as Christians, of course to make God our aim in everything we do (God is to be the centre of our lives), yet we all, or most of us, suffer from the temptation to treat God as somebody, are prey to the grammatical illusion that "God" is the name of somebody. Then we get ourselves a false, illusory, God. That is the God we have to reject, to ignore in all our works. What Eckhart is doing is alluding to - or himself succumbing to - this temptation, and then throwing it off, throwing off the implications it has for the motives of our actions and the way we act. Then, if we do not act so as to aim at this false God, if we aim at nothing with our works, then we will be aiming at the true God. Eckhart's paradoxicality is simply a demonstration of the peculiar grammar of "God". In particular, it shows that to make God your aim is not to make *somebody* or *something* your aim. (I wonder whether many of the 'mystical paradoxes' of certain religious thinkers and texts are not to be treated in a similar way.)

Laying Up Treasure

Closely related to the idea of seeking a reward from God is that of laying up treasure in heaven. So if I am right about what it means to seek a reward from God, we should get a similar result from looking at what it means to lay up treasure in heaven. We read in Matthew:

> Do not lay up treasure for yourselves on earth, where moth and rust disfigure and where thieves break in and steal. But lay up treasure for yourselves in heaven, where neither moth nor rust disfigure, and where thieves do not break in or steal. For where your treasure is, there too will be your heart.(6:19–21)

Note again the old point that there is no hint of a possibility that you might store up treasure *both* on earth *and* in heaven. If you lay up treasure on earth then, *ipso facto*, you do not lay up treasure in heaven; and if you lay up treasure in heaven, then, *ipso facto*, you do not lay up treasure on earth. If you want to amass treasure in heaven, therefore, you need do no more – within the general context of a Christian way of life – than *not* amass it on earth. That is, as far as Otto can see when he is trying to learn how to use all this language about God and heaven, the way to amass treasure in heaven is not to amass treasure anywhere, not to amass treasure at all. There are many activities that we might want to describe as treasure-amassing behaviour: storing up money under the bed, keeping as much as you can in high interest bank accounts, investing in antique silver, being careful to get the kind of qualifications that lead to the highest paid jobs. And we might want to add, in the case of certain religious people, piling up 'merit', or something similar. Whatever such activities we can think of, the one who lays up treasure in heaven does not perform any of them.

So here is another way in which heaven is not like Wimbledon. We already know that, though you can lay up treasure in Bayswater and in Wimbledon (you can have a bank account in both), you cannot lay up treasure in Bayswater and in heaven. Connected with this is the fact that there is both laying-up-treasure activity which is laying-up-treasure-in-Bayswater activity and other, different, laying-up-treasure activity which is laying-up-trea-sure-in-Wimbledon activity. If I am laying up treasure in Bayswater and I want also to lay up treasure in Wimbledon, I have to do something *else*, perform additional laying-up-treasure activity. And if I want to lay up treasure in Wimbledon instead of in Bayswater, it is not enough for me just to stop my laying-up-treasure-in-Bayswater activity. Again, I have to do something else. I don't just have to close my account in Bayswater, but have also to open one in Wimbledon, or bury a treasure chest on Wimbledon Common; I have to perform some other laying-up-treasure activity. But if I want to lay up treasure in heaven instead of in Bayswater, there is nothing else – no other laying-up-treasure activity – that I have to do. All I have to do is to stop laying up treasure in Bayswater, and everywhere else. The activity, if there is one, that we call "laying up treasure in heaven" is not a species of laying-up-treasure activity.

There is indeed a kind of activity that is called "laying up treasure in heaven", but it is not a matter of amassing riches anywhere – it is a matter of giving them away. So Jesus says in Luke:

> Sell your possessions and give alms; make yourselves purses that do not wear out, an unfailing treasure in the heavens, where no thief comes near and no moth destroys. For where your treasure is, there too your heart will be. (12:33f.)

Those who are encouraged to lay up treasure in heaven are those who have a choice about it. It is not that they do not lay up treasure on earth because they have no income, no treasure, to amass. They do have wealth and income, and so their not amassing it means giving it away – as alms to those in need. To those in need: it is this that makes giving treasure away into laying up treasure in heaven. It cannot just be a matter of giving it to your friends or your family, whether they need it or not. The important point is not just that you get rid of it, unburden yourself of it, but that you use it in ways consonant with the gospel. Giving away your treasure, if it is to count as laying up treasure in heaven, must be part of your whole way of life, one that can be characterised as an attempt to follow the gospel. That is why the rich young man is asked by Jesus not only to sell his possessions and give the proceeds to the poor, but also to follow him (Matthew 19:16ff.) The following of Jesus, becoming a disciple, would mean that the man lives the kind of life that gives the initial act of giving to the poor a context, a context that makes it appropriate to describe that act as laying up treasure in heaven.

Once, in the context of discipleship, you cease to lay up treasure on earth, there is nothing further you have to do that would count as laying up treasure in heaven. But there remains the possibility that this is because, by a peculiar mechanism, if you cease to lay up treasure on earth, that very act is also a laying up of treasure elsewhere, in heaven. It remains a possibility that laying up treasure in heaven is after all a form of laying-up-treasure activity, even though it does not look like it. Ceasing to lay up treasure on earth might not after all be a ceasing, but a trade or a transferral. It might be as if the very act by which I close my account at Bayswater is also one which opens one up for me in Wimbledon, as if treasure in heaven really were treasure somewhere, which I acquire at the price of all the treasures I have at the moment, here on earth. And there is much biblical language that seems to support such a view; for example:

> The kingdom of heaven is like a treasure hidden in a field, which somebody finds and hides, and he goes in his joy to sell all he has and buys that field. Again, the kingdom of heaven is like a merchant looking for fine pearls. When he found one very precious pearl he went and sold everything he had and bought it. (Matthew 13:44–46)

Does not language like this make it look as if Christians really are in search of treasure somewhere and believe that they have been taught a reliable technique to enable them to acquire it?

Yes, until we look at how such language actually functions, what place it occupies in the lives of disciples. What we actually *see*, and what Otto sees, is that those who are in the process of laying up treasure in heaven, those of whom it can appropriately be said that they are laying up treasure in heaven, are not laying up treasure, but giving it away, as part of life as a disciple. We do not see the heavenly treasure that they gain by such means, and neither do they. That in itself is not decisive, for I also have treasure that neither I nor anybody else can see, or of which nothing more can be seen than an entry in a ledger in a bank. But I *can* go and get the cash out of the bank; and if I can never do that, then I do not after all have any treasure in the bank. If I have treasure on earth, then I *can* see it. But nobody ever sees treasure in heaven. You might want to say of somebody that it can be seen *that* he has treasure in heaven, but you could never say that because you saw any treasure that he had. You might say it if you saw that he was a generous man, that he gave away what he had to the poor, but not because you saw that he *had* something, as one has possessions. Treasure in heaven is not a kind of treasure, not something you possess. Treasure in heaven cannot be transferred to Wimbledon, as treasure in Bayswater can. It cannot be mislaid or stolen, neither can it be eaten by worms, as Chippendale chairs can. But that is not because it is so extremely well protected. It is because nobody would know how to set about stealing it, because nobody could even try; there is no such task as stealing it. So also there is no such task as protecting it. There is nothing to protect.

Treasure in heaven is like a pearl of great price. But the man who acquires it is the generous man, not the shrewd merchant. We know how to distinguish between the one who is generous and the one who is calculating, the one who is simply entering into a profitable bargain; and it is of the former, not the latter, that we say that he has treasure in heaven. If treasure in heaven were a kind of treasure, the man who has it, being a generous man, would want to give that away too. But treasure in heaven cannot be given away, any more than it can be stolen, for there is nothing to give away. And so you cannot hang on to it, either. If anybody wanted to keep it, he would not be generous, and so would not have it in the first place. And he would in any case be making a logical mistake, in thinking that treasure in heaven is a kind of treasure. You cannot want to keep it, for there is nothing to want to keep. The merchant who goes in search of fine pearls and finds one and sells all he has to buy it is in effect transferring his acquisitiveness and his possessiveness from one object to another. He is saying: I would rather have that (the fine pearl) than this (all my money). But the one who wants treasure in heaven has not simply transferred his acquisitiveness from one object to another. He has ceased to be acquisitive. To want to lay up treasure in heaven is not to want to lay up treasure elsewhere; it is not to want to lay up treasure at all. It involves a change of attitude, from acquisitiveness to generosity, a conversion. Treasure in heaven is the treasure you acquire by not being interested in acquiring any treasure.

This was well understood by the rich young man. Jesus tells him, "Go, sell what you possess and give to the poor, and you will have treasure in heaven; and come, follow, me". And Matthew says that "when the young man heard this, he went away sorrowful; for he had great possessions" (19:22). Going away sorrowful is not the reaction of somebody who has just been presented with a marvellous bargain, an opportunity to gain a great deal by trading one possession for another. Neither are we to imagine that his sorrow was one as of a merchant disappointed that the deal was not quite good enough for him to accept. And it wasn't, either, because he didn't really trust Jesus to fulfil his half of the bargain, that he did not really believe that he would have treasure in heaven; it is not that he was held back by 'lack of faith'; he did not go away mistrustful. What held him back was that he was tied to riches, to possessions. So Jesus comments that it is impossible for the rich enter the kingdom of heaven (cf. Mark 10:24; in some manuscripts it is those who trust in riches who will not enter the kingdom), not that it is impossible for those of little faith to enter the kingdom (v.23f.). In promising the rich young man treasure in heaven, Jesus was not just offering a bad deal; he was not offering *any* deal at all. He was not promising him that he would get something, but asking him to give everything, not appealing to his acquisitiveness, but asking him to be generous; that is why he went away sorrowful.

There was no deal, neither a good one nor a bad one. With heavenly treasure, there is no question of assessing whether what is offered is worth what is being asked for it. If that were so, if there were a bargain involved, then it would be a matter of indifference whether you decided to enter into it or not. If you offer me your Picasso, it is up to me to assess whether it is worth the Chippendale chair you are asking in return, and I may perfectly properly decide either way. But it is not in the same way a matter of indifference whether you in fact prefer to hang on to your earthly possessions and are not really interested in heavenly treasure. It is not up to you to make any such assessment of the relative worth of earthly and heavenly treasures. Heavenly treasure is worth more than any treasure on earth. But that is not a conclusion anybody ever came to, not an assessment that anybody ever made. It is rather something we have been *taught*, as part of the concept of heavenly treasure. We have learned, largely through the parables of Jesus, that heavenly treasure is supremely valuable. When we start to hear of heavenly treasure at all, we learn that it is worth more than anything (even if we are not told precisely what it is). It is not part of the teaching that it is up to us, confronted with a choice between earthly and heavenly treasure (you cannot have both, of course) to decide which is more valuable, which we prefer. You cannot believe in the existence of heavenly treasure at all without believing that it is more valuable than earthly treasure; if you don't see it as such, you don't see it as heavenly *treasure*. That is to say, heavenly treasure cannot be assessed as valuable (or as not valuable) within an existing scale of values. It can't be valuable as silver, Chippendale chairs, good health, friends or a quiet life are valuable. It is not just an earthly treasure, in a different place, or of a special kind. We cannot see that it is valuable through some relation it has to the things that we already consider valuable: we cannot *assess* it as valuable. We have to be taught it as valuable. We are taught a *new* value, and taught to change our values, to live in a different way. And that new way is not to try to acquire something different, but to give.

So once again, just as with seeking a reward from God, success is assured. There is nothing that counts as trying to amass this treasure and failing; there is no heavenly equivalent of stock market crashes, bank failures, backing the wrong horse, unforeseen expenses, thieves breaking in. The kingdom of heaven is not like a man *trying* to find treasure, but like one who finds it; the merchant too finds his pearl of great price. There is no question of failure, because there is no task. You cannot fail to gain, because you do not attempt to gain. The man who gives to gain a heavenly treasure does not give with a view to getting something else in return. Since he does not hope for anything else, he has no hope to be disappointed. He does indeed hope for heavenly treasure, but that is not to hope for a kind of treasure; and his hope is fulfilled, not as a result of his giving, but *in* his giving. His giving does not aim at anything beyond itself; generosity seeks no recompense.

Since he who lays up treasure in heaven by giving does not give with a view to laying up treasure of any kind, he gives just because he is confronted with need. His giving is a response to need, not a response to the prospect of a good deal. His concern is not for himself, but for the one in need. So he cannot say, "If it were not for the good return that I am getting by giving you this, I would not be giving". If he does say that, the return he seeks is an earthly one connected with idolatrous religion. It is a mark of idolatrous religion that its gains can be *sought*, just as ordinary secular gains can be sought. They appeal to our acquisitiveness, and do not demand conversion, but simply a redirection of our desire to possess, to be rich. This is connected with the fact that the gods of idolatrous religion can be thought in the way that ordinary secular things can. They *are* ordinary secular things, mere bodiless creatures (or even embodied ones), or would be if they existed. (This paragraph can be seen as a comment on the use of the words "idolatrous religion".)

There are such strains of idolatry in some forms of deviant Christianity. Sometimes people are encouraged to give, not out of generosity, but in pursuit of gain, of earthly rewards. American evangelists, for example, sometimes promise you success, principally lots of money, if you send a regular monthly contribution of $10, or something similar. It is no doubt a matter of great interest to many people whether spending a mere $10 a month can guarantee them riches, so maybe the claim should be investigated. It would certainly be extraordinary if it turned out to be true. But if it did turn out to be true, it would still have nothing to do with Christianity, in orthodox eyes. To the orthodox, if everybody who gave $10 got rich it would merely be a series of extraordinary coincidences, or hint at the existence of some bizarre new law of natural causation; there would be nothing supernatural or spiritual about it. That is because this deviant Christianity centres around laying up treasure on earth, not in heaven.

To lay up treasure in heaven, then, just is to give in response to need (within the context of the other practices of the disciple: it is in the first place the Christian who lays up treasure in heaven). So we find in the book of Sirach:

For the sake of the commandment help the poor, and
because of his need do not turn him away empty. Lose
money for a brother and a friend, and let it not rust
away under a stone. Lay up your treasure according to
the commandments of the Most High, and it will profit
you more than gold. Lock up almsgiving in your
treasuries, and it will rescue you from all evil. (29:9–12)

Helping a poor man for the commandment's sake is the
same as giving to him because of his need, and by this giving
in response to need you lay up treasure, and the treasure you
lay up is almsgiving. Again it could be said: giving is its own
return. And that is to say: giving does not seek a return.

Getting to Heaven

What is the point of seeking a heavenly reward, or of laying
up treasure in heaven? So that it will be marvellous when we
get there. One way to sum up the Christian ambition is to
say that Christians want to get to heaven. And that will be
wonderful. It is the ultimate success, the ultimate happiness.
There are all kinds of pictures of what heaven might be like:
being in the bosom of Abraham (Luke 16:22), being with
Jesus (Philippians 1:23), living in a city made of gold and
jewels, full of light (Apocalypse 21:9–22:5), being invited to
a wedding feast (Matthew 22:1ff.; 25:10), being given an
extra talent (Matthew 25:28); or, more popularly, being
reunited with friends and loved ones. But these are 'only'
pictures; their point is not to give an accurate description of
the reality, but to present it as attractive – to advertise
heaven as *the* place to be.

Everybody knows that these are *only* pictures, that things
start to go wrong if we try to take them as descriptions of
what heaven is really like: wouldn't being in Abraham's
bosom for ever get *very* boring? Wouldn't all that light be
oppressive, all that chanting of alleluias rather mindless?

And if I adore Charlie but he can't stand me, will we be united for ever or not? But there is a sense in which they are not *only* pictures: we cannot be shown the original, and neither can we be given an adequate picture, a picture that doesn't start to go wrong if we take it too seriously as a description. There is nothing we would call a "literal description" or "adequate description" of heaven; there is no 'what heaven is *really* like'. So the descriptions of heaven that we do have are not *in*adequate, either. That is to say, it is not that our descriptions fail where others might succeed. It is part of the *concept* of heaven that there are no adequate descriptions of it. Of heaven, there are *only* advertising posters, catchy slogans, designed to appeal. All we know about heaven, the place of God, is that it is a place in the sun. We will find it good to be in, *whatever* our tastes – if we can get there, if we aim for it, and live in such a way as to get there. That is to say, we cannot properly ask whether heaven is really the kind of place we want to go to (except as a joke); we can only ask that of somewhere *earthly*, somewhere we might have a literal description of. Whereas in other, earthly contexts a distinction is often made between literal and metaphorical descriptions, we only allow metaphorical descriptions of heaven.

We are introduced to the concept of heaven as somewhere desirable; we are *taught* to want to go there. If we learn the concept rightly, we cannot doubt that we want to go there. Heaven cannot be assessed in terms of our ordinary values; learning about heaven means learning *new* values. We can only assess pictures of heaven, not heaven itself, for the pictures are all we have; and if we find one picture unappealing, there is another designed to attract us. And even if we do not find any of the pictures attractive, still we are told to find the prospect of heaven attractive, to want to go there. We could only judge heaven, independently of being taught that it is good, by taking some picture of heaven as a literal description, and judging that. But such a heaven would therefore be describable, and a putative part of the world; it would be the place of a god that was part of the world, and therefore an idol; it would be a false heaven. This is part of the point of saying that we *only* have pictures, *only* have metaphors – to block such a move, the attempt to say what heaven is really like, and so put ourselves in a position to judge it as it really is. In Christianity, nothing *counts* as knowing what heaven is really like. It is not that we might know, but that our powers of perception or thought are too weak. But this is the same as saying that there is nothing to know. Heaven is not really like anything. There is no literal description that might be true. All we know is that to be in heaven is to enjoy supreme bliss; that is to say, we have been taught heaven as a supreme goal.

But this goal is a spiritual goal, a heavenly goal, one that we learn about in connexion with God. Pursuing that goal is going to be different, logically, from pursuing any other goal. To begin with, heaven cannot be simply added on to the list of things that are my goals in life. It is incompatible with other goals, *all* other goals. That is not just because you can only have one final goal in your life anyway; for that is not true. What I count as success in life may consist of a combination of things. I may set myself just to achieve fame, and care about nothing else; but I may seek fame, wealth, and to be the world's best hockey player, all at once, and without seeking any of these as means to any of the others. I can want to be rich independently of wanting to be famous, and yet still want to be both rich and famous. I can also, at the same time, want to be the world's best hockey player, even though there is no money in it and nobody has ever heard of any hockey players making the headlines. It may be that my goals are incompatible, that as a matter of fact I cannot pursue them all at the same time with any hope of success. It may be that all the time I have to spend juggling with stocks and shares in order to get rich, or being seen in the right places so as to make my face well-known, leaves me with insufficient time to practice my hockey. So if I think of success in these terms I may be doomed to partial failure. But that is only an unfortunate accident. The way things happen to be, it may be that if I am to achieve my life's ambition of becoming the world's best hockey player I have to content myself with being poor and unknown. But things could be different: a tobacco company might decide to take up sponsoring hockey, so that I can appear on television and the sports pages, land contracts for advertising lager, have autobiographies written for me, and so end up achieving all the goals I have set myself in life.

Earthly goals, that is simply goals – the kind of thing we learn to call "goals" when we learn English – may be only contingently incompatible. But they may be more than that. I may, if I am strange enough, want to become the fattest man in the world and want to become the thinnest man in the world. There is more than a contingent incompatibility between these goals: I logically cannot do both at the same time (except by killing all other men). But here time comes to my aid: I can try to achieve both aims in sequence, and I can form a plan to do so. I can decide to fatten myself for ten years, or until I am fatter than anybody else, and then eat practically nothing until I am thinner than anybody else. (I may well kill myself doing all this, but that again is only an unfortunate contingent fact, not a necessity.) But trying to get to heaven is not like trying to be good at hockey, not something you might do as well as trying to get famous. Heavenly success is not another form of success I might try to achieve *in addition to* any other goals I might have. This should already be obvious from what I have said about

172

seeking a heavenly reward and storing up treasure in heaven, for gaining rewards and piling up treasure are only particular forms of success, and seeking rewards and treasures only particular ways in which success might be sought. Just as seeking a heavenly reward is *not* seeking rewards. abandoning thought of reward, so trying to get to heaven means giving up trying to get anywhere, not setting yourself to achieve wealth, fame, excellence or anything else that is counted as success. If it is your ambition to get to heaven, it cannot also be your ambition to become famous, or to be the world's best hockey player. That is to say, you cannot judge the success of your life in terms of whether you achieve these things or not. If your ambition is to get to heaven, you cannot try to make something of yourself in any of these ways, try to get anywhere.

Of course, if you want to get to heaven you can have other goals as well; indeed it will be impossible to avoid them. Much of human life consists in trying to achieve things. Finishing the crossword, catching the bus, becoming an MP, learning to type, all these and many others are goals we expect people, including Christians, to pursue. But if you are a Christian these other goals cannot be your aim in life, that which gives sense and direction to your life. And that is the kind of goal heaven is for the Christian. Though life is full of earthly goals, if your aim is to get to heaven then, even if you fail in *all* your important earthly goals, your life still retains its direction. Though all your projects may fail, *you* have not failed, you can still succeed. You can succeed in your heavenly ambition even though you succeed in *nothing*. Conversely, you can succeed in all your earthly goals and still fail, if you do not live in such a way as to attain your spiritual goal.

In the New Testament what is held out to the disciples as the goal to be striven for is entry into the kingdom of heaven, and if they are going to achieve this they must give up seeking wealth, authority, security, any kind of pre-eminence, etc. They are to give up all 'worldly ambition', and that means simply that they are to give up *all* ambition, everything that might count as an ambition. And it is not just a matter of temporal incompatibility here, either. It is possible to spend half your life trying to get famous, and then the other half trying to get to heaven. But it is not possible to plan such a sequence. To begin to seek the one having sought the other cannot be to go on to the second stage of a grand plan to achieve success in all spheres; it takes the form of a conversion, the rejection of former goals as empty and worthless. If I devote the second half of my life to getting to heaven after having spent the first half becoming rich and famous, or having devoted it to achieving excellence in hockey, I cannot do that just because I recognise that my earlier goals have been achieved, so that I can now go on to others. I can only make heaven my goal if I have come to see my earlier goals as illusory, and my pursuit of them a mistake.

So heaven cannot be counted together with earthly goals; they are mutually exclusive. You make heaven your goal only if you make *nothing* your goal – if you make your goal nothing within the totality of what can be thought of as goals. But does this mean that the disciple, the one who makes heaven his goal, aims for another goal, a different one, one that is invisible, one that is unthinkable, that only the believer can know? Does the one who becomes a disciple, who is converted from worldly ambition, simply transfer his ambition from one object (wealth or fame) to another (heaven)? Heaven is held out to us as the highest conceivable bliss, indeed as beyond what is conceivable; does that mean that the disciple is immeasurably more ambitious than the worldly man? When Otto sees the way a disciple behaves, one who says, "My goal is to get to heaven, to be with God, to enjoy eternal bliss", does he see the behaviour characteristic of one pursuing an ambition? Otto has learned English. He knows what ambition is, what kind of thing is normally called "pursuing an ambition", how ambition is manifested, and how it is concealed. When he sees a disciple, does he say, "There goes an ambitious man"? And is he then simply perplexed because he does not understand what this goal is towards which the disciple's ambitious behaviour is directed?

Evidently not. The life of a disciple, if he is a good disciple, is not one of high ambition. If worldly people want to make something of themselves, want to go places, the disciple is not one who sets his sights higher than any of them, who wants to achieve status more exalted than any of them could aspire to. If the disciple understands his call rightly, then he understands that it is in part a call to the *abandonment* of ambition, to humility. This is so central to the teaching of the New Testament that it is superfluous to provide any evidence for it; and it is equally central to the whole of Christian tradition. The disciple is not one who wants to make himself great, but who is content to be small; he is not intent on going places, on reaching the heights, but is content to remain where he is. So neither can he think of himself as having achieved such an ambition; he cannot think of himself as somebody important or exalted. In fact, disciples often do think in this way, the same as anybody else, but that is when they are being *bad* disciples. When the disciple thinks as a disciple, he cannot think of his ambition as fulfilled, because he has no ambition to fulfil.

The behaviour of the disciple is not ambitious behaviour. Here the same considerations apply as when I talked about seeking heavenly rewards and storing up treasure in heaven. The principal way you get to heaven is by treating others in

175

the right way – see, e.g., the parable of the sheep and the goats, and the Sermon on the Mount. But that means that your concern is for others, not for yourself. If you, as a disciple, perform works of mercy, seek reconciliation with your enemies, that cannot be as means to an end, the end of getting to heaven; it cannot be a means to furthering your ambition. Performing such good works does not stand to getting to heaven in the same relation as, say, getting a good degree stands to landing the job you are after. You could say in the latter case, "If this degree course were not of help to me in getting the job I want, I wouldn't be doing it". But you could not say, for example, "If my forgiving you did not help me to get to heaven, I would not forgive you". For forgiveness to count as a good work, something that helps you on your way to heaven, it must be from the heart; what must be in your heart when you say "I forgive you" is forgiveness, not ambition. Christian forgiveness is forgiveness without thought of advantage. If you forgive with an eye to your own advancement (and so, to that extent would not forgive but for the advantage you derive from it) then your forgiveness is, in Christian terms, not genuine but feigned, and you are a hypocrite. So any account of heaven that makes of it a goal to be pursued, like being top hockey player only better, and to be pursued by good works such as forgiving those who have wronged you, makes Christians out to be hypocrites, just for that reason. But Christians are not hypocrites, unless they are bad Christians. They do not seek their own advantage while appearing to act selflessly. We may indeed want to say that Christians want to get to heaven, and that the way to get to heaven is to give, to forgive, etc., but that in itself shows that to seek to get to heaven is not to seek advantage; it is not to seek to get somewhere, to become someone. It is not an ambition, not even a subtle and cleverly disguised one. We may or may not want to talk of 'the ambition of getting to heaven'. If we do, then it is clear that we are using words in a strange way; for the ambition of getting to heaven is not a species of ambition. To have the ambition of getting to heaven is to have *no* ambition. A man may want to get to heaven by, among other things, forgiving those who wrong him, but that means that *he does not want to get anywhere* by forgiving others.

I talk about 'the ambition of getting to heaven', even though most of us would not want, probably, to talk so crudely, in order to bring out the point that what I am saying, here as elsewhere, has nothing to do with trying to put a ban on the use of certain expressions. We can, of course, use whatever expressions we like: it is our language. Only we have to be aware, if we are not to be in danger of misusing these expressions, that they are often related to similar expressions in peculiar and paradoxical ways. It is not a matter of a simple extension, when we talk about the things of God, of the already established use of expressions. Thus it is a mistake to say, "You know what an ambition is. You know what it is to have the ambition of getting to the top in your profession, or of becoming famous. Well, having the ambition of getting to heaven is just the same, only the object of the ambition is different". It is not as if there were an expression "to have the ambition to ...", where the dots can be filled in with any number of phrases, one of which is "get to heaven". (One way of putting this might be to say that the ambition to get to heaven lies outside the totality of ambitions. It is a *spiritual* ambition, to be contrasted with, and excluding, all worldly ambitions, i.e. *all* ambitions: as I have been using the word "spiritual", a spiritual ambition is not a kind of ambition – just as artificial cream is not a kind of cream, a glass eye is not a kind of eye, and a dumb waiter is not a kind of waiter.) To have the ambition of getting to heaven is not only not to have the ambition to reach a particular end; it is not to have *any* ambition. So in the same way we can also talk of God existing, creating the world, bestowing rewards, punishing sinners, seeing into the hearts of all men, saving sinners, doing miraculous things; but in all this we are speaking of *spiritual* things, and spiritual things are not the same as ordinary, material things, only different. We can expect our language about God to be related to our language about ordinary, material things in strange ways, and not to be a simple extension of such language, an extension that it requires no thought or observation to understand.

Being the Greatest

In this particular case, we can talk also of the ambition of Christians to be great, to be the foremost among their brethren, to be closest to God. Such language is used in the gospels themselves. For example, sometimes Jesus does not tell his disciples not to want to be great or the greatest, but rather explains to them what being great means to one who has learned to use the language of greatness properly in the context of Christianity:

> You know that the rulers of the gentiles dominate them and their great men are authoritarian. It will not be so among you, but whoever wants to be great among you will become your servant, and whoever wants to be first among you will become your slave; just as the Son of Man did not come to be served but to serve and to give his life as a ransom for many. (Matthew 20:25–28)

By all means let the disciples strive to be the greatest, but what that means in Christianity is to be what is normally, in ordinary, material contexts, called the lowest. These words of Jesus are occasioned by the request of the sons of Zebedee (actually, it is their mother who does the asking in Matthew) to be made the greatest among the disciples, that is, to be honoured above all of them, to have privileged positions: to "sit, one at your right hand, and one at your left, in your kingdom"(v.21). What has gone wrong here is that the family of Zebedee understand greatness in a material, not a spiritual sense. They know what it means to be great in earthly places, in the local village community, in the empire, in contemporary political life in general. And the mother of James and John thinks that the kingdom of Jesus can also be thought of in earthly terms: "We all know what it means to be great in the kingdom of the Persians or in the empire of the Romans; well, that's the kind of thing I want for my boys, only in your kingdom". But Jesus answers, "You do not know what you are asking". They do not know what they are asking, because they do not realise that the greatness that Jesus invites his disciples to is a *spiritual* greatness. It is not a species of greatness, but a greatness that lies outside the totality of all ways of being great. This greatness means precisely not being great, but being lowly, not occupying a position of honour and authority, but being of little or no account, like a servant or slave. What we have here is not a natural extension of the ordinary notion of greatness, but a highly paradoxical one. It is a creative misuse of it, and for the disciple a very important one.

We get the same message pushed home in Luke's account of the last supper:

> There was an argument among them over which of them was the greatest. But he said to them, "The kings of the gentiles dominate them and those who wield authority are called benefactors. Not so with you. Let the greatest among you be like the youngest, and the leader like one who serves. For who is greater, he who reclines at dinner or he who serves? Is it not he who reclines? But I am in your midst as the one who serves. (22:24–27)

Once again the disciples want to be great, and greater than each other, and once again Jesus says that greatness among them is not like greatness among the gentiles. But now he goes further. He reminds them first of one of the ways some people are greater than others: those who are waited on at table are greater than those who do the waiting. But Jesus is among the disciples as the one who serves. That is, the disciples are greater than Jesus. But it is Jesus, the one who is the inferior, who is the measure of greatness for the disciples. So for them, as followers of Jesus, to become great is to become lowlier than they are. Their greatness as disciples is not to be greatness at all, but spiritual greatness.

We are linguistic animals. Our use of language is central to our living. The disciples have to learn this new and deliberately paradoxical way of speaking as part of learning a new way of life. What is going on here is not an arbitrary game being played with language, an inconsequential joke, but is more akin to a linguistic change one may feel impelled to make as one may feel impelled to change one's way of life. Seriously to describe Jesus on the cross as great, as king, as God - to distort or change your existing language that much, and to be impelled to - is to have no choice, seeing Jesus on the cross, but to change your life. Since conversion of language is part of conversion of life, though we might be able to elucidate to Otto how this new use of language works, we should of course not expect him to see the point of changing language in this way unless he sees the point of changing his life. And that is something only his life can show him. So we cannot 'prove' to him that Christianity is true. And that is not because of our limited abilities, and a regrettable fact; it is because there is no such task. One of the ways Otto might come to see the point of changing his life is through misfortune, another by living with or seeing the lives of others - Christians - who inspire him to change his life, and so also to change his language, to become a Christian. Or it may be that he is brought to talk like this seriously by great suffering, or by some other shock to his way of living. This is the kind of thing that in fact often happens. It is not irrational. It only appears so to those who misconstrue the nature of Christian belief. If you see Christian belief as a kind of would-be science, then of course such conversions will seem madness, or at least to involve bad faith. You would after all not expect anybody to come to believe in the truth of a theory in astronomy just by seeing how certain astronomers live, nor to accept the existence of infinite numbers upon being struck down by a debilitating disease. But the fact that this kind of thing does regularly happen in religion, and that religious people expect it to happen, does not attest the irrationality of religious people and of religion. (Of course some religious people may be irrational, but they maybe highly rational and intelligent, like astronomers and mathematicians.) It indicates rather that, just because it cannot take account of that fact, the Christianity-as-would-be-science approach is seriously deficient. And of course the fact that people can also *lose* their faith through seeing how Christians live or by going through a crisis does not point to the irrationality of atheism, either, nor does it suggest bad faith in atheists. The ways people convert to and from faith support the point I have made before, that the use of religious language is intimately bound to the way people live their lives and how it is in them to live.

This revolution in the language and life of the disciples is not well described by saying that the disciples have to change their idea of what greatness is, so that they pursue one state as great rather than another; it makes the difference too small. For, as we have seen, it is not a matter of their pursuing one ambition rather than another, but of having no ambition at all. It is therefore not, either, that they pursue a *perverted* ambition, but still a material one – that they are heepish rather than napoleonic, that they strive to be dominated rather than to dominate, to be last rather than first, to sit at the bottom of the table rather than the top, to be poor rather than rich, uncomfortable rather than comfortable, reviled instead of honoured. This is simply to invert normal values, while still remaining ambitious, to see a particular state as desirable and to strive for it. It is to make poverty a form of riches, to make the last place more honoured than the first, to think in processional order. The point for a Christian, however, is not to seek *any* riches, not to compete for *any* place of honour.

This is connected with the fact that the Christian life is not competitive. To seek a position of honour is to seek a place relative to others; if you are to be at the top of the table, then others will not be at the top. To strive to be at the top is *eo ipso* to strive to exclude others from the top. It is to seek a *special* place. But then also to strive to be at the bottom of the table is to strive to exclude others from the bottom. It is still to insist on achieving your own end, your own ambition, in competition with others, so making yourself great in your own eyes, even if you have a strange idea of greatness. And it is still to prefer yourself to others. But the point about Christian greatness is that it is not the object of an ambition, not a way of being great. It is to prefer others, not yourself; to be a servant, at the disposal of others, not insisting on your own way:

> Be devoted to each other with brotherly love, excel each other in showing honour. (Romans 12:10)

> Do nothing from ambition or vainglory, but humbly think of others as better than yourselves, each one not looking to his own interests, but to those of others as

well. (Philippians 2:3f.)

Love does not seek its own way. (1 Corinthians 13:5)

So also it is not to insist that others be available to be 'served' by you – not to insist on helping old ladies across the road whether they want to go or not, or on being last through the door. It is to be content to be in a place of others' choosing, to be in a place determined by others' needs – even if that place be one of authority – rather than by your own ambitions. Thus, in Christianity, *everybody* can be at the bottom, since all can be at the disposal of others. And hence everybody can be at the top, too. And getting there is done precisely by not trying to get anywhere.

Hence the disciple is also in a sense one who is going nowhere in particular. While he may move (since he is alive), it is not towards a goal. He may say that heaven is his goal, but then it is a spiritual goal. That is, if heaven is his goal he has no goal. (Incidentally, an alternative to this is to say that, though the Christian has a goal, he is not going anywhere because he has already achieved it. This is somewhat the line taken in Ephesians, in which we are said to be already raised up with Christ and made to sit with him in the heavenly places (2:6). So it is possible to talk of trying to get to heaven or of already being there, and both kinds of talk can be put to work to express that the Christian is not going anywhere. Once again, it is the actual use to which words are put that is the important thing, however much the actual words may vary from person to person or from time to time.) We know what it is to seek a goal, what kind of activity can be described as goal-seeking activity; and the one who has heaven as his goal does not exhibit goal-seeking behaviour. For example, if somebody is intent on reaching a goal he is reluctant to be taken out of his way. Other people can interfere with his achievement of his goal, not only by being in competition with him, but also, even if there is no competition, by making claims on him which distract him from his goal-oriented activity. If you want to be a successful businessman, the demands of family life may make it difficult if not impossible to achieve your aim; or if you want to finish an essay in time for an imminent tutorial, you do not want to be distracted by somebody dropping in for a chat – and if all he wants is idle chatter, to pass the time, then the interference becomes annoying. The disciple, however, is not to be reluctant to be taken out of his way:

> If anybody forces you to go one mile, go two with him. (Matthew 5:41)

That is to say: Do not be forced. For if you give more than is asked, then you give it freely. And if you go somebody else's way freely, that means that you do not see going his way as an interference in the pursuit of your own way. So your way is not the road to a goal. Since there is no goal, there is no goal to be interfered with, either. So, if heaven is your goal, nobody can interfere with your achieving it. The demands of others do not make it difficult of achievement. Indeed, it is just by looking to the needs of others rather than your own that you get where you want to go. And it is by insisting on your own way that you do not get there: naturally, for if there is a way to insist on, the way to a goal, it is not the way to heaven. It is only a false heaven that there is a way of achieving; it is only a material goal that can be attained by following a method, and whose attainment can therefore be interfered with. The way to heaven, on the other hand, is a spiritual way; that is, it is not a way, but involves the abandonment of all ways.

CHAPTER 6
PRAYER

Talking to God & God's Being There

Christians pray. The term "prayer" may be used to cover many things, but that Christians pray means at least this: that they talk to God. Does this not mean that Christians believe that there is somebody whom they call God and to whom they talk when they pray? After all, I can only talk to Charlie, or try to, if I believe that there is somebody called Charlie there for me to speak to. Is the case not the same with God? Do I not here have to abandon any talk of God as nothing, as not an existing person? If God is nothing and nobody, then, though Christians may say they talk to God, yet in reality there is nobody there to be talked to. That may in fact be true, but it is surely not what Christians believe.

I can talk to Charlie. I can also talk to Bill. I can also talk to Charlie *and* Bill, together. There is no limit to the number of people I can address. But I cannot talk to Charlie *and* God. If I talk to God, I am not talking to people; if I am talking to people, I am not at the same time talking to God. I can of course pray to God in the presence of people, just as I can talk to people in the presence of God, and I can lead a whole group of people in a joint prayer to God. I can also use the form of a prayer, pretend to be praying, while really addressing my words to those assembled with me. But I cannot actually talk to God and to people together. God cannot be a member with others in a list of those I am talking to. This is not because we are not supposed to talk to God and Charlie at the same time, or because we have found that God will not listen to us if we are talking to people as well. It is because we do not *count* anything as talking to people and to God at the same time. It is part of how we teach people about talking to God. What Otto sees when he sees people talking to God (that is part of how he learns what it is to talk to God, how he learns the use of the words "talk to God", "pray") is that they are talking but there is nobody there they are talking to. If Otto can see there is somebody there they are talking to, then they are not talking to God.

Normally, if Alvin is talking to somebody Otto can identify who it is he is talking to. This he will sometimes do by asking Alvin who he is talking to, and sometimes he will just be able to see or hear who it is. Sometimes what Otto sees and what Alvin says may not correspond. Alvin may come up to Otto at the party and tell him he has just been talking to the famous Diana, whereas Otto, who has seen them talking, knows that it was in fact the obscure Brenda. If you are talking to somebody, there arises the question of the identity of the one you are talking to, and you can get it wrong. But if you are talking to God, the question of the identity of the one you are talking to does not arise in the same way. If Alvin says he has been talking to God he cannot be mistaken about *who* he has been talking to. He cannot mistake somebody else for God as he can mistake Brenda for Diana. Neither can he speak to God under the mistaken impression he is talking to Herbert. If Alvin says he has been talking to God, what he says is decisive. That is the way this part of our language works, differently from our talk about speaking to Charlie. God is not a bodiless Charlie.

Now suppose somebody wanted to say that that is just what God is, so that when Otto sees Alvin speaking when there is nobody he is speaking to, that means only that things are not as they appear. Can we say that Otto needs the information that there is in fact somebody there who Alvin is talking to, only he is invisible and otherwise undetectable? Of course, God is there; but does that mean that there is *somebody* there? If we are trying to teach Otto the way we talk about God, then there is this immediate point: Otto can see no difference between there being somebody invisible there and there being nobody there. But to learn the use of this part of our language, as to learn the use of any words, he needs visible or otherwise discernible criteria to be able to determine when the words are being properly used and to be able to use them properly himself. He needs to be able to *see* or otherwise detect when it is correct to say that somebody is talking to God. Talk of invisible or bodiless persons is not going to help him learn the language, to be able to use it. (Indeed, he will first have to learn what is meant by such a phrase, when it will be correct to call somebody or something an invisible person or a bodiless person, and there is problem enough there.) Whether there are any such invisible persons around will be quite irrelevant to the use, and so the meaning, of the language.

If I am to talk to Charlie, he has to be there; and he might not be there. There are criteria for establishing whether he is there. He has a recognizable body, and I can by and large easily tell whether he is there in the same room as me. But things can be a bit more complicated than that. When we talk about somebody being 'there', we do not necessarily mean that they are in any particular place. You do not have to be in the same place as somebody to be able to talk to them – there are telephones. And when we say that somebody is there, we can mean not so much that he is in a particular place, as that he is present as a person at an event, is part of what is going on. To be there – at the party, at the conference – is not just to be in the place where the party or the conference is going on, but to be party to the occasion, to be doing something. Talking to people is an occasion. When two people talk together, it is not enough that they both be there. The two have to do things – to speak, listen, and so attend, make gestures, give appropriate replies to what has been said. (So we may say to somebody who does not react in the appropriate way when we speak to him, who seems inattentive, "Are you there?" or of him, "He's miles away".)

But, however complicated our talk of people's being there, there are criteria for whether Charlie is there or not when we talk to him. There are no such criteria for establishing the presence of God. (This is so in Christianity; it is easy to imagine how there might be such criteria in other religions. For example, it may be said that God is present in or through an image, so that you can only pray and be heard in the presence of the image – and that need not be a matter of distance, but of whether you are within the confines of the precinct, however large it may be, where the image is contained. Or you may want to talk to a particular rain god who is only present when it is raining, so that you can only pray and be heard when it's raining.) In Christianity, when you talk to God, nothing counts as God being absent. God is always present when you pray. And nobody ever discovered that. It belongs to what we are taught when we are taught about God. It is part of the concept of God in Christianity. It is not a piece of wonderful knowledge (we did not have to wait for philosophers to prove it to us, before we could be sure of it); it belongs to the language. So you can feel a fool if you are talking to Charlie and realise that he is not there – that the criteria for establishing his presence are not after all fulfilled, as you had thought they were. But you cannot feel a fool by realising that God is not there, for there are no criteria of God's presence that can fail of fulfilment. It is of course possible to come to feel that prayer *in general* is foolish, but that is to believe that there is no God, that God is not there to be talked to. But that is to reject the entire *practice* of prayer. If you accept the practice, there are no occasions on which you feel foolish because you discover that God is not there listening, even though on most occasions he is there. By contrast, when you feel foolish because you realise that Charlie isn't there, this is not a matter of rejecting the entire practice of talking to people, or of talking to Charlie, coming to believe that Charlie does not exist. It is rather to be embarrassed at noting that, on this occasion, the rules governing the practice – which you accept – have not been adhered to.

If God is always there, this is not as a brute presence, as a book might be present; he is always there *to be talked to*. He is there as part of the context you establish by talking to him. He is always attentive; there are no criteria for establishing whether he is attentive. Again, this is part of our language about God; nobody ever found it out. So he is always attentive, however many people are talking to him at the same time. God's face is always turned to you, even though it may also be turned to a million others; and he has only one face. This too we know, not through some marvellous discovery, but because it is part of the way we talk about God, and part of the way we use language about talking to God – language which, it is already beginning to be clear, functions in a rather different way from our language about talking to people.

In Matthew's gospel, Jesus gives some teaching on talking to God, and part of what he says is this:

> Whenever you pray, do not be like the hypocrites, for they love to pray standing in synagogues and on street corners so as to be seen by men. Amen, I say to you, they have had their reward. But when you pray, go into your room, close your door and pray to your Father who is in secret; and your Father who is in secret will reward you. (6:5f.)

The disciples are enjoined to go and pray in private, alone. So I can talk to God in private just as I can talk to Charlie in private, and I can go and be alone with God just as I can go and be alone with Charlie. Here are more similarities between God and Charlie; but there are differences that surface here, too. If I am alone with Charlie, then Charlie is alone with me; but if I am alone with God, God is not alone with me – we do not *say* of God that he is ever alone with anybody. So too Charlie and I may be alone together, but God and I are not alone together. More importantly, if I am with Charlie, even if I am alone with Charlie, then I am not *alone*. But if I am alone with God, then I am alone – indeed, I may contrive to be alone precisely so that I can be with God. In the context of prayer, God is the one I am with when I am with *nobody*.

We may say that God is always there. But does that mean that I am never alone? It certainly does if God is an invisible somebody; for, after all, if I say Charlie is always there (he is keeping guard over me) that does mean I am never alone. I may frequently talk about being alone, express a desire to be alone, hate being alone, etc. Do I not really mean all that, if I am a Christian, if I believe that God is always there? Or when I say I want to be alone, do I, as a believer, mean something different from Freddie the atheist when he says he wants to be alone? When I use the word "alone", do I always mean "alone, apart from God"? No. I use the word in exactly the same way as Freddie does, so I mean the same as he does. And when I say "alone" I do not mean "alone with God", for I make a distinction between being alone and being alone with God; I will use the two phrases in different circumstances. I can be alone, and then I can be alone with God, if I start praying, talking to him. That does not suddenly make God appear – for God never appears. It can still be said of me that I am alone. It is not that I am really not alone, that there is somebody else there with me, only he is invisible. I really am alone, and my being alone with God is not incompatible with my being alone in the way that my being alone with Charlie is. Though we might say, "God is always there", that does not mean I am never alone.

But Christian language is extremely fluid, and there might, as well, be contexts in which I would want to say that – because God is always with me – I am never alone. Think here of John 16:32, where Jesus says:

> Behold, the hour is coming – it has already arrived – when you will be scattered, each to his own, and you will leave me alone. But I am not alone, for the Father is with me.

God is the one who is with him though *nobody* is with him, when everybody has abandoned him. And what that means is that he will not react as one abandoned. "God is with me" is not used as a report that somebody is with me, but as an expression of confidence in peril. So that God is with me can never be a matter of indifference to me, as it might be a matter of indifference to me if Charlie is with me. "God is always there". This sentence has a use in the context of prayer. It means I can always pray. When I speak to God he is always there to listen, so I can pray even when I am alone, when there is nobody there to listen to me. And there may well be other contexts in which we would want to say that God is always there. But, at least when I pray, he is present as we might say that a person is present at an event, taking part in what is going on; he is there in the context of my prayer. He is not just there as a brute presence, just being there but having nothing to do with my prayer, not attending to me, not listening to me. Do we want to say that God is also sometimes present as a brute presence, just hanging around, as a book might just be there? I can pray when I am alone. God can be with me when I am alone. But

191

if he could just be there, independently of any context that is established by what I do, that would appear to imply that, contrary to what has already been established, I am never really alone after all, even when I and everybody else think I am.

There is also this: I may pray when alone, but I also do private things and shameful things when alone, things that would make me ashamed, or just embarrassed, if anybody saw me doing them. So these are things that I have to make sure I am alone before I do them; I make sure nobody is there, apart from me. Then, when I do them, have I forgotten that 'God is always there'? And do I then remember it again when I turn to prayer? No. When I pray, it is no part of what I do that I remember that God is there, as if I had forgotten it. This is established, if it needs to be established, by the fact that I can pray alone at set times; I can set myself to pray at a certain hour; this is a traditional Christian practice. But I cannot set myself to remember something I have forgotten at a certain hour. I might of course prepare myself for prayer at that hour by first doing what I might want to call "remembering God" or "remembering that I am in the presence of God"; but that I can do that at set times only shows that remembering that I am in the presence of God is not a case of remembering something I have forgotten. What I do when I pray, then, is not remember something I had previously forgotten, but establish a context. And when I finish praying, it is not that I promptly forget again that God is there; I dissolve the context in which God was present with me. (How could I, in any case, be plausibly supposed to have such a gymnastic memory?)

If I am doing something shameful when alone, I may suddenly remember that God sees me, that God is there, as he always is. (So here is another context in which we use the sentence "God is always there".) And if I do not remember that God sees me, that does not mean that I have forgotten it; if you want to do something shameful, how could you forget that there is somebody there with you, who can see what you do – especially if that somebody is one you know is *always* there? If my wife is always there, always with me, I will certainly not forget the fact if I want to steal from her purse or commit adultery. If I remember that God sees me, it is not that I have recovered from a temporary lapse of memory, and my reaction is not the same as if I remember or realise that *somebody* can see me. If I remember that God sees me, then I react with shame at what I am doing; I regret doing it, and am brought to judge my action as shameful. But if I realise that *somebody* can see me, I may or may not regret doing it. What I regret primarily, in the realisation that they can see me, is just that I have been seen, been caught at it; of course, for it is because I knew I would regret being seen that I tried to make sure I was alone when I did it. And I may regret only my being caught at it, not my action itself: I may consider that I am doing something quite acceptable in having an affair with my secretary, and regret only being caught doing it by the wife, who is tediously narrow-minded about these things. Or I may be a hardened petty thief with no conscience at all, simply a desire to do my deeds without being seen. The thought "God sees me" necessarily leads me to a judgment on my action in the way that the thought "Somebody sees me" does not. Being seen by God is not the same as being seen by somebody. And God can see you when you are alone; God is the one who sees you when *nobody* sees you. And it is precisely when I am *alone* that God sees me. If God were somebody who was there with me, he would not see me when I am alone.

Talking to God

When I speak to God, I do not have to attract his attention, as I have to when I begin to speak to somebody; I do not have to address him by name, or make gestures in his direction, or raise my voice (I do not actually have to speak at all). All these things, that I normally have to do when I begin to talk to people, are part of what makes it true that I am talking to one person rather than another. In addition, while I am talking to somebody, I attend to him, what I say is directed at him, I *mean* him; and while I am talking to him or with him I do not normally attend to somebody else. There is a difference between my attending to him and my attending to somebody else, and this is manifested in a number of ways. Generally, I am closer to the one I am talking to than to others, and if I am not, I will generally raise my voice to speak to him; we will look at each other, and may both carry on a play of gesture; when I am talking he will give signals when he wants to interrupt, and I will look out for them. All these things can be seen or heard; other people can normally tell when I am attending to, talking to, one person rather than another – it is not a matter of something that goes on privately in my head.

There is behaviour characteristic of talking to God, but it is not the behaviour characteristic of talking to somebody. Not only do I not have initially to attract God's attention, but neither do I do any of the things that I do when I talk to somebody. If I do all these things with Charlie, they are part of what makes my talking a talking with *Charlie*, this man here, rather than with Bill, Matilda or Sebastian, who are scattered about other parts of the room. If all these things are missing in prayer, what makes my prayer talking to *God*? What makes it true that in my talking I mean, attend to, God? How do I know that my attention has 'found the right mark'? When talking to people I sometimes devote my attention to the wrong one by mistake. How do I know that I do not similarly make a mistake with God? Of course, these are not real questions. When I think I am talking to God I can't get it wrong, but that is because I can't get it right either. My attention does not aim at any mark. (Or if it does, it is not aimed at God, the one I am praying to. I might while praying fix my attention on a statue or a painting or a crucifix; but if I do I am not praying *to* it, but *before* it.) Attending to God is not attending to somebody or something; it is not a kind of attention.

In talking to somebody, attending to them and having their attention go together. If it is a real question whether my attention 'aims at the right mark', so it ought to be a real question whether God is attending to me. But, as I mentioned before, this question does not arise; I don't have to attract God's attention when I start to pray, and neither do I have to hold it. In the teaching on prayer in chapter 6 of Matthew, which I have already referred to, Jesus is critical of the hypocrites. What is wrong with them is that they try to attract attention when they pray, to exhibit themselves as praying. What the disciples are to do is not to exhibit themselves; they are to pray in secret, to have no thought of being seen. You can tell when somebody is praying in order to be seen. He does it on street corners, makes extravagant gestures, adopts particular poses when and only when he sees people around. His behaviour is exhibitionistic. The disciples are not to behave in this way; they are not to seek the attention of men, but to go and pray in private, where nobody sees them. Then God will see them and reward them. But they are not seen by God because they behave in such a way as to attract *his* attention. In going into their room to pray, they are not exhibiting themselves to somebody *else*, namely God; they are not exhibiting themselves at all. They are not trying to attract anybody's attention; they just go and get on with it. That is why God sees and rewards them. So when you pray, the situation is quite unlike when you go to talk to somebody. If, when you talk to God, you do not begin by attracting his attention, that isn't because you do not have to, because God is already attentive. It is because you are not concerned about being attended to; you are not showing yourself.

We normally think of prayer as something people do to get what they want, making requests which will or will not meet with a response. A lot of prayer is like that, and Jesus himself says, "Ask, and it will be given you" (Matthew 7:7). But note that the prayer that Jesus is talking about in Matthew 6 is not like that. It is *ritual* prayer, prayer that is enjoined as a practice. It is a good practice, one for which God will reward you when he sees you do it (but only, of course, if you do not do it so as to be seen, for the sake of a reward). It is not a way of getting things by asking for them; what you get is a reward for a practice *seen*, not a response to a request *heard*. It is simply a practice that forms part of the life of a Christian disciple and that seeks nothing beyond itself, has no goal. In this respect it is like almsgiving, and so is treated immediately after it in Matthew (followed in turn by fasting, another ritual practice to be performed without thought of attracting attention.)

If I know how to talk to Bill, then I know, more or less, how to talk to Charlie. But I have to be *taught* how to talk to God, even if I can already talk to Bill. So Jesus teaches his disciples to pray by giving them the words of the Lord's Prayer (Matthew 6:9–13. In Luke he gives the words of the prayer in response to the request of the disciples, "Lord, teach us how to pray, as John taught his disciples". (Luke 11:1)) Talking to God is a different practice or range of practices from talking to people, and one of the differences is that in talking to God I can regularly use formulas, even nothing but formulas, such as the Lord's Prayer. And though I might get bored doing that, God does not get bored as people would. (How can I say that with such confidence? – Because he displays no signs of boredom. And that is because we do not have the language for him to display signs of boredom; there is nothing that *we* are prepared to *call* "an expression of the boredom of God". God escapes boredom, not because of the remarkably full life that he enjoys, but because there is no place for talk of the boredom of God in our language.)

I can use formulas when talking to God. I can even read them from a book, like the psalter or other collections of prayers. What then is the difference between my praying such prayers, speaking to God with them, and simply reading them? If I really mean them as prayers, how do I mean them? It is not that when I am praying I am attending to somebody called God. My attention is not on anybody; it is on the prayers I am reading. (I can, and should be, also attending to God, but that is not attending to somebody, and it does not conflict with my attending closely and exclusively to the prayers.) I might be reading the prayers for all sorts of reasons – to enjoy the language, as part of a study of English grammar, because I have been given the task of memorising them, as part of a study of Christian beliefs and practices. Or it might just be a whim, to help pass a few idle moments. What shows what I am doing is partly what I say if asked, and partly the context that surrounds that activity. If I am praying the prayers, they play a different part in my life from the one they have if I am, say, memorising them for use in a stage play. If my reading the prayer is also praying the prayer, that may be for a number of reasons: it may be part of an attempt to live a more Christian life, to express penitence, to ask forgiveness, a way of getting something I want, or it may be simply a practice that I have been taught constitutes prayer when it is done in the context of a Christian life, that is, a ritual that forms an element of the lives of Christians. Whatever account is given here, whatever it is that makes reading or saying words prayer, as opposed to anything else, it is clear that it is not that my attention is directed at somebody called God.

One of the ways my words must relate to the rest of my life if they are to count as prayer comes out in the distinction that Christians sometimes make between real prayer and empty, merely formal prayer. Though I may say I am praying when I speak or read the words I do, and though the context shows it is not part of a study of English or an attempt to learn a stage role, yet it can still be said of me that I am not *really* praying. You really pray for what you really want. For example, I pray every day that the plight of the poor in third world countries may be alleviated. But in the rest of my behaviour I show that I do not really want that. I will not support charities that are carrying out sensible aid programmes, I will not buy goods from poor countries even when they are of good quality, I oppose all national and international schemes devoted to helping the poorer nations, I buy shares in companies notorious for exploiting them. Now it may be said of me that I am not really praying for the poor, that my prayers are an empty sham. Or if I pray to be freed from a besetting vice but make no attempt at all to stop my vicious activities, do not show myself uneasy about them, and actually take great delight in them, then I show by my behaviour that I do not want to escape this vice. My prayer is not a genuine petition, expressing what I want; again, it is a sham.

Asking God for Something

Suppose somebody does pray for something as a means of getting it, asks God for it because he really wants it. For you can ask God for something because you want it, just as you can ask Charlie for something because you want it. In general, I ask Charlie for what I want because I want it and because I think it is in his power to give it to me and that he will give it to me, if I ask, and because I think it proper to ask him. I ask, both because I assume he does not know what I want or when I want it unless I ask for it, and because he will not give it to me unless I ask for it. And one of the reasons he will not give it to me unless I ask for it (there may be others) is that he does not otherwise know what I want or that I want it. That is, it is in general part of the function of my request to inform him of what I want. (But this will not always be true. Consider, for example, the situation in which a child is being taught the *practice* of asking for things. Then the mother may know perfectly well what the child wants and be only too happy to give it to him; but he has to be brought to ask for it first.)

Much of this does not apply to my asking God for things. To begin with, God already knows what I want before I ask for it; there is no question of informing God of what I want. It is indeed part of the practice of prayer to make our requests known to God (cf. Philippians 4:6), but that is not the same practice as making our requests known to Charlie. Neither is it true that God will not give me what I want unless I ask for it. There are many things I want, things which I might pray for, for which however I do not pray, and which yet God does give me. And I do not have to use many words in prayer, even if I want many things; whatever and however much I may want, I can always pray using the same formula – the Lord's Prayer (cf. Matthew 6:7ff.); I may even pray without words (cf. Romans 8:26f.). Asking God for something, then, is quite unlike asking somebody for something, even though similar forms of words may be used. What we are doing with the words is different. When I learn English, I also learn what it is to ask somebody for something, and when it is and is not appropriate to ask for it. I learn the place that the making of requests has in people's lives. And asking God for something, making a request of God, does not have that place in my life; whatever place it does have, whatever function asking God for something has in my life, it is not that one. It would be a misleading account of prayer to say, "You know what it is to ask somebody for something; well, here it is just the same, only it is God you ask". Asking God for things is a different practice from asking somebody for something. God is not one more person whom we might ask for something.

So also persistence in prayer, in asking God for something, is not like persistence in asking somebody for something. We learn by experience the results of persisting in asking people for things, and the results vary according to who we are asking, what mood he is in, what we are asking for, what is polite. And very often it is a sign of social incompetence to persist; it is the kind of thing we are taught not to do. But we are taught to persist in asking God for things (the parable of the widow and the unjust judge, Luke 18:1ff.). And we have to be *taught* this persistence. We do not learn from experience that it produces results. Indeed, this teaching of Jesus seems to be occasioned by people's experience that such persistence does not produce results, for the parable is told "to the effect that they ought always to pray and not to lose heart". Persistence in asking God for things occupies a different place in people's lives from persistence in asking people for things. It is part of a separate practice that is taught. – And the practice taught could have been different. Jesus could have told a different parable, say, to the effect that having asked for something once there was no need to carry on asking for it. (In fact there seems to be something like this in Matthew 6:7.) And would such teaching then be false? Would it fail to 'correspond to the facts about God'? There are no such facts, apart from the teaching. There are no facts about God that govern whether it is wise for us, e.g. to persist in asking him for something, as there are facts about other people that tell us whether it is wise for us to persist in asking them for something. The practice of asking God for things is in large measure separate from, independent of, the practice of asking people for things. That is why it has to be taught, even to those who already know how to ask people for things, and why many different practices of prayer may be taught.

Answered Prayer

To investigate what people mean when they say God has answered their prayer, we have first to make a simple distinction between two different senses of "answer" or "response". If I ask you for the salt, you can pass it to me, saying something like, "OK. Here you are". You answer my request both by acknowledging it and assenting to it verbally, and by what you do, by actually passing the salt. But this combination of words and actions is not necessary. You could just pass me the salt in silence, and that would equally count as a positive response to my request. Sometimes it is part of an answer to a request for action of some sort to say you are acting in response to a request, and sometimes the action stands on its own. When God is said to answer prayer, he is said to answer it in the second sense. God does not in any ordinary sense use language when answering people's prayers. If you pray for rain, God is not said to answer by saying, "OK. Here it comes", and sending rain; he simply sends the rain.

If I pray to God, there may be occasions on which I want to say that God has answered my prayer. Do I mean that *somebody* has answered me? If Charlie answers my request positively, he gives me what I ask for. If I ask him for a particular book, he gives me the book. (Let us say he hands it to me in silence, or sends it without a covering note.) But he also gives it to me *because* I ask for it. In the typical case, that means that he gives it to me *when* I ask for it – certainly not before I ask for it; and if he gives it to me some time after I ask for it, we give an account of the lapse of time in between, so that the giving and asking are given some mutual connexion – and we would speak of a *delayed* response to my request. That there is a temporal relation of this kind between the asking and the giving is part of what makes the giving a *response* to my request, rather than a random act of generosity. And the same goes for God. It is part of what makes what happens God's reply to my request that I receive from him what I do, having asked for it. And generally that means *soon* after I have asked for it (though here too we will want to allow delayed response, giving something that counts as an account of the lapse of time between the asking and the receiving). That is part of what distinguishes it from random generosity. It is because I have asked that what happens is a reply, a response; the request provides a context for what happens that makes it appropriate to describe it as an answer.

But, as already noted, there is a difference between God's reply and Charlie's reply. If I had not asked, Charlie would not have given, at least in the standard case; that is part of the function that asking plays in our lives, that it brings it about that other people do things they would not otherwise do, or at times when they would not otherwise do them. Part of the reason I ask Charlie to give me the book is that I believe he will not give to me *unless* I ask him for it. But God would have given anyway. My prayer makes no difference to what happens, in this sense: I may pray for something to happen because I want it to happen, but not because I believe that God will not grant me it unless I pray for it, that my praying is a condition that God imposes before he will give me what I want. If I ask God to cure my son, it is not because I believe that God will not cure my son unless I ask him to. And so if I pray for something to happen, and it does happen, I may say that God has answered my prayer, that it happened because I prayed for it; but that explanation does not function in the same way as the explanation that Charlie gave me the book because I asked for it.

If I pray for rain, and it rains, then I say that God has answered my prayer. Freddie the atheist may see me praying for rain, and see it rain soon after, and yet be unimpressed. From his point of view it is not an answer, for it would have happened anyway: it was a perfectly natural event, with ordinary antecedent causes that can be traced by a competent meteorologist, so there is no need to invoke my prayer and an answering God in order to explain it. That may be all perfectly right, and I may readily agree that the rain has ordinary, 'natural' causes, so that it would have happened anyway, even if I had not prayed. But I may still insist that it was the answer to my prayer. And here it is not that one of us must be wrong and the other right; it is that one of us has prayed and the other has not. If I pray for an event to happen, and it happens, then ordinarily I cannot but see that as the answer to my prayer; that is part of what prayer is. (Just as, if I ask Charlie for the book and he gives me it, I cannot but see that, ordinarily, as the response to my request.) And if I pray for something to happen, say, for it to rain, that does not mean that I have temporarily forgotten that events have natural causes. I may be inclined to say, even to insist, that *all* events have natural causes, and yet still pray for an event to happen. Indeed, I may pray for an event to happen of which I myself will be a principal natural cause, if it happens; I may, for instance, pray that I will get a good mark in the examination, or be able to swim ten miles to safety when my boat capsizes, or that my wife will bear me a child. And that does not show that I am hopelessly irrational. (I may be irrational, but I may be highly rational, and it is the rest of my behaviour that will show that.) It shows that asking God for something is not to be construed completely on the model of asking somebody for something; God is not somebody whom I ask for things.

This is connected with another important difference between the way that Charlie gives me things and the way that God gives me things. If I ask Charlie for a book and he gives it to me, there are two features of what happens that make us want to say that Charlie has answered my request. First, I get the book, having asked for it (and normally, soon after). Second, Charlie *gives* it to me; he performs some action that results in my receiving the book, and he performs it so that I may receive the book. If I write a letter to Charlie asking him to send me a book, and I receive it, having asked for it, the first of the conditions is satisfied. I will assume, reasonably enough, that Charlie has given it to me. But it may nevertheless not be true that Charlie has given me the book. For it may be that Charlie received my letter and decided to refuse my request, or forgot all about it, but that by coincidence my Aunt Matilda decided to send me a copy of the same book (anonymously) at the same time, for a surprise present. Or it may be that Charlie decided to send the book to somebody else, but posted it to me by mistake, or that the postman delivered it to me by mistake, instead of to the person it was intended for. Only if it is true both that I get the book having asked for it and that Charlie has performed some appropriate action directed to that end, and because I asked for it, would we want to say that Charlie has given me the book in answer to my request.

But things are different with God. If I ask God for something, and get it, there is no further doubt, no question to be raised, as to whether God gave it to me. If I ask for rain, and it rains, then God has sent the rain in answer to my prayer. There is no possibility that God decided to refuse my request but that my Aunt Matilda made it rain, or some other spirit did, or that God really intended to send snow but sent rain by mistake, or that he intended to send rain elsewhere, but it arrived here instead. How do I know that all these possibilities are ruled out? It is not because I have reflected upon the omnicompetence of God or on the incompetence, in this respect, of my Aunt Matilda. It is rather that the second of the two features mentioned above in connexion with Charlie's giving does not apply to God. If I receive rain, having asked for it, to establish that this is in answer to my prayer it does not also have to be established that God performed some appropriate action directed to that end. What answers my prayer is not that I get what I asked for and that a particular agent, viz. God, does something that constitutes his giving it to me. What answers my prayer is simply that I get what I want. The question of agency does not arise. What happens that constitutes the answer to my prayer is not something that is done by a particular agent. What I pray for when I pray for something is not that a particular agent do something with the intention and result that I receive something; I pray simply to receive it. It is not that I want somebody to do something, but that I want something to *happen*.

This can be brought out in the following way. If I ask Charlie for something, it can be because I want it, he has it, etc. But it can also be because I want *him* to give it to me. If he has taken some money of mine, I may demand it back, and demand it from *him*. I may say to his friend who offers to repay out of his own money, "No, I don't want it from you. It isn't just the money. He took it: *he* must give it back; he must right his own wrongdoing". Or what I want may be something that I can easily get from any number of people, but it is important to me that the one I love give it to me. And so on. But if I ask for something from God, it is not that I am concerned that God *and no other* give it to me. I may pray, "O God, give me the book I have been searching for all these years"; but I will not add, "And I will accept it from you and no other, as a sign of your love, because it was your fault I lost it in the first place, etc." I know very well the ways that books come to people: they buy them in shops, get sent them for Christmas. And this may be just the sort of thing I have in mind when I pray for the book. I will not reject the book when my Aunt Matilda sends it to me for Christmas, on the grounds that I insist on getting it from God and no other.

There are circumstances where it looks at first sight as if something like that might happen, as if somebody might insist on God being the agent. For example, if I am a member of a certain kind of religious sect, I may pray for the life of my son who is dying from some disease, and I may in a sense insist that the cure come from God and no other; I may on religious grounds refuse to allow any medical assistance to be given to the boy. But if he then lives, though I may say that this is the answer to prayer (for I did pray), that God saved his life, this is not because I have established that one particular agent and no other has saved him. I have only established, if I have been careful to keep the doctors away, that, though he is now better, *nobody* cured him. I have not established that a particular agent, called God, has performed certain actions that constitute the answer to my request. What I know, and all I need to know, is that I have received what I prayed for. There is no reason to suppose that I do any inferring here. And it is not mere haste on my part if I neglect to wonder whether the cure might have been effected by, say, a cheeky demon who overheard my prayer and wanted to play a practical joke on me, making me think it was God who had done it, when in reality he had refused my prayer. To say that God has given me something in answer to my prayer is *not* to say that a particular agent has given me it; it is not to say that anybody has *done* anything. But certainly God does things; I know that, since I pray for things and he gives them to me.

So we can also say that God is an agent. But God is not somebody who is an agent, somebody who acts. When God acts, it is not that *somebody* acts, not that somebody *does* something that results in my getting what I pray for. If we want to call God an agent, then he is a *spiritual* agent. We speak of God's agency in a different way from the way we speak of the agency of Charlie or my Aunt Matilda; and this logical difference is obscured if we list him together with them as somebody who acts.

This is connected with the fact, already noted earlier, that when I ask God for something I ask for something to *happen*. I pray that it may rain, that my son may live, that I may become a better person, that the people I love may fare well, that the starving may be fed, that the nations may live in peace. Here there may be no thought of agency at all. In fact, it is hard to see how there could be agency in some cases; it does not rain because somebody *does* something (not yet, anyway). And where there is agency involved, the agency is not the agency of some invisible being called God, but of quite ordinary, material agents: the starving will be fed if *the rich* provide them with food; the nations will live in peace if *their governments* work hard for mutual understanding; I will become a better person if *I* learn to cope better with the pressures of life, or become less selfish. I may pray that somebody do something, but that somebody is not an invisible agent called God. What God does in response to prayer is either what just happens or what is done by somebody material like Charlie. That is to say, what God does in answer to prayer is not something that is done by anybody; it is what happens.

Praying for a Rise

I work for Sebastian. Being in need of money, I pray to God that Sebastian give me a rise, and what happens if my prayer is answered is that I get my rise, and that Sebastian gives it to me. My prayer is answered, not by any invisible agent's doing something, but by Sebastian's doing something. There is nothing going on behind the scenes when my prayer is answered, nothing hidden. I can *see* when my prayer has been answered.

It might be replied that there is indeed something going on behind the scenes here, something hidden, an invisible act by an invisible agent: God inspires Sebastian to give me the rise. But this is no real answer. It may be right and proper to say that sort of thing in the context of theology or of ordinary religious discourse, but it is not relevant to the philosophical question of how the concept of God's answering prayer works. It simply substitutes for it the question of what we mean when we say that God inspires people to do things. Maybe it is correct to say that theologically the answer to how God answers prayer must include talk of how he inspires people. So maybe the concepts hang together. But bringing in talk of inspiration here will not help us understand the concept of the answer to prayer unless we already understand the concept of inspiration; and we don't. It certainly cannot be assumed that when we say that God inspires somebody we are talking about some invisible activity of an invisible person. (This may be a temptation, but think of the parallel temptation to think of thoughts, sensations, etc., as hidden, invisible occurrences, and see the way Wittgenstein treats it in *Philosophical Investigations* and *Zettel*.)

If we are trying to understand how the concept of God's answer to prayer works, that involves seeing in what circumstances we *say* that God has answered prayer. It cannot be one of those circumstances that God has inspired Sebastian to give me the rise, for this is not something we see, and we need visible criteria for the application of concepts, if we are to learn how to use them. If we had to know that God had done something undetectable, namely inspire Sebastian, in order to have the right to say that Sebastian's giving me the rise was an answer to prayer, that is, in order to use correctly the concept of God's answer to prayer in this instance, then we never could use that concept correctly. It cannot be that the correct use of a concept, that is, the correct use of words, has to be grounded in a belief about what is in principle undetectable. What decides whether I have used words correctly are the visible circumstances in which I have used them and the general practice of the use of the words in question. And if there is a practice of the use of words, there must be a correct use of those words, that is a use of those words in conformity with that practice. It might be a matter of argument here just what are the circumstances in which it would be correct to say that God has answered my prayer if I pray for a rise and Sebastian gives me one. There may be no generally agreed practice; it is a feature of religions that people recommend different uses of language to each other; that is part of the nature of theological and doctrinal disputes. But in no case can it be that to use the concept correctly it has to be established beforehand that an event has taken place whose occurrence cannot, by definition, be established. If I pray for a rise and am given a rise, and I say that God has answered my prayer, that is because I have prayed for a rise and have been given one. It is because certain visible events have occurred; they are my criteria. It is not because, as I believe, some hidden, unseen event has taken place. I have no grounds for supposing that such an event has taken place, either.

It cannot be countered here that I say that God has answered my prayer because I *infer* that God's inspiration has taken place in Sebastian's heart. For on what grounds would I base such an inference; from what would I infer the occurrence of such an event? It cannot be said that I infer it from the fact that Sebastian has given me a rise, for precisely what is in question here is whether Sebastian's giving me a rise is indeed the effect of God's action, and so is indeed the answer to my prayer. Besides, I do not know what I am supposed to be inferring here; I would not know what the inspiration of God looked like if, *per impossibile*, I saw it. All I know about it, all I *can* know about it, is that it is what is responsible for Sebastian's giving me a rise when he does so as a result of God's answering my prayer. Here again what Wittgenstein says in the philosophy of mind is applicable, *mutatis mutandis*:

> If you say he sees a private picture before him, which he is describing, you have still made an assumption about what he has before him. And that means that you can describe it or do describe it more closely. If you admit that you haven't any notion what kind of thing it might be that he has before him – then what leads you into saying, in spite of that, that he has something before him? Isn't it as if I were to say of someone: "He *has* something. But I don't know whether it is money, or debts, or an empty till". (*Philosophical Investigations* 294)

The inspiration of God, construed as an event which takes place within Sebastian, inaccessible to me, is like Wittgenstein's private picture (only more so, since the inspiration of God is also inaccessible to Sebastian). It is, as far as an investigation of the concept of answered prayer is concerned, useless; it is another beetle in the box. That is, talk of the inspiration of God is not to be construed in that way, as a hidden event whose occurrence has to be inferred.

In any case, what evidence is there that I do actually make an inference here? And why should it be thought that I have to make one? The reason I say that God has answered my prayer when I have prayed for a rise and Sebastian has given me one is just *that*, not anything that I infer from it. So I may be very impressed and grateful to God that he has answered my prayer, and what I am impressed by and what I am grateful for is not that some undetectable event has occurred in Sebastian's soul, but that I prayed God that Sebastian would give me a rise, and he did. What impresses me and what I am grateful for are visible events, not invisible ones. And I am not impressed by those visible events as *evidence*, from which I can infer unseen events. I am impressed and grateful because of the importance of those visible events in my life: I needed a rise badly, and now, in desperation, I put my trust in God. If I say, "God has answered my prayer", that is more like a *reaction* to a sequence of (visible) events than a *conclusion* based on an (unjustified) inference to the occurrence of some (invisible) event.

It is because everything here is visible that I can be *certain* that God has answered my prayer, as religious people very often are; there is no inference involved that would infect everything with uncertainty, no possibly rickety steps from premises to conclusion. I can of course also be uncertain about whether my rise is a matter of answered prayer. It may be part of a subtle trap to bring about my downfall (Sebastian has never been so generous before, and he has always disliked me); it may be that he has heard, as I have not, that a rival is about to try to tempt me away to a better position, and has given me this unexpected rise so that I will feel morally obliged to stay with him. But what gives rise to my doubts are possibilities of the way things may go later –

visible things; they are not doubts about the validity of an inference to something invisible. So I may later, because of events I can see, come to revise my opinion and say that it was nothing to do with my prayer at all that he gave me the rise. (I *may* do that, but I need not. Once again we have to note that religious language is used very variably. I may want to say, for example, that although he gave me the rise from purely selfish motives, or even out of malice, yet God used his motives to give me a rise in answer to my prayer, or something similar. What I say in such circumstances will probably depend on my general views on prayer and the linguistic practices I would recommend in connexion with it. But in either case doubts about the occurrence of an invisible, unidentifiable event do not enter the picture here.)

If I am not making any doubtful inferences, neither am I caused to doubt by the consideration that if Sebastian gave me a rise after I prayed to God, that might after all have only been a *coincidence*. For instance, I do not think anything along these lines: Perhaps when I prayed to God that Sebastian would give me a rise God, for his own purposes or because of my iniquity, refused my prayer, refused to cause Sebastian to give me a rise; but it just so happened that around that time Sebastian decided quite *independently* to give me a rise. If I prayed for something to happen, then I do not see whether it happens or not as a matter of chance: that is part of the concept of prayer. The event's happening or not happening is not something that I can see as independent of God. If it happens, God has brought it about; and if God does not bring it about, it does not happen. There is no question of other agents intervening or just by chance bringing about the same result. And that can only mean that when I am certain that God has brought about a certain event in answer to my prayer I am not certain that any particular agent, as opposed to others, has brought it about.

There is, because I have prayed, no question of having to identify the correct agent; I am just not interested in agents here. And that means that when I speak of God as an agent, I do not speak of *another* agent, one additional to those in whose existence Freddie believes. If God were such another agent, then it would after all be possible for what looks like an answer to prayer to be only a coincidence; that is, it would be possible for me, having prayed, to wonder whether my rise had anything to do with God or was a mere coincidence, attributable solely to Sebastian or to other human agents in addition to Sebastian. (Though we would still be left with the problem how the two cases could be distinguished. There would be no visible criteria, no criteria by which one who prayed could distinguish between them. And that means also that there would be no criteria by which a learner could learn to distinguish them. They could not arise as separate concepts. Since they *are* learned as separate concepts, it *is* possible to distinguish between them; so God cannot be a separate, additional agent.) In fact, the notion of coincidence has no place within the language of prayer. To raise the possibility of coincidence here is not to throw doubt on whether in the particular case what happened was the answer to prayer, as it seemed to be; it is to bring into question the whole idea that God might answer prayer, the whole *practice* of prayer. If I pray for something, I cannot regard the outcome as a matter of chance, which might or might not yield a coincidence; if I do see it as coincidence, then I do not pray, and if I am inclined to see it as a matter of chance then I am inclined not to pray. If I pray for something and it happens, and I say, "Perhaps it was just a coincidence", rather than, "God has answered my prayer", that marks a loss of confidence in a particular form of expression, and hence also in the practice – prayer – and the way of life in which it is embedded. If I doubt, my doubt

213

is not whether a particular agent brought about what I prayed for. It is about whether my prayer had anything at all to do with what happened. – 'Had anything to do with': not that I postulate some causal relationship. There is an obvious, though not causal relationship: that what happened is what I prayed would happen. The question is now whether this relationship any longer constitutes for me a satisfactory explanatory one; that is, whether I would be happy to offer "Because I prayed for it" as an answer to the question, "Why did this happen?" That will no doubt depend on the general state of my religious beliefs, how firmly I believe in God, and what I believe about God.

Wrong Praying

But there is some place – a different one – for talk of coincidence with respect to prayer. Alvin really hates Christopher. Most of the time he tries, as a Christian, to be nice to him and to wish him well. But one day it all becomes too much for him. He prays, "O God, please let Christopher lose his wife, his job and his home, let him be struck blind and then die slowly and in agony of a horrible and incurable disease". And behold, soon Christopher does lose his wife, his job and his home, is struck blind and then dies slowly and in agony of a horrible and incurable disease. Alvin is grateful and triumphant, and tells Brian how God in his goodness has answered his prayer. Brian is horrified.

A: I prayed for it, and what I prayed for happened. What more do you want?

B: But God just doesn't answer prayers like that.

A: Yes he does. He just has.

B: It was just a coincidence.

A: Now you're talking like an atheist. You yourself have prayed for things, and when they happened you didn't talk about coincidence. You believed your prayer was answered and gave thanks to God. I'm doing the same.

B: No. I prayed for peace, and I prayed that the drought might come to an end. Our Lord teaches that peace and the relief of suffering are good things in God's eyes. So they are good things to pray for; and they are in accordance with the command to love. That is why I can say God answered my prayer. Your prayer was not loving. It was a terrible thing you prayed for, and it was a terrible thing to pray for it.

A: I know Jesus says that, and of course God will not answer prayers if they are not in accordance with his will. But if I pray for something and it happens, especially such an unusual thing, how can I *not* believe that God has answered my prayer? It must be that Jesus is wrong here.

B: You can't think that Jesus is wrong, surely – not to mention the whole tradition of the Church. It is only because you accept them that you pray at all. However impressed you might be, you have to accept that this is a coincidence. The fact is, you shouldn't have prayed such an awful prayer in the first place.

A: I see your point. But I *did* pray this prayer, and what has happened has made me think again. It has revealed to me something new about God. I can't just go on believing what I have been told.

B: Well, I'll pray for you.

This inconclusive exchange illustrates a number of points. First, the importance in religion of what is authoritatively said. Although here Brian is not an authority for Alvin, he can appeal to authorities they both accept; this is part of the procedure of persuasion in religious arguments. But what has happened to Alvin, inclining him as it does to heterodox beliefs, also makes him in part inclined to reject those authorities.

Second, since Alvin has prayed for something to happen and it happened, he cannot, of course, see it as coincidence. His position here is exactly the same as that of one who claims to have had an orthodox prayer answered. It is perfectly reasonable, given what has happened, for him to say what he does, even to be compelled to say it. But for the orthodox Brian it cannot but be a coincidence, a mere chance conjunction of events with no significance. What is or is not to be called a coincidence is determined by your system of beliefs, and what happens to you can incline you, perhaps compel you, to change or abandon your beliefs.

Third, because of this, orthodoxy is connected to orthopraxy. Because Alvin is bound to be impressed if he prays this prayer and Christopher does suffer all these things, it is important that he not pray this prayer. Forbidding prayers like this is not only a way of stopping people doing bad things; it is also a way of preserving beliefs. What is at stake here are fundamental beliefs about the nature of God. If you can believe that God will answer *that* sort of prayer, you cannot believe that he loves all his creatures, particularly people, in the way that Christian orthodoxy maintains. Because *this* opinion is not to be held, *that* act is not to be done. Roughly, what God *will* not do (what it is against his nature to do) is what it is wrong to pray for. This is only a special instance of the general point, raised before, that what you believe and what you can believe hangs together with how you act or are prepared to act. It also has relevance for talk about the place of morality in Christianity. You are less likely to pray a prayer like Alvin's, and so come to believe the things that Alvin does, if your life is solidly grounded in the Christian virtues. In Christianity, virtues are not just a matter of living well, but are also linked to believing well. The correct description of the place of the virtues in Christianity must bring out this link with doctrine. There can be no question, for example, of saying that Christianity is 'really' only a form of morality, that doctrine can be interpreted as a kind of disguised moral teaching. Because there is a close link between doctrine and morality, they cannot be the same thing.

CHAPTER 7

MIRACLES

A Boulder

Time and again we have seen that "God" is not to be construed as the name of a person or a thing. It functions in our language quite differently from "Charlie", and the functions are brought no closer by the suggestion that God is a person who lacks a body, or is an invisible something. But there seems to be a problem here: God does things. As Christians believe, he performs miracles, he keeps the whole universe going, and he created it in the first place. We say that he does things in answer to prayers. It is surely no longer possible when we get to this point to say that God is nothing, that "God" is not the name of some being. For you have to be something before you can do anything. If hurtling boulders stop short, suspended in mid-air, inches from some poor child lying helpless in their path, that must be because somebody or something has stopped them, somebody or something with at least as much reality, as much power, as the boulders themselves. And if we attribute such events to the agency of God, hail them as miracles, then we must mean that God is somebody or something, a powerful, if invisible, agent. If we are minded to say that God sustains the whole natural order, as probably most Christians would be, then we are similarly talking about some very powerful, indeed indefinitely powerful (since we do not know the extent of the universe) agent, in whose existence we believe. And if we say – and what Christian does not? – that God created the world, we must also be committed to saying that God is an agent, somebody with the power to bring something out of nothing. It may indeed be very difficult to conceive how anybody might bring something out of nothing, but this much is surely certain: what is nothing cannot bring something out of nothing. From nothing and nothing there can only come nothing. This seems to be the crunch.

Suppose, then, that there is a child lying helpless at the foot of a mountain. (He has broken his leg, and his foot has been trapped in a crevice, or has been tied up and left there by a wicked uncle.) There is a landslide, and one particularly large boulder starts hurtling down, heading straight for the child. It is not deflected by an outcrop of rock, nor is it slowed to a halt by an intervening line of trees. It keeps on down, gathering more and more murderous speed, takes one final leap and is about to descend upon the boy, smashing him to pulp, when, suddenly, it stops dead in mid-air, just six inches above the boy's nose. Everybody who sees it (it happens near an alpine resort) is astounded. The boy is dragged out from underneath, and the whole thing is hailed as a miracle, for which God is thanked and praised. (Nobody thinks it would have been much better, would have saved everybody some very uneasy moments indeed, if God had arranged for the boulder not to have fallen from the mountain in the first place. Is that because they do not consider the matter carefully enough?)

Most reports of miracles are quite difficult to investigate, but not this one. Not only did many people see it happen, not only was the whole event captured on film, but the boulder now remains poised in mid-air, just hovering there, for some weeks. And despite all attempts to move it, it will not budge. This gives ample opportunity not just to verify that what is claimed to have happened did in fact happen, but also for people to investigate this boulder. An investigation is organised by the local church authorities, who are very careful with reports about miracles. First, somebody throws a large bag of flour over the whole area; if there is anything or anybody invisible holding the boulder up, this will render it visible. But nothing is revealed – no large hands attached to powerful arms stretching up into the sky, or to arms attached in turn to some nearby, huge, invisible and evidently benevolent monster whose existence has hitherto been unsuspected; no invisible struts supporting the boulder from underneath; no invisible but extremely strong and quite inelastic rope tied round the boulder with its other end attached to the top of the mountain. Second, the scientists are brought in with their most sensitive and sophisticated instruments to see if any kind of force field can be detected that might account for the boulder's being held where it is (not that you would need very sensitive instruments to detect such a large force). This also reveals nothing. Other objects, even other boulders, are brought next to the boulder and let go; they drop to the ground in the normal way. The boulder is subjected to all known tests to find what it is made of, and its composition turns out to be exactly the same as that of other boulders in the area which fall to the ground normally. The scientists also perform all sorts of other tests I cannot think of. After weeks of investigation it is concluded that no cause can be discovered why this boulder should remain suspended in the air. The miracle is finally confirmed by the church authorities, bells are rung, *Te Deums* are sung, prayers of thanksgiving are said, the boy enters a remote monastery. Eventually the boulder sinks gently to the ground, where despite the best efforts of the guards to protect it, it is broken up by enthusiastic crowds come in search of relics.

Otto follows all this closely; he is on holiday there at the time and sees it all happen. That, he will be told, is a miracle if ever there was one. Thus he will begin to learn the use of the word "miracle"; and he will also be told of other miracles that have been reported throughout the ages. Some of them, perhaps, he will believe, and others not, but he will now know the kind of thing a miracle is supposed to be. He will also know that a miracle is ascribed to God: a miracle is what happens when God intervenes in the natural course of things to safeguard the innocent, to thwart the plans of the wicked, to confirm the truth of the faith. Though God acts in many and often secret ways, here are instances where his agency is evident.

If Otto now believes in miracles, and believes that the incident with the boulder is one, then he believes that it was God who saved the life of the boy by stopping the boulder from crushing him, suspending it in mid-air. But does that means that he believes that somebody or something held the boulder up, prevented it from falling to the ground and killing the boy? Well, he has seen and heard that it has been established at great length that there was *nobody* and *nothing* preventing the boulder from falling to the ground. Not only that, but it was just *because* it was established that nobody and nothing was preventing it from falling to the ground that it was concluded that its not falling was a miracle. If the flour had revealed a normally invisible giant holding it up, that would have been very surprising indeed, and a great find, but it would have meant that the incident was not, after all, a miracle. It was a miracle, not because it was, *per impossibile*, discovered that there was an invisible, undetectable agent called God who was, it was also discovered, responsible for the boulder's not falling on the boy, but because it was discovered that there was *no* cause for the boulder's not falling on him. To be justified in calling it a miracle, we do not have to establish *both* that there was no cause for its not falling *and* that there was one after all, namely God. That conjunction could not be established, for it is a contradiction. And it does not help here to appeal to any distinction between natural and supernatural agents, detectable and by definition undetectable ones. If God is a natural cause, then the scientists, establishing that there are no natural causes involved, establish also that God is not involved. If, on the other hand, God is supposed to be a supernatural cause, then again it cannot be established *both* that no natural agents are involved *and* that God is involved, since God, being a supernatural cause, is by definition undetectable. So, however many scientific tests were carried out, they could only confirm the first half of the conjunction, leaving the second untouched; so it could never be established that we had the right to call any event a miracle.

But, more directly, that is not in fact how the word "miracle" is used. It is not applied to events when it has been established, *per impossibile*, that an undetectable agent was responsible for them, but when it is believed – has been established or is simply presumed – that *no* agent is responsible for them. Presumed: for in some cases no very thorough investigation may be made, or the claim that an event is a miracle may be made before any investigation is undertaken. If an investigation is made at some later stage and a cause for the event is discovered, then the claim that the event is a miracle may well be abandoned. Or, if a miracle is still claimed it will be a different kind miracle. It may be held to be a miraculous *coincidence* that the boulder was stopped by this newly discovered force just inches from the boy's head; or that the boy was lying just inches away from certain death. (Again, nobody who called this a miracle would reflect that a lot of anxiety would have been spared had God arranged for the boy to be lying three miles away; for nobody would think of using the word "coincidence" if the boy were so far away, and it is only when you have a coincidence that you can have a *miraculous* coincidence, only then that you might think of God being involved at all.)

And so it because *no* agent is responsible for the event (or so it is believed) that it is said that *God* is responsible for it. To establish, or simply to presume, that an event is a miracle is of course to establish or presume that God is responsible for it. But to do that is not to say that somebody *else*, apart from all the agents that have been ruled out, is responsible for it. To say that God brought it about is not to say that *somebody* brought it about. God does what *nobody* does; God causes what *nothing* causes.

(And so we might want to call God an 'internal' cause. Causes act *on* things, so we can say that they are external to them. We say that God caused the boulder to stay suspended in mid-air when *nothing* caused it to stay suspended, as far as we can discover. That is, nothing acted on it. And now we do not want to say that there was after all a cause acting on it. If we say God was the cause, we don't mean that. So, we might go on, God is not an external cause but an *internal* one; he acts not *on* things, but *in* them. And by that we would not mean that God would be revealed by breaking open the boulder. Roughly, to say that God is an internal cause would be to say that he is *not* an external cause. Compare this with the way sensations and thoughts are said to be internal. We would not expect to find a thought or a sensation inside somebody if we opened him up. But on the other hand we certainly do not expect to find a man's sensations outside him, either. The similarity here is related to the fact that, just as "pain" is not the name of something, so neither is "God".)

God causes what *nobody* causes; is this not, after all, what makes a miracle so impressive? What is so astonishing is that an event can happen without a cause. If we wanted to say that there was after all a cause, would not that make it less impressive? What impresses is not that God is discovered to be the cause of events, for Christians believe that anyway. It is no discovery for *them*, and atheists on the other hand would refuse to be impressed, refuse to call any event a miracle. They would, for the most part, because they believe that *every* event must have a cause (compare what I said about ghosts). Some Christians also believe that every event must have a cause, and are therefore also very sceptical about the occurrence of this kind of miracle; but they are none the less convinced for all that that God does act in the world.

But now suppose an atheist were prepared to allow that an event could happen without a cause. Suppose that in this particular case Freddie did accept all the scientific investigations as conclusive, and came to the conclusion that the boulder remained suspended in mid-air for no reason whatever, that nothing caused it to stay like that. What would be the difference between him and the Christian who said that the event was a miracle, that is, was caused by God? For the Christian the event certainly has a significance that it does not have for Freddie. That the boulder stopped dead just when it did, just when it was about to kill the boy, will be a sign of God's care for people, a vivid confirmation of what he has always believed. It will not be a *proof* of what he believes, for the event only has significance in the context of belief; it does not impress Freddie, who does not believe, as a proof of anything (and that need not be because Freddie is too dull to follow the proof). As such a vivid confirmation, the event will have its effect on the way the believer views the rest of his life: since God is here shown dramatically to care for people and to cause particular events to happen to show his care, the believer can come to see his own life and events surrounding it more vividly as a manifestation of the loving care of God for him. He may not in fact see it like this; there are other possibilities. But the difference between this event for him and for Freddie is that it can connect with the believer's life and beliefs in any number of ways in which it cannot connect with Freddie's life and beliefs. However the difference may be put, it does not consist in this: that Freddie believes that nobody and nothing is responsible for the event, and the believer believes that after all somebody, viz. God, is responsible for it. Of course the believer does believe that God is responsible for it, but to believe that is not to believe that *somebody* is responsible for it. We may say that the Christian believes there is more going on here than Freddie does, but that does not mean that he believes there are more agents involved (and that he can correctly identify who the extra agent is); rather, he sets the event in a wider context. And it is by placing events within a context, fitting them into a scheme, relating them to other things that happen or to things we believe that we understand them. Freddie, who has no context available to him to fit the event into, therefore simply finds it baffling. At most, he can say that it *must* fit into the scheme of natural causes, even if apparently it does not and he cannot see how it might. (If he finds such a position unconvincing and is not content just to remain baffled by it, then he may be tempted to become a Christian in an attempt to get a more satisfactory view of it.)

I mentioned the matter of the correct identification of the putative extra agent. Here the following question arises. If the Christian thinks there is an extra invisible agent involved in all this, how can he say so confidently that that agent is God, the God of Christian religion? Might it not be one of the gods recognised in Polynesia, or in Africa, or among the North American Indians? The miracle takes place during an international conference, and is witnessed by North American Indians, Africans and Polynesians, as well as by Christians. They all say it is a miracle, and they all say that it was brought about by their respective gods. Should not the

225

Christian at least hesitate over his identification of the agent? And if he should not (for after all we know that Christianity is true and that there are no other gods but ours), then should not the others hesitate? In fact, none of them do hesitate, even though they are all very rational and thoughtful men, much concerned in their daily lives with establishing the identity of agents (it's an international conference of detectives). It is not that they are over-hasty in settling, each according to his own prejudices, the question of the identity of the invisible agent. There just is no such question here. They can each react with certainty because there is no question that can give rise to doubt. They do not make different assumptions, different inferences or different hypotheses. They each place the event in a different context, the context of a different faith, of lives lived out within different faiths. Since they ascribe the miracle to different gods, we can say that they are in disagreement, but whatever is going on here – and it can be difficult to characterise religious disagreements – it is not a dispute about the identity of an agent.

I have made all this up, to keep the story simple. But there are genuine reports of miracles (not necessarily reports of genuine miracles). Think of the shrine of Lourdes, where, it is claimed, people are sometimes miraculously cured of their diseases. Often close to death, they are suddenly restored to health. Brain tumours shrivel, cancers disappear, and the recovery is claimed as a miracle. How are such claims investigated, and what is taken to establish that a recovery is indeed miraculous? Much of the investigation is concerned with *ruling out* possible causes for the cure, showing what has *not* caused it; and it is certainly not proved to be miracle by the discovery of the cause for the cure and its subsequent identification as God.

A Rescue

Now take the case of a sheer coincidence. Some people want to say that some coincidences are miraculous, that they are brought about by God. If they say that, do they mean that *somebody* brings them about, arranges them?

Simon, a desert explorer, has foolishly gone off into the North African desert on his own. His Land Rover breaks down hundreds of miles from anywhere. He decides to try and walk back to civilisation, which he knows lies due north. Unfortunately, his compass has gone wrong, and it leads him off in the wrong direction, deeper into the desert. This would not be so bad, but his canteen of water develops a hole and all the water runs out into the sand. He struggles on for a couple of days until his strength is exhausted. He is about to lie down and die, but then, for no particular reason, he makes one last huge effort and drags himself round the corner into the next wadi. It is wednesday. Hugo is an eccentric millionaire. On thursdays he normally flies from his home in Wigan to one of his islands in the Mediterranean, just for a quick afternoon dip. This week, just on a whim, he decides he will go instead for a picnic lunch in the North African desert, where he has never been before. Furthermore, on another whim, he thinks it might be nice just this once to go out on a wednesday instead of a thursday. Thus it is that when Simon, almost dead, rounds the corner into one last wadi, he beholds a banquet spread before him. There is also a first-class medical team, well equipped with every modern facility (Hugo is very nervous about his health). Simon's life is saved, and Simon, being a Christian, gives thanks to God, whose hand he sees in the preservation of his life. He sees it as a miracle.

What does he believe when he says it's a miracle? There are no strange, uncanny events here, no violations of the laws of nature, no specific elements in this whole complex of

227

events that leap to the eye as being due to the agency of God. What is remarkable here is not any particular event, but the conjunction of them that resulted in the saving of Simon's life. If it is a miracle, it is a miraculous *coincidence*. Nobody has been coordinating it all, supervising operations to make sure that Simon and Hugo did meet up here. Simon and Hugo took their own decisions, quite unknown to each other and independently of each other. All this is implicit in calling it a miraculous *coincidence* in the first place. If somebody had been supervising everything, then, if it had been well planned, it would not have been a coincidence that Hugo and Simon met up; Simon's delighted surprise would have been misplaced, and he would have got over it as soon as he realised that it wasn't a coincidence. (And if somebody did plan it all, then is not Simon over-hasty in being so thankful for the preservation of his life? Could not the supervisor have arranged things to spare him so much anxiety and suffering? Could he not have arranged it so that Simon was never endangered in the first place – that his Land Rover did not break down but brought him safely and without incident back to town, or that Simon decided not to make this particular trip into the desert at all?) The assumption of a hidden supervisor behind the scenes is out of place here. We know what it is for people to plan things, to supervise and direct events – that is the kind of thing we see in battles, police manhunts and rescue operations. But that is just what we do *not* see here. And it is not that Simon, in calling it a miracle, assumes that is an *invisible* supervisor who issues coordinating instructions to the parties involved, or otherwise directs their actions, without their knowing it. Indeed, what is astonishing about the whole thing, and the reason why it is called miraculous, is that totally *uncoordinated* events should have produced this highly desirable result, and should have produced it as the outcome of a highly undesirable situation – somebody being lost and about to die in the desert.

This fact, that the good result is brought out of a bad situation, is an important one. If we are tempted to say that everything has been arranged, then, as I said, it seems that it could have been a great deal better arranged – to avoid danger, anxiety, etc. But if it had been better arranged, if the situation had not been bad in the first place, then Simon's not dying would not have struck anybody as a miracle, because nobody would have been struck by any coincidence. This kind of coincidence has to be a close shave. That is to say, if we are to call it a coincidence, and a miraculous one, then things must already have been *badly* managed – if we think of them as managed at all. What we would have to say then is: How miraculous that things turned out so well – when they had been so badly botched. Just *because* things have come to this pass, just because it required a miraculous coincidence to remedy things, we cannot say that things were arranged to come out this way.

If we say that what happened was a miracle, we may also want to say that it was arranged by God. But that is not to say that *somebody* arranged it. God is the one who arranges when *nobody* arranges. God's arrangement of events is not a species of arrangement of events. That is why when God arranges a conjunction of events we can still call it a coincidence; whereas a conjunction of events that somebody arranges is *eo ipso* not a coincidence. It is also why it is not over-hasty to thank God for arranging things in this way. It would be quite out of place to say that after all things could have been differently arranged so as to produce less stress all round. They could not have been arranged differently, since they were not arranged at all.

For the same reason there does not arise any problem over the identity of the one who arranged this coincidence, since nobody did. Hugo is a Hindu, so while Simon attributes his miraculous delivery to the Christian God, Hugo attributes it to Siva. Hence we may say that the two disagree. But their disagreement, whatever its nature may be, is not over the identity of an invisible supervisor.

Now suppose things are different. Suppose the whole thing *had* been arranged. Suppose Charlie, for reasons known only to himself, had arranged for the mechanic to put a faulty part in the Land Rover so that it would break down in the middle of nowhere, had replaced Simon's excellent compass with a dud, and had drilled a hole in his canteen. He had arranged for Simon's progress on foot across the desert to be monitored from a discreet distance, and had asked his friend Hugo to change his usual plans so as to allow Simon's dramatic rescue to be staged. Simon enters the wadi and exclaims, "Thank God! It's a miracle!" After he has been somewhat restored, Hugo lets him in on the secret. What is Simon's reaction going to be? He is not going to be overcome with gratitude to Charlie. He has been playing with his life. And even if it is explained to him that he was never in any real danger (had he collapsed before reaching Hugo, a medical team was ready on hand to rush to his assistance), still Charlie has played a very cruel practical joke on him. One does not thank such. – Yet he was ecstatically grateful to God when he thought his rescue a genuine coincidence, when he thought it had been arranged by God.

Once he realises the whole thing was arranged by Charlie, he realises also that it was not a genuine coincidence. There are two points here. First, he has to be told, or he has to surmise, that it was all arranged by Charlie, or arranged by anybody at all. If he thinks it was a coincidence, he does not have to be told or to surmise that it was due to God. "It's a

230

miracle!" is not a conclusion but more akin to an exclamation, a reaction. So neither is his gratitude to God, who is by definition responsible for miracles, the result of any inference. "God is responsible for this" does not work like "Charlie is responsible for this". Second, if he realises it was all arranged by Charlie, that means it was not a coincidence after all; it was not what it appeared to be. And that means it was designed to appear other than it really was; it was a *trick*, a *deceit*. But if he thinks it is all due to God – and perhaps he even says, "It was all arranged by God" – that does not mean that he thinks it was not after all a genuine coincidence. On the contrary, it is the *coincidence* that he thinks has been brought about by God, and for which he thanks him. So it was not other than it appeared to be; there was no design, no trick, no deceit. It is not that God made the whole thing *look like* a coincidence. It really was what it appeared to be; that is why it was ascribed to God. Simon took it at face value, and was right to do so. He did not think about what must be going on behind the scenes before thanking God.

The moral of all this is: God is not an invisible Charlie. Hence Simon does not behave inconsistently in thanking God for what happened when he thought it was a miraculous coincidence and cursing Charlie for what he did when he realised it was not. (So neither is there any need to find explanations for any supposed inconsistency in his attitudes. We do not have to suppose, say, that it has been drummed into Simon from his early childhood that God can do what he likes and is always right, that it is blasphemous to criticise him in any way. That is, we do not have to suppose that Simon would curse God if only he were able to think straight, to free himself from his preconceptions and prejudices, just as he curses Charlie. That would be to give a psychological explanation where a logical, philosophical one is called for.) A clue to the difference between God and

Charlie here is that it is natural to say that Simon curses Charlie for what *he did*, whereas he thanks God for *what happened*. Agency is attributed to Charlie in a way it is not attributed to God. And here it is not a matter of a mere form of words. Simon may also thank God for what he did, but the point is that this is equivalent to thanking him for what happened. And there is not the same equivalence in the case of Charlie: he is cursed for what he did, and *not* for what happened. He is cursed when it is realised that all these events did not just *happen*. And he is cursed because it is all a matter of what *he* did. So in the case of God, an event, what happens, is not *mere* event; it is equivalent to deed, what God does; whereas in the case of Charlie, mere event is opposed to deed, what he does. This connects with what I said earlier about prayer. Praying God to *do* something is praying that it *happen*. So if Simon prays God to save him, he prays simply to be saved. And when he thanks God for answering his prayer, for saving him, he thanks him because something has happened.

It is important to bear all this in mind when it comes to other things Simon might say when he attributes his rescue to God. For he may say that the conjunction of events that led to his rescue was not really a coincidence, that it was a sign, even a proof, of the loving care of God. It was not an accident, a random conjunction, but was brought about by God in his mercy. But here 'not *really* a coincidence' means: not *mere* coincidence, something devoid of significance. It does not mean that it was not what it appeared to be, not a coincidence but a carefully worked out plan rigged up to look like one (and the one who did the planning and the rigging was God.) No, it was because it was believed to be a genuine coincidence that it was ascribed to God in the first place. But now: because it is ascribed to God it is not really a coincidence, not a *mere* coincidence. And this is not to deny the original premise, but to say that what is a genuine coincidence is, *in a deeper sense*, not really a coincidence at all. It is not that it has been discovered to be something other than it appeared to be. It remains what it appeared to be, only the words "not really a coincidence" express a *deeper insight* into what it is, into what it appeared to be. (So in religion generally, if we say that things are not what they appear to be, it is not that they are something *else*, so that appearances are deceitful; it is that you need insight, a deeper understanding – of things as they appear to be – to see them as they *really* are. Here is a glimpse of the function of the words "real", "really" in a religious context. When we say, "God really exists" or, "God is what is ultimately real", etc., what is going on in those sentences is not likely to be unrelated to my remarks here.)

So Simon may say that, because his rescue was due to God, it was not really a coincidence. And if, as a result of his experience, he gives up exploring deserts and becomes an evangelist or a theologian, he may develop whole theories of God's providential care for mankind, as manifested in, among other things, miraculous coincidences. But however highly developed these theories may be (and they may be good or bad ones, confused or unconfused) the basic logical difference between God and Charlie remains. If he wants to say that God watches over us all like a loving father, guides our lives, arranges our circumstances providentially, helps us out when we are, or are about to be, in trouble, that does not mean that *somebody* watches over us all like a loving father, guides our lives. So the questions that would arise if it were said that Charlie was doing all of this do not arise here: Why does he not do a better job of it? Why does he wait until sare in such a mess before helping us out? Why does he not always help us out? How can he allow such dreadful things to happen? Does it not degrade us and

233

deprive us of our freedom that he should treat us like children and guide (here we should prefer: manipulate) us all the time? Etc. And so also it is not irrationality or inconsistency on Simon's part if he urges us to be grateful to God for all this, to love him and thank him, whereas if Charlie were doing it all Simon and we would be indignant, resentful, etc. Perhaps much rebellion against and rejection of God, much indignation and resentment against him, comes from this kind of confusion: feeling imprisoned, degraded and dominated by a God who mismanages things to produce so much suffering – feelings that come from wrongly assimilating God to Charlie.

Miracles & Holes

What is going on in these stories of miracles is roughly this: Events take place of a kind that we would normally attribute to an agent, one who either acts directly (the boulder) or who guides, supervises and coordinates the actions of others (the desert rescue). They do not strike us as random but as significant, since they produce highly significant results, such as the saving of human lives. So we would normally attribute them not just to an agent but to an agent who is concerned with human welfare, who does roughly the kind of thing we hope we would do if we were in a position to. But: there is no sign of any such agent's being involved here. We do not discover an agent of an unusual nature, whom we call God, and we do not on that basis call the event a miracle. Rather, there is an established or presumed absence of any agent. It is not that an invisible and otherwise undetectable agent is inferred, either, and that the event is called a miracle on the basis of that inference. We have no reason to believe that people do typically make such inferences in situations where miracles are spoken of; and, as we have seen, such inferences would in any case be out of place.

The making of inferences is a much less common activity than some philosophers think, but there may be a special reason why it may be thought here that people *must* be making inferences, even though there may no evidence that they actually are. For, it might be said, even though we see no agent involved in these miracles, there *must* be one – and if not seen, then inferred. And the reason why there must be such an agent is the question: But how *could* a boulder suddenly stop still in mid-air, unless somebody or something very powerful stopped it and held it there? But to this it can be answered that there is another possibility: such a thing could also happen if *God* held it there. And that is in fact the explanation we give in this case, since we have already satisfied ourselves through our investigations that the boulder does *not* remain suspended in mid-air because somebody or something very powerful is holding it there. (It would be a mistake to say here that our investigations might not be conclusive, so there might after all be something holding it up, and that something might be God. Any possible uncertainty is not what makes room for our talk of God. On the contrary, to the extent that we doubt the exhaustiveness of our investigations, to that extent do we doubt that what has happened is a miracle, that God did it. If you like, our investigations are empirical, natural, and any room they might leave open is for a natural agent, not a supernatural one.)

These events are called miracles, not because an invisible agent is inferred, but because there is, it is believed, *no* agent involved. In particular, events like these are ascribed to the agency of God in the absence of any agent called God to whom they might be attributed. "God" is not the name of an agent. I am not, of course, saying that it is in any way wrong to call God an agent. Of course God is an agent, for he does things; for example, he saves the lives of people by means of miracles. But in calling God an agent we are doing something quite different from what we are doing when we call Charlie an agent. We cannot without causing confusion say, "You know what it is to do things, to be an agent; after all, you have seen Charlie doing things, being an agent. Well, it's just the same here, only it is God who is doing things, being an agent. Acts are acts, whether it is Charlie or God who performs them".

But there really is a temptation to do this, to say: Agency is agency, no matter whose agency it is. Part of the reason for this temptation is perhaps the great similarity between situations in which we say that God acts and circumstances in which we say that people act; e.g. that things behave in ways that we normally attribute to an external cause (boulders suddenly stopping); and that these situations issue in humanly significant events, such as the saving of a life. These similarities are impressive, despite the *obvious* differences – in particular, that there just is no agent around (we can see there isn't), nobody doing the things we would normally attribute to somebody. And this absence is itself part of the trouble, for it seems to leave a hole in the situation, one that demands to be filled. But holes do not make any demands; *we* demand that they be filled, since otherwise the situation seems so difficult, even impossible, to understand. There seems to be nothing for the understanding to grasp. Well, are not situations in which we speak of God *supposed* to be difficult, even impossible, to understand, mysterious? Does not postulating an agent to fill the gap, an agent of a type we can understand and are familiar with (an agent we can choose from a list of possible agents), mean that such situations are made to seem too much like ordinary situations? Does not saying "agency is agency" make God too much like Charlie? To fill in the gap by postulating such an agent does not so much complete for

236

us what is there so that we may understand it better, as give us a different situation from the one we started with, and one which does not have the same significance for us:

> Mere description is so difficult because one believes that one needs to fill out the facts in order to understand them. It is as if one saw a screen with scattered colour-patches, and said: the way they are here, they are unintelligible; they only make sense when one completes them into a shape. – Whereas I want to say: Here is the whole. (If you complete it, you falsify it.) (Wittgenstein, *Remarks on the Philosophy of Psychology* I 257)

Part of the difficulty we have in understanding the action of God properly is that we try to understand it in the wrong way, because we are so tempted to fill in the picture; and we fill it in with something we can already understand, something ordinary, an agent like Charlie. We understand things better if we leave what seems to be the hole and content ourselves with what we see. God is not to be understood by trying to strain beyond what can be seen, by 'transcending the world of the senses', but by resisting the temptation to do that, by learning to be happy with what we have. God and God's activity are to be seen, if at all, in what can be seen and described, not by any attempt to look beyond or behind it:

> Here we come up against a remarkable and characteristic phenomenon in philosophical investigation: the difficulty – I might say – is not that of finding the solution but rather that of recognising as a solution something that looks as if it were only a preliminary to it. "We have already said everything. – Not anything that follows from this, no, *this* itself is the solution!"

> This is connected, I believe, with our wrongly expect-
> ing an explanation, whereas the solution of the diffi-
> culty is a description, if we give it the right place in our
> considerations. If we dwell upon it, and do not try to
> get beyond it.
> The difficulty here is: to stop. (Wittgenstein, *Zettel*
> 314)

If we still cannot rid ourselves of the feeling that there is a
hole to be filled, then we may also still feel that this hole,
even though it would be a mistake to fill it, makes the
situation hard to understand. But that may be because we
cannot get used to the idea that there is so little to
understand. It is said that God is incomprehensible. What
this investigation of miracles suggests is that if God is
incomprehensible, that is not because he is so very *difficult*
to understand, but because there is nothing that *counts* as
understanding God; *there is nothing to be understood*. We
may indeed have a use for the phrase "understanding God",
but it will not be applied to the resolution of intellectual
puzzles concerning God. The things of God must be
understood in a different way, and that will include not
trying to understand them by postulating agents like
Charlie, only invisible. It will involve understanding that –
in this sense of understanding – you do not understand.
Here, as so often, what Wittgenstein has to say in the
philosophy of mind is as illuminating in the philosophy of
religion. (Here for "thinking" read "God"):

> Compare the phenomenon of thinking with the phe-
> nomenon of burning. May not burning, flame, seem
> mysterious to us? And why flame more than furniture?
> – And how do you clear up the mystery? And how is
> the riddle of thinking to be solved? – Like that of
> Flame?

Isn't flame mysterious because it is impalpable? All right —but why does that make it mysterious? Why should something impalpable be more mysterious than something palpable? Unless it's because we *want* to catch hold of it. – (*Zettel* 125f.)

CHAPTER 8

THE ACTIVITY AND CREATIVITY
OF GOD

A Storm Stilled & A Rolling Ball

Look first at a another miracle, or a miracle story, this time one which actually does involve an agent, where a miracle is recounted as being performed by a human being. Matthew tells of this miracle performed by Jesus:

> He got into the boat and his disciples followed him. And behold, there was a great storm on the sea, so that the boat was hidden by the waves. But he was sleeping. And they came and woke him saying, "Lord, save us; we are perishing". And he said to them, "Why are you afraid, men of little faith?" Then he got up and rebuked the winds and the sea; and there was a great calm. But the men were astonished, saying, "What sort of man is this, that even the winds and the sea obey him?" (8:23–27)

Jesus speaks, and the storm subsides. How are we to understand this story? Are we to suppose some causal mechanism here, if we are to make sense of what is going on? Surely not. To begin with, no such mechanism is as much as hinted at. (Do we even know what such a mechanism would look like if we saw it? Can we even say how a man would go about controlling the weather so that he could cause a storm to subside?) The story is not told in causal terms at all. It is not a matter of cause and effect, but of command and obedience. And so the question of the wondering disciples is not, "How did he do it?" but, "What sort of man is this, that even winds and sea obey him?" The disciples are not impressed by the ability of Jesus to manipulate the weather, but because he commands and is obeyed; that is, he orders the storm to subside, and it subsides. What is revealed here is not the power of Jesus, but his *authority*. What Jesus does here he does by issuing a command, not by operating a causal mechanism.

In fact, it is an essential feature of this story, not incidental, that there be no causal mechanism involved. To see why, imagine a simpler, non-religious case. Suppose somebody (perhaps in the course of a variety act) says to a ball, "Roll over there", and the ball actually does roll to the right spot, the spot the magician points out. What we would suspect immediately is that this is not the whole story. We would think that there must be some *cause* for the ball to roll. That is, we do not think of a command as a cause in situations like this. The case when the ball rolls after he says, "Roll over there" is quite different from the case when he says, "Roll over there", and at the same time hits it with a cricket bat. In the second case we do not think of his hitting the ball as an extra cause of its rolling, in addition to his command; it is the sole cause. The command does not even approach being a cause, even an ineffective cause; jumping up and down or blowing might be thought of as an ineffective cause, but not giving an order. The point is not just that the command seems to us useless as a way of getting the ball to roll, but that we do not see how it might ever have anything to do with the rolling of the ball at all, for the rolling of a ball can only be the effect of some cause, not a response to a command. That is why we think there must be more to it when all we see is that he says, "Roll over there", and it does. We think there *must* be something hidden from us. So we would search for some secret mechanism that would explain why the ball rolled. And we might discover, for example, that at the same time as he says "Roll over there" he switches on a transmitter in his pocket that

241

activates a motor within the ball that makes it roll, or some other motor to which the ball is attached by an extremely fine thread. That is to say, our response to the situation is to ask, "How did he do it?" and to try and find the answer. And even if we can't work it out, even if we cannot find any hidden mechanism, we assume there must be one.

If we do discover one, we have discovered his *trick*. He has set up the situation to make it look as if it is other than it really is. In particular, he makes it look as if his words have a purpose, when they do not. Even if the motor is triggered by his voice, that is, by a particular pattern of sound waves, still that is just how he has set up the mechanism: what is actually *said* – the fact that these sounds are *words* that have meaning as part of a language – is irrelevant to what happens. This is true as well if what he says is a signal to some hidden accomplice who then pulls on the string. For such a signal, *any* words would do, or some other pre-arranged sign, like scratching his nose. His words do not function in the way he wants us to think they do: they are not a command to the ball to roll over there. (At the word "there" we might imagine him pointing to the place where the ball then rolls – making what would normally be a meaningful gesture, but which here only looks meaningful, which serves no purpose, except perhaps a covert causal one, or as a secret pre-arranged signal to an accomplice. It would not indicate to the ball where to roll.) Whatever the function of his words and gestures, they have no relevance *as command*. Yet the point of the trick is to make it look as if they did have such relevance. There would be no interest or entertainment otherwise. How then does he make them look relevant? Simply in this way: he says, "Roll over there" – and the ball rolls over there. His words have the form of a command, and what happens is what is commanded. That is all. It is because we are convinced that inanimate things do not really obey commands that we think there is a hole in the picture we are given by his words and what happens; we think there must be some hidden causal mechanism in operation. It would be the *absence* of such a mechanism that would force us into revising our ways of thought, admitting that inanimate objects do under certain circumstances obey commands, or perhaps that they are not inanimate after all. This would amount to accepting the initial picture as complete, without any gaps in it that demand to be filled. Convinced as we generally are that there is a gap, that inanimate things really are inanimate, and that they do not obey commands, we are sure also that it is a trick, and our question is, "How did he do it?"; not, "What manner of man is this?" We do not think he is a man with authority. He exercises power, not authority.

It is otherwise in Matthew's story. Here Jesus speaks, and the storm subsides. That is all. There is no question of filling in the story by reference to a hidden causal mechanism (perhaps operated by a hidden or bodiless accomplice). Even if we knew what such a mechanism would look like, to postulate one would be to undermine the entire point of the story. It would be to make the words of Jesus, *considered as command*, irrelevant. And it would make the appropriate question not, "What manner of man is this?"; but, "How did he do it?" If we believe this story, what impresses us is very simple, and it impresses on account of its simplicity. It is that all that happens is that Jesus commands the storm to stop, and it does. We are not impressed by his ability to operate a causal mechanism. We do not infer a causal mechanism; and if we did, that would rob the story of its impressiveness. If we thought there was an answer to the question "How did he do it", that is, if we thought such a question appropriate in this context, we could at most think of Jesus as performing a very clever *trick*, a difficult manipulation: a trick, because it is made to look as if his telling the storm to subside has something to do with its subsiding, whereas in fact it has nothing to do with it. It is the simple conjunction of command and the occurrence of what is commanded, set in this particular context, that impresses. Jesus impresses as one with *authority*, not power or skill.

But we are reluctant to believe, in normal circumstances, that wind and waves are the kind of thing that anybody can have authority over. They are inanimate, and if they change their natural course, that must be as the effect of a cause, not in response to a command. So this story of Matthew's is strange, and difficult to believe. What can make it easier to believe is if we say that the conjunction of command and what is commanded is just a coincidence. That would mean that, though we may accept that things happened as Matthew describes them, that was just a lucky accident, to which we attach no particular significance. But one thing this cannot mean here is that it must have been a coincidence because we can find no causal connexion between the command and what is commanded. For, as we saw, it is a mistake to look for any such connexion here in the first place.

If the disciples do attach significance to the conjunction of events, it is not because they infer that something is going on behind the scenes. The link between command and what is commanded, which provides that conjunction with significance, is not provided by any hidden causal chain but by the context. The disciples are in peril and they ask Jesus to save them. Then he speaks and the storm subsides. In that situation, they could not but see themselves as saved by Jesus, and the wind and waves as obedient to him. The conjunction is significant partly because it produces a humanly significant result – the rescue of the disciples from peril – and partly because they look to Jesus in the first place for their deliverance. For them to understand what happened as a mere coincidence would be for them to regard their own salvation as a matter without significance, or for them not to have asked Jesus to save them. The conjunction gets its meaning from the prayer, a prayer in peril.

But surely, we might think, we can test whether or not it was a coincidence, or we know what it would be like to conduct such a test: Take Jesus and put him in other storms and ask him to still them. If he can, then in all probability it was not a coincidence the first time; if he can't, it was. But here precisely the conditions that made the conjunction significant in the first place are lacking. This would not be an appeal to be saved, but a request for a display of power as part of a scientific test. Whatever happened, whether the conjunction was repeated or not, the result could not be seen as a miracle. It was the human peril and the appeal to Jesus for salvation that formed the context that linked together the command and the occurrence of what was commanded, that made it possible for Jesus's words to be seen as command, and the subsiding of the storm as a response to it. These elements are an essential part of the description of what Jesus is reported to have done. He *could* not, logically, do the same except in such a context.

So the reaction of the men in the boat is not over-hasty. It is not based on any assumption or hypothesis about what would happen regularly. And it may be remarked here that parallel considerations apply to the case of the boulder. An essential part of the meaning of that case – an essential part of its being a miracle – is that a boy's life is saved because the boulder stops. It is not the stopping of the boulder alone that constitutes the miracle – that would be simply be an inexplicable wonder, strange enough in itself perhaps, but devoid of religious significance, not miraculous, not making you want to speak of God. So in the case of the boulder, we do not have two miracles: first, the stopping of the boulder without means; and second, the miraculous coincidence of its stopping just before it got to where the boy was. Its stopping just before where the boy was is an essential part of the description of the situation, an essential part of the one miracle. It would be a totally different situation, religiously, if the boulder was stopped without means just *after* it had got to where the boy was and smashed him to pulp. So, in the case where the boulder is stopped by means, such as a small intervening clump of trees, it may still be possible to talk of a miracle – the miraculous coincidence of this small clump being in exactly the right place, in an area where there are hardly any trees – but that does not mean that in this second case we have only one miracle, while in the first case there are two. The first, like the second, is only one miracle; the two are just different types of miracle.

To return to the stilling of the storm, the request to 'do it again' only makes sense if what is going on is conceived in causal, quasi-natural-scientific terms. This kind of testing only makes sense if you think that you should be able to reproduce the same effect by repeating the cause. But the stilling of the storm is not that kind of situation. Jesus does not *act upon* the wind and the waves, or pretend to. In that sense, he does not do anything, so he cannot be asked to do it again. The great calm is not brought about as the effect of some cause, for as far as we know they are not being operated on by any cause; if they were, the whole thing would be a trick, to which the actual words of Jesus would be irrelevant. Jesus does not do anything to the wind and the waves: he commands them to be still. And the great calm that follows is not the *effect* of his words, but an obedient *response* to them. And what makes it possible to understand

246

the events in this way is the context of human peril and entreaty.

It may in fact be impossible for many people to understand the story like that, for example people who cannot conceive themselves reacting to a situation of such peril by entreaty. And in any case, wind and waves do not after all have a soul, or any hearing, so they cannot respond to a command. In order to be able to accept this story, we have to be able to see the inanimate world as subject to authority. If we cannot do that, then the story becomes unintelligible. Hence the temptation to try to make it more intelligible by filling it in with reference to some hidden causal nexus. But to do that would be to destroy its meaning. Once again: here is the whole. If you complete it, you falsify it. In order to understand the story properly, we have to rest content with what can be seen, with what is described – the human context, and within that the command of Jesus and the occurrence of what he commands. To believe it is to recognise Jesus as having not power over nature, but authority over it, which is also authority to save. To reject it properly is not to do so because 'we cannot think how he did it' – there is no how – but because we can do nothing with the idea that what is inanimate can be commanded.

The actions of Jesus are believed by Christians to image in some way the activity of God. And indeed what we have drawn from the story of the stilling of the storm confirms what was said about God's activity earlier: that God does not act upon things, does not affect them, do things to them; so if we want to retain anything like that kind of language, we might say that God acts *in* things rather than on them. But the stilling of the storm reminds us also of an alternative kind of language that has always been prominent in the Christian tradition, namely the language of command and obedience. God is said to create by command. For example:

> And God said, "Let there be light"; and there was
> light. (Genesis 1:3)

> By the word of the Lord the heavens were made, and
> by the spirit of his mouth all their host...

> For he spoke and they were; he commanded, and there
> they stood. (Psalm 33:6,9)

He commands the elements and the powers of the sea:

> Praise the Lord from the earth – sea monsters and all
> oceans, fire and hail, snow and frost, storm-wind doing
> his word. (Psalm 148:7f.)

This kind of language, though it carries its own difficulties
with it, has at least one advantage: it makes clear that God
does not do anything to things, does not act upon them,
does not interfere with them, make them different from
what they would otherwise have been. There is no temptation to postulate an invisible agent behind the scenes who
brings about events as causes bring about their effects. To
understand events as having been brought about by God is,
on this model, to see them not as effects of somebody with
great power, great strength, but as signs of somebody with
great authority.

So the greatness of God is seen in a different way, too. The
greatness that comes from power, from strength, is in a sense
impersonal. A strong person is a force to be reckoned with,
just like a natural force. To worship one who is powerful in
this way can seem a very dubious thing to do; it comes close
to power-worship. But authority is essentially personal. If
somebody has authority then, in so far as it is not backed by
power, it is *he* who impresses, not the power that he can
wield. In a sense, *anybody* can wield power, just as anybody
can operate a causal mechanism. You don't have to be an
impressive person to do that, but merely a strong or a skillful

one. Personal greatness is manifested in authority. For that reason, it often stands out particularly clearly when the great one is weak, when he can exert no powers of compulsion. The recognition of somebody's authority is freely afforded; even if you say, "I can't help seeing him as authoritative", you are not under compulsion. But the recognition of power, in the sense of strength, does have an element of compulsion about it; to refuse to recognise power, to defy it, is to risk being hurt by it. To acknowledge somebody's power is to submit to them, but it is not to recognise their greatness, for it is possible to be powerful and petty. But to acknowledge somebody's authority is to see him as great; and that, without resigning your freedom.

And so God is worshipped as great. He is not simply worshipped as immensely powerful (indeed, omnipotent), with it being left in doubt what kind of person it is who exercises all this power – so that he might turn out to be rather nasty and petty. He is worshipped as *great*; that is, *he* is worshipped, not his power. And when it is said that God is manifested by or in the natural world, that means that he is manifested as great, not as merely powerful. So the Christian response is to worship and praise God in freedom, not to cower as if compelled. The language of authority, then, brings out the essentially personal nature of God in Christian belief and worship, an aspect of it that can easily be lost sight of if God is spoken of only as a cause producing effects.

Commands of God

All this shows a lot about the action of God not just in miracles but generally. It shows that in talking about God's acting in the world we are not positing some invisible agent who affects things in a way we do not understand; we do not make inferences to something hidden. It might seem that with this talk of authority we do after all have to infer

249

something, only an invisible commander instead of an invisible cause. But that is not so. We do not infer an invisible commander, any more than we infer that boulders, winds and waves do after all have souls, that they are capable of hearing and responding to commands. To say that the wind and the waves calmed down because Jesus commanded them to is not to deny that there may have been perfectly good causes for the dropping of the wind and the smoothing of the waters. We may in fact insist that there must have been. And we don't go around ordering inanimate objects to move as a way of trying to affect their behaviour. If we do, we are, like Canute, unsuccessful. Things just do not respond to our commands. And that is just why the response of the wind and waves to the command of Jesus is a miracle; it is also why we are inclined to be sceptical about this miracle story and others in the gospels.

The ordinary, inanimate constituents of the world, then, are not susceptible of command. If Charlie orders the snow to fall, it will not. But if God orders it to fall, it does. Here then is one difference between God's commanding something to happen and *somebody's* commanding it to happen. And it is not just a matter of God's being so much more authoritative than Charlie. We might say: we do not even know what it would be like for Charlie to command the snow to fall and for the snow to fall *because he commanded it*; which is to say that we would not count any words that Charlie uttered as constituting a genuine command to the snow to fall, even though his words have the form of a command. We do not have the institution of commanding inanimate things. But that the snow falls because he commands it is just what we do say of God. God is the one of whom it makes sense to say that he commands the natural world, and of whom it makes sense to say that the natural world does what it does in obedience to him. That is to say, *we use* this kind of language to characterise the relation between God and the natural world. (So the christological point of the story of the stilling of the storm can be put philosophically like this: The story says that it makes sense to say of Jesus – as it does not of Charlie – that he commands the natural world, and to say of the natural world that it obeys Jesus. But it only makes sense of God to say that he commands the natural world. The story proposes that we take this way of talking, which we can use only of God, and use it of the man Jesus.)

When Charlie gives a command, there is something that constitutes his giving a command; he speaks, shouts, sends a note, gives a signal. But when God gives a command there is nothing that constitutes his giving a command. We see nothing, except that what happens happens. The command of God is not another event, one hidden from us. When Charlie tells me to sit down, and I sit down, we can ask about the relation between these two events. It may be that I sit down in obedience to his command; or it may be that Charlie has no authority over me at all, so I did not obey him, but I was going to sit down anyway; or perhaps I didn't hear him, and sat down of my own accord; or it may be that I thought that Charlie told me not to sit down, and that I sat down to spite him, as an act of defiance. But we cannot ask this sort of question about the relation between the command of God that it snow and its actually snowing, since they are just not two separate events. I cannot suspect, for instance, that the snow is not really obeying God but was going to fall anyway, or that it misheard or misread the command. Again, if I obey Charlie I can obey eagerly, reluctantly, quickly, slowly, unsurely; and there are characteristic signs of this in my behaviour. But when the snow obeys God, none of that can happen; if it falls slowly, that is not because it is reluctant, but because God has commanded

251

it to fall slowly. There is no gap between the command and the obedience that would allow any *manner* of obedience to creep in. That can be put this way: any manner that belongs to a description of the event also belongs to the description of the command. What happens is what was commanded, and what was commanded is what happens. Command and event commanded have quite a different relation to each other in the case of God and natural inanimate objects from that in the case of Charlie and me. How do I know this? It is not a matter of special inside knowledge about the relation between God and the world. It is a matter of the language we use, what we say about God. It has nothing to do with God having more authority than Charlie or the natural world being so much more obedient than I am. The *logic* of command-talk with reference to God and the world is quite different from the *logic* of command-talk with reference to Charlie and me. To say that God commands the snow to fall is not to say that *somebody* commands it to fall. Any more than to say that the snow obeys God is to say that it obeys *somebody* (for we know that snow, having no soul, cannot – logically – obey anybody. – But it does obey God).

One of the points raised in all this opens an area that is very important in discussing religion, one which I do little more than mention here. I said, "We do not even know what it would be like for Charlie to command the snow to fall and for the snow to fall because he commanded it". This is as much as to say: we could not understand somebody who said that this is what had happened. But this is altogether too sweeping. For might we not make sense of things that we do not in fact make sense of? Consider the *terzettino* from *Così Fan Tutte*:

> Soave sia il vento,
> Tranquilla sia l'onda,
> Ed ogni elemento

Benigno risponda
Ai nostri desir.

(Roughly: May the wind be gentle and the sea calm, and may each element respond kindly to our desires.) We can understand that the characters might express the wish that the wind be gentle and the sea tranquil. But can we understand how the elements might respond to their desires? We will of course say that this is not meant seriously, but what is it that is not meant seriously? What would it be like for them to use these words seriously? Well, suppose the wind was gentle, the sea calm. Might not they say, "We expressed the desire that this happen, and it happened"? And that is all. There need be no causal explanation of the fact that it happened when they had expressed the desire that it should. (It would be a mistake to look for one.) Is that not a plain use of language, one that we might understand? To say that we do not understand it is to say that, as Christians, we do not say that. We do not (not cannot) make that connexion between our desires and what happens. So we would not, for example, *thank* the elements. We would thank God. What we say is that God responds (or does not) to our prayers, not the elements to our desires. It is to God that the elements respond. But we can imagine others acting and speaking in different ways, including praying to the elements. Then it would be the prayer that made the connexion, which we do not make, between their desires and the elements, and that made the behaviour of the elements a response. So we could also make sense of the idea that the elements behave in the way they do because Charlie so commands them. Only, we do not.

The importance of this idea of making connexions goes far beyond how we might talk about the weather. People do in fact quite often make such (non-causal) connexions between their desires, thoughts, actions, and so on, and

what happens. Suppose a young man is having a heated
argument with his father. Overcome with anger, he spits at
him, "I hope you die"; then he storms out. And then, soon,
his father dies, through accident or some disease. Can we
not easily understand his making a connexion between his
wish and his father's death? (would not many of us make
such a connexion?) – even though he might be able to give an
explanation of the death in natural terms. Only he does not
give that explanation, and is not impressed by it. He feels
guilty. Why? – "I wished my father dead, and he died". The
description of his wish is the same as the description of what
happened. That is all. That is the explanation of his feeling
guilty, not any causal connexion that he hypothesises
between his wish and his father's death. It is not that his
father dies, that he knows the medical causes, but that he
wonders whether there is in addition any causal connexion
between his wish and his father's death (why should he
wonder such a thing?), concludes that there is (how could he
reach such a conclusion?), then feels guilty. We might want
to draw his attention to the natural causes of his father's
death. But perhaps his attention is not to be drawn. It is fixed
on the fact that he wished his father dead.

A similar case, though one where the expression of a
desire is in action, not words, is mentioned by Wittgenstein
in his *Remarks on Frazer's Golden Bough*:

> The same savage who, apparently in order to kill his
> enemy, sticks his knife through a picture of him, really
> does build his hut of wood and cuts his arrow with skill
> and not in effigy. (p.4)

The point is that the savage has a perfectly good idea of
causal efficacy; he knows the difference between sticking his
knife into his enemy and sticking it only into a picture of
him. So if he does nevertheless stick his knife into a picture
of him, it is not because he mistakenly thinks that that will

result in his death, just as if he were to stick it into his enemy himself. Nevertheless, there must be, for him, some connexion between what he is doing and his enemy's death. The way that Wittgenstein puts the connexion is:

> The description [*Darstellung*] of a wish is, *eo ipso*, the description of its fulfilment. And magic does give representation [*Darstellung*] to a wish; it expresses a wish. (ibid.)

It is not that we cannot understand all this, but that as Christians we do not make these connexions. What happens, if it happens, is the fulfilment of a prayer to God, not of, say, a wish. So it is a response from God, not from the elements, nor does it come from our magic powers, or from the power of thought. We might put this by saying, "As Christians we do not believe in the spirits of the elements or in magical powers". That is to say, words like these get their sense from our adopting some practices and rejecting others. They are not a way of saying that practising magic and the like is irrational because it has been shown that it has no causal efficacy. We pray to God, so we do regard some things that happen as God's response to prayer; but we do not pray to the elements, and we do not stick pins into effigies, so we never see anything that happens as the work of elemental spirits or the effect of witchcraft. It is the practice (or its rejection) that is primary, not the words. And religious practices are not by and large enjoined because they have been found to work or rejected because they have been found inefficacious. It is interesting to note here that plenty of such practices are forbidden in the Old Testament:

> There shall not be found among you one who passes his son or daughter through fire, who works divination, a soothsayer, one who reads omens, or a sorcerer, one who works spells, a medium, a shaman or a

necromancer. For everybody who does these things is
an abomination to the Lord, and on account of these
abominations the Lord your God is driving them out
before you. For these nations you are driving out listen
to soothsayers and diviners. But not so with you; the
Lord your God has not allowed you. (Deuteronomy
18:10–14)

It is quite clear that these things are not being scorned
because they do not work. They are not unintelligent or
laughable; they are *blameworthy*, abominations. It is not
that the Israelites, being causally *au fait*, will of course not
practise them; they are not *allowed* to. What we have here is
not a piece of primitive scientific insight, but a religious
commandment.

Ashtrays & Explanations

If we can find some causal connexion between the one who
commands and the event that is commanded, then it is all
exposed as a trick. Not necessarily a shoddy trick: in the
story of the stilling of the storm, if we discovered 'how he
did it', so that the meaning of his words became irrelevant to
what actually happened, still we could say that he did save
the lives of the people in the boat, and that is commendable.
But his action now becomes in a sense *ordinary*. It is not
miraculous any more, but has found a place within the
normal, natural scheme of things. We may praise Jesus for
saving his disciples, and admire his immense skill in being
able to manipulate the weather, but we will no longer think
of his action as imaging that of God, giving us a glimpse into
the realm of the divine, the mysterious. We have been able to
explain what happened, so that we can live with it more
comfortably, and so it is less awe-inspiring, less disturbing.
And that also means that we have been able to describe what
happened without distorting or disturbing our *language*,

without saying, "The storm subsided because Jesus commanded it" – without saying of Jesus what it makes sense to say only of God. Indeed, if we can find a causal connexion we don't have to talk about God at all here. (But first we have to *look* for one, and if we do that, react to the event in that way, that already shows a disposition not to talk about God. Naturally, for to talk about God is already not to think only in terms of the natural scheme of things; it is already to introduce a disturbance into our language and into our lives.)

This is an important point. In his *Remarks on Frazer's Golden Bough*, Wittgenstein says:

> How could fire or fire's resemblance to the sun have failed to make an impression on the awakening mind of man? But not "because he can't explain it"(the stupid superstition of our time) – for does an "explanation" make it any less impressive? (p.6)

The final question here is obviously rhetorical, but if we took it seriously and tried to answer it, we would surely have to say: yes. It is often part of the way explanation, particularly scientific explanation, is used that it tends to make the phenomena less impressive, less wonderful, by bringing them within the sphere of the natural, the ordinary. They may remain beautiful or frightening, but they are no longer mysterious, they no longer speak of God. This *need* not be part of the function of scientific explanation: it used to be said that scientific laws showed the wonderful ways that God had ordered his creation. But the spirit of some more recent science has been different. It is as if scientists said when confronted with awe, "There is no need to wonder at this phenomenon; there is nothing mysterious about it; it can all be explained perfectly satisfactorily by the laws of physics; etc". Wittgenstein himself says something close to this, commenting on a remark of Renan about how primitive peoples wondered at natural phenomena:

> ... is it being assumed that men, as it were, suddenly woke up and, noticing for the first time these things that had always been there, were understandably amazed? – Well, as a matter of fact we might assume something like this; though not that they become aware of these things for the first time but that they do suddenly start to wonder at them. But this again has nothing to do with their being primitive. Unless it is called primitive not to wonder at things, in which case the people of today are really the primitive ones.... As though lightning were more commonplace or less astounding today than 2000 years ago.
> Man has to awaken to wonder – and so perhaps do peoples. Science is a way of sending him to sleep again. In other words it's just false to say: Of course, these primitive peoples couldn't help wondering at everything.... It is like supposing that they had to be afraid of all the forces of nature, whereas we of course have no need to be afraid..... We cannot exclude the possibility that *highly* civilised peoples will become liable to this fear once again; neither their civilisation nor scientific knowledge can protect them against this. All the same it's true enough that the *spirit* in which science is carried on nowadays is not compatible with fear of this kind. (*Culture and Value*, p.5)

And this is also part of the spirit behind Frazer's *Golden Bough*: to say that though primitive peoples may have wondered at certain phenomena, we nowadays have no need to do so, since we can give them all good scientific explanations. I have already tried to show that to talk of the activity of God is not to be doing pseudo-science, is not to postulate an invisible and otherwise undetectable agent in order to account for the phenomena. That is to say, those like Frazer who attack such talk because they see in it a kind of pseudo-science are mistaken. In that sense, religion and science are not in competition. But there is a conflict between talk of the activity of God and 'the spirit in which science is carried on nowadays' [sc. 1930], in so far as that spirit is one which seeks to dispel wonder. For that wonder, which has always been recognised as important in religion, is not just a contingent psychological accompaniment of talk about God. In some cases at least, such talk is the *expression* of such wonder at what happens.

To take an absurd example: Suppose I come into my room one day to find an ashtray there. That strikes me as very odd: I have never seen it before, I don't smoke, so I would have no reason to have one; and none of my friends, whom I question about it, have any knowledge of it. So it's a bit of a puzzle. Then I discover that a new neighbour who has just moved in a few doors away, and who does not know me, brought it round while I was out and left it for me, thinking I might like it. Now it is no longer odd that it is there (though I might think it an odd thing for an unknown neighbour to do). Everything is now satisfactorily explained. But suppose that kind of explanation is ruled out. Suppose the ashtray suddenly appears in my hut, in which I live alone on an otherwise deserted island hundreds of miles from civilisation. I may perhaps suspect that somebody else has arrived on the island unknown to me, and go off to check. (The island is easily small enough, without caves or hollows, and its vegetation sparse enough, for me to be able to establish with certainty whether anybody else is there.) A search reveals nothing. Perhaps an animal brought it up from the beach, where it had been washed up. But I know that there are no animals on the island capable of carrying such a thing, which in any case looks brand new and has no signs of being worn by sea or wind. Now my attitude to the presence of the ashtray is different from what it was in the first case. It is now no more a puzzle; it no longer makes me curious, itching to fit it into the normal pattern of my experience. For now I have established to my satisfaction that it *cannot* be fitted into the normal pattern of my experience. I am no longer curious, but uneasy; its presence is uncanny, no longer a source of itch but rather of uncertainty, fear, perhaps even wonder or terror. If I am so inclined, I might say to myself that a ghost or a spirit brought it – because I have already established that *nobody* and *nothing* brought it.

I might see that as a kind of explanation, but if I do it is a quite different kind of explanation from that which arises in the first case; a ghost is not like a new and hitherto unknown neighbour. Attribution to a neighbour solves the puzzle, removes the oddity, makes everything normal again. But if I say that a ghost brought it, that does not dispel the fear, make the phenomenon less impressive, less odd; it does not make everything normal again, but expresses its abnormality. I give myself that explanation because the phenomenon is strange, impressive, weird. The oddness the phenomenon has for me I express by talking in terms of an odd (that is uncanny, weird, not merely surprising) cause or agent. And so, in the first case, if I am surprised by the sudden appearance of an ashtray in my room, if I say, "How strange that ashtray just appearing like that", you might answer, "No, it's perfectly explicable: that new neighbour must have brought it". But you would not answer, "No, it's perfectly explicable: a ghost must have brought it". That a ghost brought something is not a perfectly good explanation for its appearance, even though one that is often or almost always wrong . To try to explain something by reference to ghosts is not to try to make it appear normal again, even if unusual; it is to confess its abnormality, and to express an attitude towards it as weird, uncanny, because it does not fit in.

Another way to put the same point is this: If I am told that a new neighbour brought the ashtray, I might say, "Ah, now I see"; and now I *understand* how it got there. But if I am told, or myself say, that a ghost brought it, I do not in this case say, "Ah, now I see", and I do not now think that I understand how it got there. All I know is that it did not get there in any normal way, any way that I can understand, that it got there in a *weird* way. I do not get here the feeling of relaxation, of satisfied itch, of enlightenment, that I get in the former case. The puzzle has not been solved but turned into mystery.

Acts of God

Something similar happens when an event is attributed to the agency of God. As I said before, God is not a ghost, and there will be big differences between statements attributing events to the agency of God and those attributing events to the agency of ghosts. But there are nevertheless similarities. Though in some contexts it might be said that 'theoretically' all events are attributable to the agency of God, that God as creator and prime mover is involved as agent in all change, yet in fact people tend to talk about God doing things, either in the Bible or in ordinary life, when the events concerned are in some way striking, impressive. But the way these events impress is different from the way the actions of ghosts impress. Sometimes events are attributed to God, as they are to ghosts, when no cause can be found for them, as in miracles. But whereas if an event is (said to be) caused by a ghost it is something spooky, if it is caused by God it is significant, and may be either wonderful or terrible. That is partly a matter of the nature of the events themselves that are attributed to God. God may save the lives of innocent children by stopping boulders in mid-air, for the lives of children have an obvious human importance. But he does not go round making ashtrays suddenly appear. We can know that in advance, without having to find out, because we would refuse to associate the name of God with such a trivial event. The acts of God can be significant in a number of ways; they may show us things about our moral or spiritual lives, or about God himself. Hence, though they may be wonderful, terrible, or awe-inspiring, they can never be simply weird. An act of God can make you change your life, or fall to your knees, or shout with joy to the heavens, but it cannot just make you go goose-pimply and send shivers down your spine.

Despite these differences it remains true that to say that something has been done by God is, often, to react to it in a particular way. The events that are called "acts of God" are impressive, significant; and that means that if you call an event an act of God you behave as one impressed, to whom a sign has been given. It is not, as we have seen many times now, to infer that the event in question was brought about by an undetectable agent with a particular identity. So also, to deny that an event is an act of God is not to deny that there is any unseen causal nexus leading to an unseen agent; it is to be unimpressed, not to see any particular significance in it.

After the archbishop of York confirmed the appointment of David Jenkins as bishop of Durham, York Minster was struck by lightning and badly damaged by fire. Those who opposed the appointment of Jenkins saw this as an act of God, or at any rate some of them did. That is, they saw it as significant, and what it signified was that the appointment should not have been made. Those who favoured the appointment of Jenkins thought that that was nonsense. It was not an act of God, but was due to entirely natural causes, and it had no significance at all. The dispute was not about whether it was possible validly to infer the involvement of an unseen agent in the coming of the lightning and the burning of the minster. It was about what significance, if any, the events had. The fact that the pro-Jenkins party could appeal to natural causation may seem to contradict this, but the appeal was to what the anti-Jenkins party already knew, and these latter could perfectly well accept that an explanation in terms of natural causes could be given and yet still say that it was an act of God. On the other hand, neither would the appeal of the pro-Jenkins party to natural causes be upset by a Christian with a philosophical turn of mind saying that God was, as prime mover, causally involved in all events, so must be in a sense responsible for these ones, too. That would not be enough to make it an act of God, since it would not make it significant: if God is causally involved in all events, then he is causally involved both in significant ones and in trivial ones, so his involvement in the minster fire does not make it anything special. So the question is not about invisible agents or the lack of them, but about whether the events did have any special significance, any meaning for Christians. The appeal to natural causes does not have the function of a claim that the events were due to one set of causes rather than another, but of saying, "Don't wonder at them, don't think of them as significant or extraordinary. They are perfectly ordinary, so don't pay any particular attention to them". The conviction that they are perfectly ordinary is expressed by explaining in natural terms how they happened. For it is one thing to say that an account in terms of natural causes is possible – as both sides in the dispute might do – and another actually to give such an account. To admit the possibility of such an account is to say, "Yes, it is possible to look at what happened in that way". But actually to give such an account, and to insist on it, is to say, "Look at it like this".

An explanation of an event makes it ordinary, makes it fit in with our normal view of things. So if you wonder why there was lightning and are told that it was a result of various things going on up in the sky that we know how to talk about in terms of the laws of physics, then that makes the lightning intelligible. You can say, "Ah, now I see"; now you understand. But if you are told that the lightning was made by God or sent by God, that is not an explanation in the same way. This explanation does not make the lightning ordinary, does not make it fit in with the rest of your experience. You do not say in this case, "Ah, now I see". Or at least you would not say it in the same tone of voice. You might say, "Now I see" if you come to see the lightning as an act of God, but not because somebody told you it was, imparted that information. That it was an act of God would have the character of something *revealed* to you (as by God or an angel), not something told you (as by any human agency); so that you say, "Now I see" – You were in darkness, blind to the truth, and now your eyes have been opened to see the lightning for what it *really* is. (It is not that you have found out more about it.)

The attribution of the lightning to God does not solve the puzzle of where it came from; it does not address itself to that problem and indeed, there was no such problem here in the first place. Rather, it says, "See this event as significant; don't think of it as ordinary but as charged with meaning, and be impressed with it". And then there may follow an account of what significance it has; e.g., "Don't you see? This is a sign of God's anger that the Church of England has abandoned traditional teaching, that an unbeliever has been appointed to watch over his flock". Notice what a great deal is necessary to create the possibility of understanding the lightning in this way. You have to be a Christian, deeply concerned about the Church of England and Christian tradition, and you have to have views on David Jenkins, views that will be shaped by your beliefs about and attitudes towards what he says and stands for. That in turn will depend on your views about what is right in a number of areas, and maybe also on your opinions about 'liberalism' and 'modern society' in general. And all this will be linked to the way you live, your habits, what you actually do, as well as what you normally say.

Seeing significance in events is not an arbitrary thing. It depends on the wider context of a person's life. The whole dispute about whether the lightning did or did not come from God as a judgment on events in the church will seem amusing, if not laughable, to an atheist (or indeed to any Christian who thinks the Church of England too insignificant to merit such special attention from God). For him there is simply no question that the lightning could have had any such meaning. And this is just what we should expect. He cannot so much as entertain the idea that it has this significance because his life has not been such as to provide a context that would make it possible for him to see it like that.

Being Punished

This kind of thing is important for some Christians at a more personal level, too. For example, a believer might have his marriage ruined, or go blind, or contract a serious, even fatal disease, and say, "This is a punishment from God". What is going on here? clearly, being punished by God is logically very different from being punished by Charlie. First, God is a righteous judge; though we have talk of being wrongly punished by Charlie, we do not similarly speak of being wrongly punished by God. And God's judgement is linked to the judgement of others. Unless you feel you have done something worthy of punishment, you cannot acknowledge you are being punished by God. So you can say, "Charlie is punishing me for doing this, but actually I didn't do it"; but not, "God is punishing me for doing this, but I didn't do it". And you can say, "Charlie is punishing me for doing this, but I don't think there's anything wrong with doing it"; but not, "God is punishing me for doing this, but I don't think there's anything wrong with doing it". Saying "God is punishing me" involves self-judgement. This is linked to the fact that if you say, "My illness is a punishment from God," you say it with *conviction*; you say it in a different tone of voice from "My illness is a punishment from Charlie" (if you would ever say this). Similarly, somebody might say of you, "Charlie is punishing you for doing this, but I don't think you did anything wrong in doing it"; but not, "God is punishing you for doing this, but I can't see there's anything wrong with doing it". Saying "God is punishing you" is partly an expression of disapproval of you for doing what you have done.

Second, how might an illness, for example, be a punishment from Charlie? We could imagine Charlie (as opposed to Harry) injecting somebody with a virus because they have disobeyed him. No such thing is in question in the case of punishment from God. Suppose you have crossed Charlie and you find yourself ill. It would not normally strike you that your illness is punishment from Charlie. Evidence that he is into viruses and that somebody has injected you recently, or some other causal story linking your illness to Charlie, might convince you that he has done this to you, as a punishment. But you would need some such evidence, otherwise it would simply not occur to you. No such considerations arise in the case of God. You do not need to be convinced that any *particular* process has occurred by which you have become ill. *Any* process would do. (Though there is a point of importance here: sometimes what are called punishments from God are closely related to *your* particular activities: you might, for example, get this sexually transmitted disease through sexual activity you see as culpable. The sin is punished *via* the sin. So it is punished through what *you* do, not through what somebody else does; whereas when you sin against Charlie your sin is punished through what Charlie or his agents do.)

Third, you can say "God is punishing me" when there is *nobody* punishing, when there is no detectable agent doing anything to hurt. Simply, something bad is happening, like an illness. Since there is no question of agency, neither is there question of the identity of an agent. If somebody says, "I am being punished by God" you may try to persuade him he is wrong. But you will not do it by saying, "Could you be mistaken? Are you sure it's *God* who is punishing you, and not somebody else?" God is not one agent among others. You can be mistaken about the identity of somebody who is punishing you, but you cannot make that sort of mistake when you say God is punishing you. The special nature of the persuasion here is also important. Trying to persuade somebody that God is not punishing him is a different enterprise from persuading him that Charlie is not punishing him. (Things may have been set up to look as if Charlie is punishing him, but it is really somebody else, or a cruel joke, or a move designed to estrange him from Charlie.) It is getting him not to see what is happening as punishment – deserved punishment – getting him not to condemn himself. You are persuading him about himself. Here one may use theological arguments, arguments from the nature of God: God is loving and forgiving, not vindictive. So what one says about the nature of God is intimately linked to a project of getting people (perhaps including yourself) to see themselves in a particular way.

Where Did All This Come From?

But it is not only unusual, extraordinary events that you can

267

see like this. You can react in a similar way to quite ordinary events and to quite ordinary things. These, too, it is possible to treat as extraordinary. For example, you can look around at a perfectly ordinary and familiar environment – an environment through which you and everybody else would ordinarily pass without comment – and stare with wonder, awe-struck, and ask, "Where did all this come from?" Here you are not asking for a causal account of the origins of everything you see – the lamp-posts, the trees, the rubbish on the pavement, the hole in the road. You may know, or at least be able to conjecture, all the causal explanations. And you are not puzzled or curious, as if seeking an explanation that will be satisfying, that will set your mind at rest and make you see the environment as ordinary again. You are not asking for a form of words to which you will react with, "I see" or, "So that's where it comes from", and then pass on your way again. The question is more like the expression of a reaction – of wonder or of awe. And so too is the statement "All this is made by God", which might be offered, or which you yourself might formulate, in answer to it, or which might be exclaimed instead of it. Just as the question is not a request for information about causal origins, so neither is the statement an answer to one. To say "God made it all" is not to supply information about where things come from. It is an expression of wonder at them. (So we could imagine Freddie walking along the street, suddenly being wonderstruck and saying, "Now I understand what all these Christians are talking about when they say the world is made by God". And he would not have to say this because he has suddenly been struck by a new causal argument.) It is not ordinarily a possible answer to a question such as, "Where did this puddle come from?" It is not a possible answer to such a question, not because we want to deny that God creates puddles, but because "God made it" is not the kind of answer we are normally looking for when we ask where something comes from. It is not a causal explanation. (And this is true even if there are puddles in the street when we stop and exclaim "Where did all this come from?" or "God made all this".) So saying "God made it all" does not make it fit in with our ordinary experience, make it normal. Indeed it is here of ordinary things, things that do not need to be fitted in, that we say, "Where did it all come from?" Part of what is meant in saying "Where did it all come from?" or "God made it all" is that we now see even the ordinary as extraordinary, that that is how it *should* be looked at, not taken for granted. If I say, "Where did all this come from?" the things I see around me are not a puzzle but a mystery; and saying, "God made it all" does not dispel a difficulty, solve a puzzle, but rather expresses a mystery.

It is not an unimportant point here that if I say, "God made all this" I am speaking of my environment, or the scene before me, as a whole. I am not giving an account of the origin of the things that go to make it up; I am not saying that God made this lamp-post, God made this hole in the road, God made this old tin can. I know that all these things have diverse origins. And so neither am I giving an account of the origin of my environment considered as the sum of its components. Since I know that its components originated in many different ways, and that they came to be here together as a result of many different causes, I know that there is no single unitary account of my environment considered as the sum of its components. In asking "Where does all this come from?" I am not, therefore, asking for such an account, and in saying "God made all this" I am not giving myself one. "God made all this" does not give an account of anything.

It is a mistake to start talking at this point of surprise or puzzlement at there being anything at all there. To begin with, surprise is normally a reaction to something unusual

269

within an environment: a crocodile in the bathroom, a cockroach in the soup, an interesting programme on channel X. If somebody showed the normal expression of surprise when there was only the usual plastic duck, or bits of mushroom or another repeat showing of a documentary on the problems of growing kale in Alaska, then we should think there was something wrong with him, or at least that whatever it was he felt here it was not surprise. But in the present case we are not dealing with what is unusual within an environment. Secondly, surprise or puzzlement is dispelled by explanation. I may be surprised or puzzled to find a puddle on the floor of my room which was not there when I left it five minutes ago; but when I realise from other signs that my neighbour's dog has visited my room in the meantime, or discover that one of the pipes overhead is leaking, then I am no longer surprised, merely annoyed. But what I am confronted with when I say "God made all this" need be nothing unusual, nothing that creates surprise or puzzlement, and the effect of "God made all this" is not to explain, and to dispel any feeling, but rather to express it. So neither is "Where did all this come from?" an expression of puzzlement or surprise which is dispelled by the answer "God made all this". (The two expressions are not related as question and answer.) The feeling that makes you say "Where did all this come from?" or "God made all this" may well be one that takes you by surprise, but it is not itself a feeling of surprise.

Creation & Pots

If I say "God created the world", am I saying that somebody made it? It certainly seems so, for it looks as if I must be saying that the world comes from somewhere, was brought into existence. And if it was brought into existence, that must have been done by somebody (or something). It may be difficult enough to imagine that the world was brought into existence by somebody out of nothing (if there was already something, there was already a world), but it is surely impossible to think that it might have been brought into existence out of nothing by nobody.

If I say "Charlie made this pot", there is quite a lot that has to be presupposed for this to make sense. First, I have to know that pots are artefacts; I have to know that they are the kind of thing that are made, that they do not occur naturally. If I say, "Charlie made this pot", I may be making a mistake, for the pot may have been made by Harry instead. But if I say, "Charlie made this tree", I am not just mistaken; it is not just that the tree was made by somebody else, by Harry. Trees are simply not the kind of thing that are made; nobody at all made them. And that is not just an accident, a contingent fact about the way trees occur. If something is made, it cannot be a tree; that is, we would not call it a tree. I might be shown a tree-like structure and told, "Charlie made that", but that tells me that what I see is not a tree. And this has nothing to do with any supposition that Charlie is not clever or skillful enough to make a tree. Charlie may be *extremely* clever. He may have the skill to make things much more complicated than trees. It is not that it takes such tremendous skill to make trees, but that it does not take any at all, since trees are not made. If Charlie has made a tree-like structure, he might call it a tree, and we might not complain, but it would be the same as calling it an *artificial* tree. And an artificial tree is not a kind of tree. Trees are *natural*. So implicit in my saying "Charlie made this pot" is the distinction between artefacts and what is natural; and it only makes sense to say "Charlie made this pot", I can only get even as far as being mistaken, because pots lie on one side of the distinction rather than the other.

Secondly, I know that Charlie is the kind of thing that might make a pot. He is a human being who knows what pots are, and who might have the physical and mental capacities requisite for making pots. I cannot, even mistakenly, say, "Trafalgar Square made this pot". One way of putting this is that I know roughly the kinds of things that Charlie would have to do to make a pot, or if I do not I could learn how to make pots by watching Charlie or somebody else making one. But I cannot say this about Trafalgar Square. I can imagine Trafalgar Square doing certain things: taking my breath away, becoming overcrowded, smelling awful. But I cannot imagine it doing the kind of thing that would be needed to make a pot, and I could not, therefore, learn how to make a pot by watching Trafalgar Square make one. So nothing would count as Trafalgar Square's making a pot. If pots mysteriously kept appearing in Trafalgar Square, then I and most of us would probably say just that: that pots keep appearing mysteriously in Trafalgar Square. I would not say that Trafalgar Square was making them, since it does not do anything that counts as making them.

This is not merely a piece of verbal legislation. Some people might indeed want to say that Trafalgar Square was making the pots that appeared in it. But then they would not be making a mistake, but creating a new use of language. For "Trafalgar Square made this pot" does not function as an explanation of the origin of a pot in the same way as "Charlie made this pot". Suppose pots do keep on mysteriously appearing in Trafalgar Square; mysteriously, because careful investigation reveals no way that they get there, nobody who brings them and no mechanism that makes them pop out of the ground. Some might then say, "How on earth do these pots appear here? – The square itself must actually be making them, somehow". But this move of course does not solve the mystery of the appearance of the pots, as "Charlie brings them by night" would. It simply reformulates it in terms of the mysterious process of the production of the pots. And the process is mysterious, not because we do not know what it is, but because there is no process to discover. The square does not do anything that would count as producing the pots. No advance, in terms of causal explanation, is made by saying "The pots are produced mysteriously, in a mysterious way, by the square", instead of "The pots appears mysteriously in the square". Nobody who said the former instead of the latter would think he had somehow solved the mystery of the appearance of the pots, made it any easier to understand. So to say that Trafalgar Square was making the pots would not be to correct somebody who said they were simply appearing in it. It would be to make language take a new turn, one which the other might not be prepared to follow. It would be to propose a use for this combination of words. Here we have to make a decision between two ways of speaking.

But to propose a use for this combination of words is not to offer another explanation, apart from all the ones that have already been found to be false. This new sentence comes into play, if at all, when *all* (causal) explanations have been ruled out. In this sense it is not an explanation at all; it serves as one way of marking that there is no explanation, that all of them have indeed been ruled out. So that if afterwards an explanation for the appearance of the pots were found, it would not function as an alternative, rival explanation to the 'explanation' that the pots are produced by Trafalgar Square; the latter sentence would now be without any use at all, since it was used to signal that there was no explanation, and now it has been discovered that there is. That the pots are produced by Trafalgar Square is not a member of a list of possible alternative explanations of the appearance of the pots. It says, "Don't understand the appearance of the pots in any of those ways". But not, "Understand it in this, other, way".

The square does not *do* anything. So we might ask: what is the difference between the pots just appearing 'while the square is around' and their being produced by the square? There is no activity of the square to link it to the pots, anything that we might call the productive activity of the square. Not that anybody would be inclined to, but it would be no use appealing to an 'invisible activity' of the square that produces the pots. It gets us no further. For this invisible activity cannot be described, except as the activity that produces the pots, and we want to know *what* activity it is that produces the pots. We would also want to know what makes that activity the activity of Trafalgar Square. Why should it not be an activity of Battersea Bridge? How do we know that the pots are not produced by Battersea Bridge in Trafalgar Square? (Rather: why should we not say that?) Of course, we would not know what to say if asked how the bridge produced them in the square, but then we would not know what to say if asked how the *square* produced them in the square, either. No. Say, if you like, "The pots are produced mysteriously by the square", but that is no closer to being a causal explanation of what is happening than "The pots appear mysteriously in the square". It does not explain how they appear; indeed, the sentence is only formulated after all possible explanations have been ruled out. It does not explain their appearance by reference to a process of production, something the square does to produce them; for it does nothing. Here you may speak, if you like, of a *mysterious* process, but a mysterious process is then not a process. (There is a parallel here with the fact that a spiritual being is not a kind of being.)

This brings out a third and related point. If I say, "Charlie made this pot", he has done something (so I believe) that counts as his making the pot; and that means that *he* has done something that counts as making it. There is a difference between his making the pot and Harry's making it or Matilda's making it. If I believe that Charlie made the pot, then I do not just believe that the pot appeared, perhaps signed "Charlie", or looking like the pots that Charlie normally makes. I believe that Charlie, and nobody else, actually did something that counts as his making the pot.

How does all this help us to understand what it means to say "God made the world"? To begin with, I can say that Charlie made this pot because this pot is an artefact; but if I say that God made the world I am not committed to saying that the world is an artefact. It is not a thing, that might be made or not, but a totality of things, some of which are artefacts and some of which are not. Most of the things in the world are not things which have been made; they are not artefacts, but natural. And yet we say that God made them. So God's making things does not mean that they are artefacts; God does not, of logical necessity, only make *artificial* trees. God also makes what is natural. We might gaze out over a landscape of trees, rivers and mountains and say, "All this world of nature, all this that nobody made – God made it". That might be a paradoxical way of speaking, but it would not be to say that after all somebody did make it. It is not to say that somebody made things that nobody made. What nobody made is not made by somebody – it is made by God. God made what nobody made.

We may also want to say that the world manifests the power and skill of God, but if we do that it is not because God would have to be so extremely powerful to make something so big (indeed, infinitely powerful to make it out of nothing) and so clever to make something as intricate as a fly's wing or as precise as a crystal. It is not just that God is so much stronger and cleverer than Charlie. If Charlie were much stronger and much cleverer, he might produce these things too; but if he produced them, they would be artefacts.

And to change his name from Charlie to God would not be enough to make his products natural rather than artificial. To say that God made the world is not to say that somebody very powerful and wise made it; it is not to say that anybody made it. God cannot be listed together with Charlie and others as one who makes things. Charlie makes things, and God makes things, but Charlie makes – necessarily – artefacts, as God does not. If Charlie has made something, then it has been made by somebody, whereas if God has made something, that does not mean that it has been made by somebody.

Generally, it is of the world that we say that it is made by God. We do not say that so much of individual things. (Perhaps that is because then it would look too much like an account of how the thing arose; but if we are asked to give an account of how an individual thing arose, we will not mention God, but rather somebody or something.) But no doubt if we wanted to make a particular point about a specific thing we might say that it is was made by God. If we tend not to say it of individual things, still less do we say it of individual artefacts. We would hardly point to a Picasso and say, "God made that" (though again it is possible to think of particular circumstances in which somebody might want to say it). Certainly we would never say, "God *painted* that". When people make things, there are processes by which they make them: they paint, fire, chop, mould, write, glue. But there is no process by which God makes things. He does not paint, sculpt, mould, extrude, compress or bake. Naturally, for these, and all processes by which things are made, result in the appearance of artefacts, and what God makes is not, by virtue of his making it, an artefact. If I say, speaking of an artefact, "Charlie made this", then it makes sense to ask how. If he made it, there must be some process by which he made it. There must be, because there must be some process by which *he* made it; if there were not, there would be no difference between his having made it and Harry's having made it. But if I say of an individual object, or of the world, "God made it", there is no answer to the question, "How did he do it?" That is not because we do not know how, but because there is no such question; there is no process by which he made it.

We can imagine God making things, tell stories about how he made things, and perhaps paint pictures of him making things. But we know 'it wasn't really like that'. If that is so, why do we not describe or paint what it was really like? – Because this is ruled out from the beginning; we rule it out of our language about God. There is no 'what it was really like'; we admit nothing as an accurate description. Nothing will count for us as being what it was really like. So there is no process of creation, and God does not employ techniques in creating. For if there is technique, it results in an artefact, and if there is a process, we can say this: there is a stage at which what is being made is only partly formed. But even if something is only partly formed, it is already something; there has already taken place the jump from nothing to something, there has already been creation.

There is nothing that God does in creating that connects him with what is created. The creation of the world is a bit like the appearance of pots in Trafalgar Square. All we can say is that, mysteriously, it is there. Just as to say that pots are produced in a mysterious way by the square does not get us any further, does not explain how they come to be there, so saying that the world is created, in a mysterious way, by God does not explain how it came to be there. A mysterious act is not an act, nor a mysterious process a process (just as spiritual being is not a being). We have not solved the mystery of the world by saying that it was created by God. Rather, the mystery of the existence of the world has been reformulated in terms of its mysterious production by a spiritual being, God. (I do not say there is no point in this reformulation.)

That is also why there is no problem about the correct identification of the agent in creation. When I say, "Charlie made this pot", I mean that Charlie *did* something to produce it, but I also mean that *Charlie* did something to produce it. That is why he made it and not Harry, who did nothing to produce it. With Trafalgar Square the same considerations did not arise. Since the square does not *do* anything to produce the pots, *the square* does not do anything. It is not distinguished from other possible agents by the fact that it did something and they did not. As far as the appearance of the pots was concerned, there was nothing to tell us, if we wanted to talk in terms of their being produced, that we should say that Trafalgar Square produced them rather than that Battersea Bridge produced them in Trafalgar Square. If we did not say the one or the other without thinking, without hesitation ("Obviously it must be the square; why bring the bridge into it?") then we would be guided by other considerations, if there were any – say, hitherto only standard-lamps have appeared in Trafalgar Square; generally it is Battersea Bridge that is festooned with pots. But there is here no question of getting the agent right or wrong. The situation is so outlandish that the pre-existing rules of our language do not cover it; they leave us with a free choice. (And we can of course also refuse to talk about agency here at all, insist on saying only that the pots simply appear, spontaneously if mysteriously, in the square.) And the same is true when we say that God created the world. Because this is not a genuine causal explanation, though it has the form of an explanation, and because there is no activity involved, the question does not arise whether it was God who created the world or somebody or something else – perhaps Brahma, or some malicious demon. In saying that God created the world we do not ascribe some causal activity to him as opposed to some other agent or agents, as we do in a genuine causal explanation. For God does not do anything to create. Again, if we insist on treating "God made the world" as a causal explanation: suppose God were around when the world began, but did not create it. Suppose God were just there, doing nothing, and the world came into existence spontaneously. Since God does not do anything to create, what would be the difference between saying that God created the world and saying that, though there at the time, he did not create it, but it simply appeared mysteriously?

If we wanted to be prosaic about creation, to describe how the world came into existence without resorting to new linguistic turns (along the lines of the new linguistic turn of ascribing productive activity to Trafalgar Square) and without using poetry, resorting to pictures that do not tell us 'what it was really like', then all we could say is: There was nothing, then there was the world. In other words, we would not be giving an account of *how* the world came into existence, but simply saying *that* it did. We would not describe God's doing something to bring it into existence, since there is no action of God to describe. God's making the world is not different from its coming into being. There is not the world's (or anything's) coming into being *and* the creative activity of God. – So God could not, as it were, *mime* the act of creation, go through the motions of creating without actually creating. There *are* no motions. There is only the thing's coming into being. So we might say: The thing's existence and God's act of creation are one and the same; the existence of the thing is an activity of God.

"God created this" does not mean the same as "This came into existence", since an atheist and a Christian could both,

279

in any particular case, affirm the latter, while the Christian would affirm and the atheist deny the former. But the difference between the two does not lie in this: that "God created this" goes further than "This came into existence" in saying that somebody called God did something, we know not what, to bring it into existence. Of course there is a point in saying "God created this", but that isn't it. And there need not be one simple point. People might say it for many different reasons. We can say this as a minimum, that the one who says it may regard – that is, treat – the thing in question differently from the one who refuses to say it. He may regard himself, for example, as not having right of disposal over it in a way that the other man may not. He may say to himself, "God made this, not me; so it belongs to him, and I am not free to dispose of it as I like" (and the thing in question may be himself). Or he may attach importance to it in some other way that the atheist does not; e.g. he may regard it as important in its own right, rather than for how it can benefit him or mankind in general. There are a number of possibilities here, but I am not concerned to enumerate them. My aim is only to show that to say that God made anything, including the world, is not to say that *somebody* made it; that the way we use sentences about God, here as elsewhere, shows that the word "God" does not function as the name of a thing or a person. That we use "God" and "Charlie" in very similar-looking sentences makes it look as if God and Charlie are logically alike; but the way sentences with "God" and sentences with "Charlie" work – what we do with them and the consequences we draw from them – shows that they are very different.

God does not employ any technique of creation. Here we are reminded again of the importance of the idea of creation by *command*: command is not a technique. What happens because it is commanded is not an action of the one who commands. It is not done by him: it happens (perhaps is done by somebody else), because commanded. So we can say truly that if Alvin commands Brian to do something and Brian does it, it really is Brian that does it: and in the sense that Brian does it, Alvin does not do it. We may say also that Alvin does it, but that means: Brian does it, because Alvin tells him to. It is not true that Brian does it only in the limited sense that he is used as an instrument by Alvin, as a hammer might be used; he is not used at all, but commanded. In that sense, Brian does not do it because he is interfered with, but does it *naturally*, even if he would not have done if he had not been commanded – it is part of natural human behaviour to do things in response to commands. So we can say, modelling creation on the pattern of command, that things come into existence and do what they do in obedience to the commands of God, and so it is genuinely they that do it, not God; like human beings acting in response to a command, they are active in what they do, and are not merely passive instruments. So we would not expect to find any activity on the part of God; God only acts in so far as things act in response to the commands of God. And so things are not used, interfered with; they do what they do naturally. As it is part of human life that people sometimes do what others tell them, so it is natural to things always to do what God tells them. – But now it should be stressed again that most things in creation are inanimate; it does not make sense to tell them to do things. If Charlie commanded the sea not to rise, we would think him crazy. And that is not just because he hasn't sufficient authority to command the sea. God is not just a more authoritative Charlie. To say that God commands the sea is not to say that somebody commands it. "God commands..." and "Charlie commands..." have to be given different explanations; they work in different ways, are appropriate in different circumstances. We know how the latter works; it is not my purpose to give a full account of the former. I say only that here is one significant difference: that it makes sense to say, "God commands the sea...", whereas it does not make sense to say, "Charlie commands the sea..."

UNCONCLUDING REMARKS

Christianity & Idolatry

Note that all the comments I have made are about Christianity, as it is, and mostly about what I take to be orthodox Christianity. They are not meant to hold for religion in general, if there is such a thing. They are a contribution to the philosophy of Christianity, not the philosophy of religion – though if any part of what I say is right, then it would be surprising if it were not also a help toward the philosophical understanding of other religions. It is easy to imagine how things might have been different, how the words and behaviour of Christians might have demanded a different account. If "God" were the name of somebody or something, if Christians showed by what they said and what they did that they believed there existed some being whom they called God, whom they worshipped, then it would be possible to exhibit your behaviour to that supposed being, as you can exhibit it to Charlie, as in fact you cannot exhibit your behaviour to God; you could seek a reward from him – as in fact you cannot seek it from God – by means of reward-seeking activity, just as you can seek a reward from Charlie. If you could seek such a reward through almsgiving, your almsgiving really would be, as it is not if you are Christian, a hypocritical display. Your concern would be for yourself, as it is now not, and that concern would be expressed by seeking to impress this other being. You would be motivated, as you are now not, by greed or fear, and if there were no promised reward or threatened punishment, that would make a difference, as it now does not, to whether you gave

alms or not. If you served such a being, you really would not
be free, as you now are; you would be in service, as you are if
you serve Charlie, and you would be anxious about his
affairs, as you are not now anxious if you are Christian. If
you feared such a being, you would be paralysed by fear,
since whatever you did you would be bound to suffer either
at his hands or at Charlie's. If there were such a being, Flew
would be right, and you really would have no grounds for
trusting in him and in his love. It really would be intolerable
to worship such a being, a form of toadying, as in fact it is
not intolerable to worship God. Worse than that, you
would be an idolater. You would be worshipping a creature,
part of the world, something that could be listed, along with
chairs, volcanoes, magnetic fields, psychological projec-
tions, and so on, as part of the contents of the universe, one
of the things that are, a something; and you would be
worshipping somebody who could be listed along with
Charlie and my Aunt Matilda as an agent.

There are perhaps idolatrous religions like that, but
orthodox Christianity is not one of them. All such idolatrous religions, if there are any, appear to be false, since we
have no reason to believe in the existence of such creatures as
they might worship – unless they are very honest about it
and worship things we can see or otherwise detect, like stars,
mountains or crocodiles. As for the invisible, intangible
ones, even if, somehow or other, their existence were
established, they could be of no religious interest to
Christians, however powerful, benign or malevolent such
creatures might be. They might be very important indeed to
us in other ways – our very lives might depend on placating
them – but we could never call them God, upon pain of
becoming idolaters. In orthodox Christianity, which forbids idolatry, "God" is not the name of anything.

An Idol Made of Wood

How might what I have said be relevant to the understanding of religions other than Christianity? Suppose I visit a remote African tribe in my work as an anthropologist. I know as yet nothing about them, their customs, work, history, ritual, beliefs. In the middle of the village there is a large building before which people bow every time they pass it. I surmise there is somebody or something very important in the building: perhaps it is where the chief lives, or it is a temple which houses their god or gods. Then there is a big festival, and out of the building is brought, in solemn procession, a carved wooden figure, which is set in the open in the sight of all. Everybody then dances around it, then bows down before it. Obviously I was right; it is a god, and what they are doing is worshipping it.

Suppose I now ask one of them why they are doing all this, that is, why this thing is their god, why they worship this image (or the spirit that dwells within it). And suppose he replies something like this: We worship him because he is our God. He watches over us and protects us from our enemies. He sees into the hearts of men and rewards the good and punishes the wicked. We pray to him for our needs and he sends us good crops and makes our cattle and our women fertile, so we thank him and hold festivals in his honour.

There is a sense in which this is all very straightforward and clear, and if there are obscurities, things I am not clear about, I can get him to go over it again, or to fill in some of the details. But there is another sense in which it is not clear at all. It is not clear to me how they can believe all this. It is all quite alien to me, and obviously false (as well as being an anthropologist, I am a believing Christian). But why is it obviously false? In the light of everything I have said up to now, it is not false because it is based on a set of false

285

hypotheses. If I reject their belief that their god makes their crops grow in answer to their prayers, this is not because I cannot discover, or even surmise, any causal links between their prayers, the idol and the quality of their crops; for to look for such causal links is to misunderstand the nature of prayer and the concept of an answer to prayer. If I cannot believe that their god protects them because I learn that they have in fact suffered many natural disasters and been heavily defeated and cruelly treated by their enemies, then I have overlooked the fact that a god can make you safe even when you are imperilled and without hope of rescue, make everything all right when nothing is right. If I am sceptical because I can discover no evidence that this god actually *does* anything – obviously, for it is only a bit of wood, and pretty cracked and worm-eaten at that – then I forget that my God too brings things about without doing anything that counts as bringing them about, that his bringing them about is not distinguishable from their happening.

If I reject their religion properly, it is not because I have such grounds for rejecting it, any more than they have grounds for believing it. I reject it because it is an alien religion, different from mine (and therefore the more similarities it has with mine the more likely I am to be broadly sympathetic to it, though I might be all the more sharply critical of its details). It may be so alien that I cannot even take it seriously, regard it as in competition with my own beliefs and practices. It may simply be, for me, an anthropological curiosity.

But now if I make my life among these people, perhaps marry one of them, and come to share their life, would not their religious beliefs and practices become a much more serious matter for me? If I become engaged in the life of that society, part of what that means is that I become engaged in their religious life, with all its expressions in word and action. Once the people become to a degree my people, they can no longer be an object of curiosity for me, and so neither can the way they live – and that includes what they say and do as part of their religion. If I am to take a full part in the life of that society, then the way that society lives must come to appear as a possible form of life for me. If at one time I reject their religion because it is alien to me, that is not to say that I reject it because I reject its intellectual foundations, for it may have none. And so if I now come to accept it, that is not a matter of overcoming intellectual objections. It is a matter of coming to share a way of life. It is not that I discover that there is after all a connexion between praying to this god and the state of my crops, or between my moral life and what happens to me. Rather, now I too, as the people around me do, *make* these connexions and others like them by the things I do, the way I live, the way I talk about my life. I make a connexion between the god and my crops by praying to him for good crops and thanking him when I get them, and by thinking there must be a reason for it when I do not get them. And I make a connexion between my moral life and what happens to me by, for instance, describing the failure of my crops as a punishment from God on account of my sins (which may be hidden from me); and so on. We may say: People do not discover religious truths, they make them.

WORKS CITED

CLARK, James M. and SKINNER, John V., ed., *Meister Eckhart: Selected Sermons and Treatises*, Faber and Faber, London, 1958.

EVANS-PRITCHARD, E. E. *Witchcraft, Oracles and Magic Among The Azande*, Oxford University Press, 1937.

FLEW, Antony and MACINTYRE, Alasdair, ed., *New Essays in Philosophical Theology*, SCM Press Limited, London, 1955.

WITTGENSTEIN, Ludwig
Culture and Value, ed. G. H. von Wright and Heikki Nyman, trans. Peter Winch, Basil Blackwell, Oxford, 1980.
Lectures and Conversations on Aesthetics, Psychology and Religious Belief, ed. Cyril Barrett, Basil Blackwell, Oxford, 1966.
Philosophical Investigations, ed. G. E. M. Anscombe and Rush Rhees, trans. G. E. M. Anscombe, Basil Blackwell, Oxford, 1953.
Remarks on Colour, ed. G. E. M. Anscombe, trans. Linda L. McAlister and Margarete Schättler, Basil Blackwell, Oxford, 1977.
Remarks on Frazer's Golden Bough, ed. Rush Rhees, trans. A. C. Miles, revised by Rush Rhees, Brynmill Press, Retford, 1979.
Remarks on the Philosophy of Psychology, ed. G. E. M. Anscombe and G. H. von Wright, trans. G. E. M. Anscombe, Basil Blackwell, Oxford, 1980.

288

WORKS CITED

Zettel, 2nd. edition, ed. G. E. M. Anscombe and G. H. von Wright, trans. G. E. M. Anscombe, Basil Blackwell, Oxford, 1981.